SUPERWOMEN

SUPERWOMEN
The Scenes in the Heroic Lives of Harriet Tubman and Sojourner Truth

By

Sarah H. Bradford
Sojourner Truth
Olive Gilbert
Frances W. Titus

Compiled, Selected and Edited
by
J. Mitchell, MA

LARGE PRINT EDITION

SUPERWOMEN
©2017
All Rights Reserved.
J. Mitchell

SUPERWOMEN

SUPERWOMEN

PREPARED FOR PUBLICATION

BY

HISTORIC PUBLISHING

No part of this revised and edited publication may be reproduced, stored in a retrieval system, or transmitted, in any form, or by any means, electronic, mechanical, photocopying, recording, or otherwise, without the prior consent of the publisher.

ISBN-13:
978-1946640413

ISBN-10:
1946640417

All Rights Reserved.
HISTORIC PUBLISHING
©2017

SUPERWOMEN

Sojourner Truth

SUPERWOMEN

BOOK ONE

Scenes in the Life of Harriet Tubman

By

Sarah H. Bradford

HARRIET TUBMAN.

SUPERWOMEN

SCENES IN THE LIFE OF HARRIET TUBMAN.

BY

SARAH H. BRADFORD.

AUBURN:
W. J. MOSES, PRINTER.
1869.

Entered according to Act of Congress, in the year 1869,
BY WILLIAM G. WISE,
In the Clerk's Office of the District Court for the Northern District
of New York. STEREOTYPED BY
DENNIS BRO'S & CO.,
AUBURN, N. Y.

Scenes in the Life of Harriet Tubman

INTRODUCTION.

THE following little story was written by Mrs. Sarah H. Bradford, of Geneva, with the single object of furnishing some help to the subject of the memoir. Harriet Tubman's services and sufferings during the rebellion, which are acknowledged in the letters of Gen. Saxton, and others, it was thought by many, would justify the bestowment of a pension by the Government. But the difficulties in the way of procuring such relief, suggested other methods, and finally the present one. The narrative was prepared on the eve of the author's departure for Europe, where she still remains. It makes no claim whatever to literary merit. Her hope was merely that the considerably numerous public already in part acquainted with Harriet's story, would furnish purchasers enough to secure a little fund for the relief of this remarkable woman. Outside that circle she did not suppose the memoir was likely to meet with much if any sale.

In furtherance of the same benevolent scheme, and in order to secure the whole avails of the work for Harriet's benefit, a subscription has been raised more than sufficient to defray the entire cost of publication. This has been effected by the generous exertions of Wm. G. Wise, Esq., of this city. The whole amount was contributed by citizens of Auburn, with the exception of two liberal subscriptions by Gerrit Smith, Esq., and Mr. Wendell Phillips.

Mr. Wise has also consented, at Mrs. Bradford's request, to act as trustee for Harriet; and will receive, invest, and apply, for her benefit, whatever may accrue from the sale of this book.

The spirited woodcut likeness of Harriet, in her costume as scout, was furnished by the kindness of Mr. J. C. Darby, of this city.

S. M. H.

AUBURN, Dec. 1, 1868.

PREFACE.

IT is proposed in this little book to give a plain and unvarnished account of some scenes and adventures in the life of a woman who, though one of earth's lowly ones, and of dark-hued skin, has shown an amount of heroism in her character rarely possessed by those of any station in life. Her name (we say it advisedly and without exaggeration) deserves to be handed down to posterity side by side with the names of Joan of Arc, Grace Darling, and Florence Nightingale; for not one of these women has shown more courage and power of endurance in facing danger and death to relieve human suffering, than has this woman in her heroic and successful endeavors to reach and save all whom she might of her oppressed and suffering race, and to pilot them from the land of Bondage to the promised land of Liberty. Well has she been called "Moses," for she has been a leader and deliverer unto hundreds of her people.

Worn down by her sufferings and fatigues, her health permanently affected by the cruelties to which she has been subjected, she is still laboring to the utmost limit of her strength for the support of her aged parents, and still also for her afflicted people--by her own efforts supporting two schools for Freedmen at the South, and supplying them with clothes and books; never obtruding herself, never asking for charity, except for "her people."

It is for the purpose of aiding her in ministering to the wants of her aged parents, and in the hope of securing to them the little home which they are in danger of losing from inability to pay the whole amount due--which amount was partly paid when our heroine left them to throw herself into the work of aiding our suffering soldiers--that this little account, drawn from her by persevering endeavor, is given to the friends of humanity.

The writer of this story has till very lately known less personally of the subject of it, than many others to whom she has for years been an object of interest and care. Put through relations and friends in Auburn, and also through Mrs. Commodore Swift of Geneva, and her sisters, who have for many years known and esteemed this wonderful woman, she has heard tales of her deeds of heroism which seemed almost too strange for belief, and were invested with the charm of romance.

During a sojourn of some months in the city of Auburn, while the war was in progress, the writer used to see occasionally in her Sunday-school class the aged mother of Harriet, and also some of those girls who bad been brought from the South by this remarkable woman. She also wrote letters for the old people to commanding officers at the South, making inquiries about Harriet, and received answers telling of her untiring devotion to our wounded and sick soldiers, and of her efficient aid in various ways to the cause of the Union.

By the graphic pen of Mrs. Stowe, the incidents of such a life as that of the subject of this little memoir might be wrought up into a tale of thrilling interest, equaling, if not exceeding, anything in her world-renowned "Uncle Tom's Cabin;" but the story of Harriet Tubman needs not the drapery of fiction; the bare unadorned facts are enough to stir the hearts of the friends of humanity, the friends of liberty, the lovers of their country.

There are those who will sneer, there are those who have already done so, at this quixotic attempt to make a heroine of a black woman, and a slave; but it may possibly be that there are some natures, though concealed under fairer skins, who have not the capacity to comprehend such general and self-sacrificing devotion to the cause of others as that here delineated, and therefore they resort to scorn and ridicule, in order to throw discredit upon the whole story.

Much has been left out which would have been highly interesting, because of the impossibility of substantiating by the testimony of others the truth of Harriet's statements. But whenever it has been possible to find those who were cognizant with the facts stated, they have been corroborated in every particular.

A few years hence and we seem to see a gathering where the wrongs of earth will be righted, and Justice, long delayed, will assert itself, and perform its office. Then not a few of those who had esteemed themselves the wise and noble of this world, "will begin with shame to take the lowest place;" while upon Harriet's dark head a kind hand will be placed, and in her ear a gentle voice will sound, saying: "Friend! come up higher!"

S. H. B.

The following letters to the writer from those well-known and distinguished philanthropists, Hon. Gerrit Smith and Wendell Phillips, and one from Frederick Douglass, addressed to Harriet, will serve as the best introduction that can be given of the subject of this memoir to its readers:

Letter from Hon. Gerrit Smith.

PETERBORO, June 13, 1868.

My DEAR MADAME: I am happy to learn that you are to speak to the public of Mrs. Harriet Tubman. Of the remarkable events of her life I have no personal knowledge, but of the truth of them as she describes them I have no doubt.

I have often listened to her, in her visits to my family, and I am confident that she is not only truthful, but that she has a rare discernment, and a deep and sublime philanthropy.

With great respect your friend,

GERRIT SMITH.

GERRIT SMITH.

Letter from Wendell Phillips.

JUNE 16, 1868.

DEAR MADAME: The last time I ever saw John Brown was under my own roof, as he brought Harriet Tubman to me, saying: "Mr. Phillips, I bring you one of the best and bravest persons on this continent--General Tubman, as we call her."

He then went on to recount her labors and sacrifices in behalf of her race. After that, Harriet spent some time in Boston, earning the confidence and admiration of all those who were working for freedom. With their aid she went to the South more than once, returning always with a squad of self-emancipated men, women, and children, for whom her marvelous skill had opened the way of escape. After the war broke out, she was sent with indorsements from Governor Andrew and his friends to South Carolina, where in the service of the Nation she rendered most important and efficient aid to our army.

In my opinion there are few captains, perhaps few colonels, who have done more for the loyal cause since the war began, and few men who did before that time more for the colored race, than our fearless and most sagacious friend, Harriet.

Faithfully yours,

WENDELL PHILLIPS.

WENDELL PHILLIPS

Letter from Frederick Douglass.

ROCHESTER, August 29, 1868.

DEAR HARRIET: I am glad to know that the story of your eventful life has been written by a kind lady, and that the same is so soon to be published. You ask for what you do not need when you call upon me for a word of commendation. I need such words from you far more than you can need them from me, especially where your superior labors and devotion to the cause of the lately enslaved of our land are known as I know them. The difference between us is very marked. Most that I have done and suffered in the service of our cause has been in public, and I have received much encouragement at every step of the way. You on the other hand have labored in a private way. I have wrought in the day--you in the night. I have had the applause of the crowd and the satisfaction that comes of being approved by the multitude, while the most that you have done has been witnessed by a few trembling, scarred, and foot-sore bondmen and women, whom you have led out of the house of bondage, and whose heartfelt "God bless you" has been your only reward. The midnight sky and the silent stars have been the witnesses of your devotion to freedom and of your heroism. Excepting John Brown -- of sacred memory--I know of no one who has willingly encountered more perils and hardships to serve our enslaved people than you have. Much that you have done would seem improbable to those who do not know you as I know you. It is to me a great pleasure and a great privilege to bear testimony to your character and your works, and to say to those to whom you may come, that I regard you in every way truthful and trustworthy.

Your friend,

FREDERICK DOUGLASS.

SUPERWOMEN

FREDERICK DOUGLASS.

HARRIET TUBMAN

SOME SCENES IN THE LIFE OF HARRIET TUBMAN.

HARRIET TUBMAN, known at various times, and in various places, by many different names, such as "Moses," in allusion to her being the leader and guide to so many of her people in their exodus from the Land of Bondage; "the Conductor of the Underground Railroad;" and "Moll Pitcher," for the energy and daring by which she delivered a fugitive slave who was about to be dragged back to the South; was for the first twenty-five years of her life a slave on the eastern shore of Maryland. Her own master she represents as never unnecessarily cruel; but as was common among slaveholders, he often hired out his slaves to others, some of whom proved to be tyrannical and brutal to the utmost limit of their power.

She had worked only as a field-hand for many years, following the oxen, loading and unloading wood, and carrying heavy burdens, by which her naturally remarkable power of muscle was so developed that her feats of strength often called forth the wonder of strong laboring men. Thus was she preparing for the life of hardship and endurance which lay before her, for the deeds of daring she was to do, and of which her ignorant and darkened mind at that time never dreamed.

The first person by whom she was hired was a woman who, though married and the mother of a family, was still "Miss Susan" to her slaves, as is customary at the South. This woman was possessed of the good things of this life, and provided liberally for her slaves--so far as food and clothing went. But she had been brought up to believe, and to act upon the belief, that a slave could be taught to do nothing, and would do nothing but under the sting of the whip. Harriet, then a young girl, was taken from her life in the field, and having never seen the inside of a house better than a cabin in the negro quarters, was put to housework without being told how to do anything. The first thing was to put a parlor in order. "Move these chairs and tables into the middle of the room, sweep the carpet clean, then dust everything, and put them back in their places!" These were the directions given, and Harriet was left alone to do her work. The whip was in sight on the mantelpiece, as a reminder of what was to be expected if the work was not done well. Harriet fixed the furniture as she was told to do, and swept with all her strength, raising a tremendous dust. The moment she had finished sweeping, she took her dusting cloth, and wiped everything "so you could see your face in 'em, de shone so," in haste to go and set the table for breakfast, and do her other work. The dust, which she had set flying only, settled down again on chairs, tables, and the piano. "Miss Susan" came in and looked around. Then came the call for "Minty"-- Harriet's name was Araminta at the South.

She drew her up to the table, saying, "What do you mean by doing my work this way, you--!" and passing her finger on the table and piano, she showed her the mark it made through the dust. "Miss Susan, I done sweep and dust jus' as you tole me." But the whip was already taken down, and the strokes were falling on head and face and neck. Four times this scene was repeated before breakfast, when, during the fifth whipping, the door opened, and "Miss Emily" came in. She was a married sister of "Miss Susan," and was making her a visit, and though brought up with the same associations as her sister, seems to have been a person of more gentle and reasonable nature. Not being able to endure the screams of the child any longer, she came in, took her sister by the arm, and said, "If you do not stop whipping that child, I will leave your house, and never come back!" Miss Susan declared that "she would not mind, and she slighted her work on purpose." Miss Emily said, "Leave her to me a few moments;" and Miss Susan left the room, indignant. As soon as they were alone, Miss Emily said: "Now, Minty, show me how you do your work." For the sixth time Harriet removed all the furniture into the middle of the room; then she swept; and the moment she had done sweeping, she took the dusting cloth to wipe off the furniture. "Now stop there," said Miss Emily; "go away now, and do some of your other work, and when it is time to dust, I will call you." When the time came she called her, and explained to her how the dust had now settled, and that if she wiped it off now, the furniture would remain bright and clean. These few words an hour or two before, would have saved Harriet her whippings for that day, as they probably did for many a day after.

While with this woman, after working from early morning till late at night, she was obliged to sit up all night to rock a cross, sick child. Her mistress laid upon her bed with a whip under her pillow, and slept; but if the tired nurse forgot herself for a moment, if her weary head dropped, and her hand ceased to rock the cradle, the child would cry out, and then down would come the whip upon the neck and face of the poor weary creature. The scars are still plainly visible where the whip cut into the flesh. Perhaps her mistress was preparing her, though she did not know it then, by this enforced habit of wakefulness, for the many long nights of travel, when she was the leader and guide of the weary and hunted ones who were escaping from bondage.

"Miss Susan" got tired of Harriet, as Harriet was determined she should do, and so abandoned intention of buying her, and sent her back to her master. She was next hired out to the man who inflicted upon her the lifelong injury from which she is suffering now, by breaking her skull with a weight from the scales. The injury thus inflicted causes her often to fall into a state of somnolency from which it is almost impossible to rouse her. Disabled and sick, her flesh all wasted away, she was returned to her owner. He tried to sell her, but no one would buy her. "Dey said dey wouldn't give a sixpence for me," she said.

"And so," she said, "from Christmas till March I worked as I could, and I prayed through all the long nights--I groaned and prayed for ole master: 'Oh Lord, convert master!' 'Oh Lord, change dat man's heart!' 'Pears like I prayed all de time," said Harriet; " 'bout my work, everywhere, I prayed an' I groaned to de Lord. When I went to de horse-trough to wash my face, I took up de water in my han' an' I said, 'Oh Lord, wash me, make me clean!' Den I take up something to wipe my face, an' I say, 'Oh Lord, wipe away all my sin!' When I took de broom and began to sweep, I groaned, 'Oh Lord, wha'soebber sin dere be in my heart, sweep it out, Lord, clar an' clean!'" No words can describe the pathos of her tones, as she broke out into these words of prayer, after the manner of her people. "An' so," said she, "I prayed all night long for master, till the first of March; an' all the time he was bringing people to look at me, an' trying to sell me. Den we heard dat some of us was gwine to be sole to go wid de chain-gang down to de cotton an' rice fields, and dey said I was gwine, an' my brudders, an' sisters. Den I changed my prayer. Fust of March I began to pray, 'Oh Lord, if you ant nebber gwine to change dat man's heart, kill him, Lord, an' take him out ob de way.'

"Nex' ting I heard old master was dead, an' he died jus' as he libed. Oh, then, it 'peared like I'd give all de world full ob gold, if I had it, to bring dat poor soul back. But I couldn't pray for him no longer."

The slaves were told that their master's will provided that none of them should be sold out of the State. This satisfied most of them, and they were very happy. But Harriet was not satisfied; she never closed her eyes that she did not imagine she saw the horsemen coming, and heard the screams of women and children, as they were being dragged away to a far worse slavery than that they were enduring there. Harriet was married at this time to a free negro, who not only did not trouble himself about her fears, but did his best to betray her, and bring her back after she escaped. She would start up at night with the cry, "Oh, dey're comin', dey're comin', I mus' go!"

Her husband called her a fool, and said she was like old Cudjo, who when a joke went round, never laughed till half an hour after everybody else got through, and so just as all danger was past she began to be frightened. But still Harriet in fancy saw the horsemen coming, and heard the screams of terrified women and children. "And all that time, in my dreams and visions," she said, "I seemed to see a line, and on the other side of that line were green fields, and lovely flowers, and beautiful white ladies, who stretched out their arms to me over the line, but I couldn't reach them nohow. I always fell before I got to the line."

One Saturday it was whispered in the quarters that two of Harriet's sisters had been sent off with the chain-gang. That morning she started, having persuaded three of her brothers to accompany her, but they had not gone far when the brothers, appalled by the dangers before and behind them, determined to go back, and in spite of her remonstrance's dragged her with them. In fear and terror, she remained over Sunday, and on Monday night a negro from another part of the plantation came privately to tell Harriet that herself and brothers were to be carried off that night. The poor old mother, who belonged to the same mistress, was just going to milk. Harriet wanted to get away without letting her know, because she knew that she would raise an uproar and prevent her going, or insist upon going with her, and the time for this was not yet. But she must give some intimation to those she was going to leave of her intention, and send such a farewell as she might to the friends and relations on the plantation. Those communications were generally made by singing. They sang as they walked along the country roads, and the chorus was taken up by others, and the uninitiated knew not the hidden meaning of the words--

>When dat ar ole chariot comes,
>I'm gwine to lebe you;
>I'm boun' for de promised land,
>I'm gwine to lebe you.

These words meant something more than a journey to the Heavenly Canaan. Harriet said, "Here, mother, go 'long; I'll do the milkin' to-night and bring it in." The old woman went to her cabin. Harriet took down her sunbonnet, and went on to the "big house," where some of her relatives lived as house servants. She thought she could trust Mary, but there were others in the kitchen, and she could say nothing. Mary began to frolic with her. She threw her across the kitchen, and ran out, knowing that Mary would follow her. But just as they turned the corner of the house, the master to whom Harriet was now hired, came riding up on his horse. Mary darted back, and Harriet thought there was no way now but to sing. But "the Doctor," as the master was called, was regarded with special awe by his slaves; if they were singing or talking together in the field, or on the road, and "the Doctor" appeared, all was hushed till he passed. But Harriet had no time for ceremony; her friends must have a warning; and whether the Doctor thought her "imperent " or not, she must sing him farewell. So on she went to meet him, singing:

> I'm sorry I'm gwine to lebe you,
> Farewell, oh farewell;
> But I'll meet you in the mornin',
> Farewell, oh farewell.

The Doctor passed, and she bowed as she went on, still singing:

> I'll meet you in the mornin',
> I'm boun' for de promised land,
> On the oder side of Jordan,
> Boun' for de promised land.

She reached the gate and looked round; the Doctor had stopped his horse, and had turned around in the saddle, and was looking at her as if there might be more in this than "met the ear." Harriet closed the gate, went on a little way, came back, the Doctor still gazing at her.

She lifted up the gate as if she had not latched it properly, waved her hand to him, and burst out again:

> I'll meet you in the mornin',
> Safe in de promised land,
> On the oder side of Jordan,
> Boun' for de promised land.

And she started on her journey, "not knowing whither she went," except that she was going to follow the north star, till it led her to liberty. Cautiously and by night she traveled, cunningly feeling her way, and finding out who were friends; till after a long and painful journey she found, in answer to careful inquiries, that she had at last crossed that magic "line" which then separated the land of bondage from the land of freedom; for this was before we were commanded by law to take part in the iniquity of slavery, and aid in taking and sending back those poor hunted fugitives who had manhood and intelligence enough to enable them to make their way thus far towards freedom.

"When I found I had crossed dat line," she said, "I looked at my hands to see if I was de same pusson. There was such a glory ober ebery ting; de sun came like gold through the trees, and ober the fields, and I felt like I was in Heaben."

But then came the bitter drop in the cup of joy. She said she felt like a man who was put in State Prison for twenty-five years. All these twenty-five years he was thinking of his home, and longing for the time when he would see it again. At last the day comes--he leaves the prison gates--he makes his way to his old home, but his old home is not there. The house has been pulled down, and a new one has been put up in its place; his family and friends are gone nobody knows where; there is no one to take him by the hand, no one to welcome him.

"So it was with me," she said. "I had crossed the line. I was free; but there was no one to welcome me to the land of freedom. I was a stranger in a strange land; and my home, after all, was down in Maryland; because my father, my mother, my brothers, and sisters, and friends were there. But I was free, and they should be free. I would make a home in the North and bring them there, God helping me. Oh, how I prayed then," she said; "I said to de Lord, 'I'm gwine to hole stiddy on to you, an' I know you'll see me through.'"

She came to Philadelphia, and worked in hotels, in club houses, and afterwards at Cape May. Whenever she had raised money enough to pay expenses, she would make her way back, hide herself, and in various ways give notice to those who were ready to strike for freedom. When her party was made up, they would start always on Saturday night, because advertisements could not be sent out on Sunday, which gave them one day in advance.

Then the pursuers would start after them. Advertisements would be posted everywhere. There was one reward of $12,000 offered for the head of the woman who was constantly appearing and enticing away parties of slaves from their master. She had traveled in the cars when these posters were put up over her head, and she heard them read by those about her--for she could not read herself. Fearlessly she went on, trusting in the Lord. She said, "I started with this idea in my head, 'Dere's two things I've got a right to, and dese are, Death or Liberty--one or tother I mean to have. No one will take me back alive; I shall fight for my liberty, and when de time has come for me to go, de Lord will let dem kill me." And acting upon this simple creed, and firm in this trusting faith, she went back and forth nineteen times, according to the reckoning of her friends. She remembers that she went eleven times from Canada, but of the other journeys she kept no reckoning.

While Harriet was working as cook in one of the large hotels in Philadelphia, the play of "Uncle Tom's Cabin" was being performed for many weeks every night. Some of her fellow-servants wanted her to I go and see it. "No," said Harriet, "I haint got no heart to go and see the sufferings of my people played on de stage. I've heard 'Uncle Tom's Cabin' read, and I tell you Mrs Stowe's pen hasn't begun to paint what slavery is as I have seen it at the far South. I've seen de real ting, and I don't want to see it on no stage or in no teater."

I will give here an article from a paper published nearly a year ago, which mentions that the price set upon the head of Harriet was much higher than I have stated it to be. When asked about this, Harriet said she did not know whether it was so, but she heard them read from one paper that the reward offered was $12,000.

"Among American women," says the article referred to, "who has shown a courage and self-devotion to the welfare of others, equal to Harriet Tubman? Hear her story of going down again and again into the very jaws of slavery, to rescue her suffering people, bringing them off through perils and dangers enough to appall the stoutest heart, till she was known among them as 'Moses.'

"Forty thousand dollars was not too great a reward for the Maryland slaveholders to offer for her.

"Think of her brave spirit, as strong as Daniel's of old, in its fearless purpose to serve God, even though the fiery furnace should be her portion. I have looked into her dark face, and wondered and admired as I listened to the thrilling deeds her lion heart had prompted her to dare. 'I have heard their groans and sighs, and seen their tears, and I would give every drop of blood in my veins to free them,' she said.

"The other day, at Gerrit Smith's, I saw this heroic woman, whom the pen of genius will yet make famous, as one of the noblest Christian hearts ever inspired to lift the burdens of the wronged and oppressed, and what do you think she said to me? She had been tending and caring for our Union black (and white) soldiers in hospital during the war, and at the end of her labors was on her way home, coming in a car through New Jersey. A white man, the conductor, thrust her out of the car with such violence that she has not been able to work scarcely any since; and as she told me of the pain she had and still suffered, she said she did not know what she should have done for herself, and the old father and mother she takes care of, if Mr. Wendell Phillips had not sent her $60, that kept them warm through the winter. She had a letter from W. H. Seward to Maj.-Gen. Hunter, in which he says, 'I have known her long, and a nobler, higher spirit, or truer, seldom dwells in the human form.'"

It will be impossible to give any connected account of the different journeys taken by Harriet for the rescue of her people, as she herself has no idea of the dates connected with them, or of the order in which they were made. She thinks she was about 25 when she made her own escape, and this was in the last year of James K. Polk's administration. From that time till the beginning of the war, her years were spent in these journeyings back and forth, with intervals between, in which she worked only to spend the avails of her labor in providing for the wants of her next party of fugitives. By night she traveled, many times on foot, over mountains, through forests, across rivers, mid perils by land, perils by water, perils from enemies, "perils among false brethren." Sometimes members of her party would become exhausted, foot-sore, and bleeding, and declare they could not go on, they must stay where they dropped down, and die; others would think a voluntary return to slavery better than being overtaken and carried back, and would insist upon returning; then there was no remedy but force; the revolver carried by this bold and daring pioneer would be pointed at their heads. "Dead niggers tell no tales," said Harriet; "Go on or die;" and so she compelled them to drag their weary limbs on their northward journey.

At one time she collected and sent on a gang of thirty-nine fugitives in the care of others, as from some cause she was prevented from accompanying them. Sometimes, when she and her party were concealed in the woods, they saw their pursuers pass, on their horses, down the high road, tacking up the advertisements for them on the fences and trees.

"And den how we laughed," said she. "We was de fools, and dey was de wise men; but we wasn't fools enough to go down de high road in de broad daylight." At one time she left her party in the woods, and went by a long and roundabout way to one of the "stations of the Underground Railway," as she called them. Here she procured food for her famished party, often paying out of her hardly-gained earnings, five dollars a day for food for them. But she dared not go back to them till night, for fear of being watched, and thus revealing their hiding-place. After nightfall, the sound of a hymn sung at a distance comes upon the ears of the concealed and famished fugitives in the woods, and they know that their deliverer is at hand. They listen eagerly for the words she sings, for by them they are to be warned of

danger, or informed of safety. Nearer and nearer comes
the unseen singer, and the words are wafted to their ears:

        Hail, oh hail ye happy spirits,
        Death no more shall make you fear,
        No grief nor sorrow, pain nor anger (anguish)
        Shall no more distress you there.

        Around him are ten thousan' angels,
        Always ready to 'bey comman'.
        Dey are always hobring round you,
        Till you reach the hebbenly lan'.

        Jesus, Jesus will go wid you;
        He will lead you to his throne;
        He who died has gone before you,
        Trod de wine-press all alone.

        He whose thunders shake creation;
        He who bids the planets roll;
        He who rides upon the temple, (tempest)
        An' his scepter sways de whole.

        Dark and thorny is de desert,
        Through de pilgrim makes his ways,

> Yet beyon' dis vale of sorrow,
> Lies de fiel's of endless days.

I give these words exactly as Harriet sang them to me to a sweet and simple Methodist air. "De first time I go by singing dis hymn, dey don't come out to me," she said, "till I listen if de coast is clar; den when I go back and sing it again, dey come out. But if I sing:

> Moses go down in Egypt,
> Till ole Pharo' let me go;
> Hadn't been for Adam's fall,
> Shouldn't hab to died at all,

den dey don't come out, for dere's danger in de way."

And so by night travel, by hiding, by signals, by threatening, she brought the people safely to the land of liberty. But after the passage of the Fugitive Slave law, she said, "I wouldn't trust Uncle Sam wid my people no longer; I brought 'em all clar off to Canada."

Of the very many interesting stories told me by Harriet, I cannot refrain from telling to my readers that of Joe, who accompanied her upon her seventh or eighth journey from Maryland to Canada.

Joe was a noble specimen of a negro, and was hired out by his master to a man for whom he worked faithfully for six years, saving him the expense of an overseer, and taking all trouble off his hands. At length this man found him so absolutely necessary to him, that he determined to buy him at any cost. His master held him proportionally high. However, by paying a thousand dollars down for him, and promising to pay another thousand in a certain time, Joe passed into the hands of his new master.

As may be imagined, Joe was somewhat surprised when the first order issued from his master's lips, was, "Now, Joe, strip and take a whipping!" Joe's experience of whippings, as he had seen them inflicted upon others, was not such as to cause him particularly to desire to go through the same operation on his own account; and he, naturally enough, demurred, and at first thought of resisting. But he called to mind a scene which he had witnessed a few days before, in the field, the particulars of which are too horrible and too harassing to the feelings to be given to my readers, and he thought it best to submit; but first he tried remonstrance.

"Mas'r," said he, "habn't I always been faithful to you? Habn't I worked through sun an' rain, early in de mornin', and late at night; habn't I saved you an oberseer by doin' his work; hab you anyting to complain of agin me?"

"No, Joe; "I've no complaint to make of you; you're a good nigger, and you've always worked well; but the first lesson my niggers have to learn is that I am master, and that they are not to resist or refuse to obey anything I tell 'em to do. So the first thing they've got to do, is to be whipped; if they resist, they got it all the harder; and so

I'll go on, till I kill 'em, but they've got to give up at last, and learn that I'm master."

Joe thought it best to submit. He stripped off his upper clothing, and took his whipping, without a word; but as he drew his clothes up over his torn and bleeding back, he said, "Dis is de last!" That night he took a boat and went a long distance to the cabin of Harriet's father, and said, "Next time Moses comes, let me know." It was only a week or two after that, that the mysterious woman whom no one could lay their finger on appeared, and men, women, and children began to disappear from the plantations. One fine morning Joe was missing, and his brother William, from another plantation; Peter and Eliza, too, were gone; and these made part of Harriet's next party, who began their pilgrimage from Maryland to Canada, or as they expressed it, from "Egypt to de land of Canaan."

Their adventures were enough to fill a volume; they were pursued; they were hidden in "potato holes," while their pursuers passed within a few feet of them; they were passed along by friends in various disguises; they scattered and separated, to be led by guides by a roundabout way, to a meeting-place again. They were taken in by Sam Green, the man who was afterwards sent to State Prison for ten years for having a copy of "Uncle Tom's Cabin" in his house; and so, hunted and hiding and wandering, they came at last to the long bridge at the entrance of the city of Wilmington, Delaware. The rewards posted up everywhere had been at first five hundred dollars for Joe, if taken within the limits of the United States; then a thousand, and then fifteen hundred dollars, "an' all expenses clar an' clean, for his body in Easton Jail," Eight hundred for William, and four hundred for Peter, and twelve thousand for the woman who enticed them away. The long Wilmington Bridge was guarded by police officers, and the advertisements were everywhere. The party were scattered, and taken to the houses of different colored friends, and word was sent secretly to Thomas Garrett, of Wilmington, of their condition, and the necessity of their being taken across the bridge. Thomas Garrett is a Quaker, and a man of a wonderfully large and generous heart, through whose hands, Harriet tells me, two thousand self-emancipated slaves passed on their way to freedom. He was always ready, heart and hand and means, in aiding these poor fugitives, and rendered most efficient help to Harriet on many of her journeys back and forth. A letter received a few days since by the writer, from this noble-hearted philanthropist, will be given presently.

As soon as Thomas Garrett heard of the condition of these poor people, his plan was formed. He engaged two wagons, filled them with bricklayers, whom of course he paid well for their share in the enterprise, and sent them across the bridge. They went as if on a frolic, singing and shouting. The guards saw them pass, and of course expected them to re-cross the bridge. After nightfall (and fortunately it was a dark night) the same wagons went back, but with an addition to their party.

The fugitives were on the bottom of the wagons, the bricklayers on the seats, still singing and shouting; and so they passed by the guards, who were entirely unsuspicious of the nature of the load the wagons contained, or of the amount of property thus escaping their hands. And so they made their way to New York. When they entered the anti-slavery office there, Joe was recognized at once by the description in the advertisement. "Well," said Mr. Oliver Johnson, "I am glad to see the man whose head is worth fifteen hundred dollars." At this Joe's heart sank. If the advertisement had got to New York, that place which it had taken them so many days and nights to reach, he thought he was in danger still. "And how far is it now to Canada?" he asked. When told how many miles, for they were to come through New York State, and cross the Suspension Bridge, he was ready to give up. "From dat time Joe was silent," said Harriet; "he sang no more, he talked no more; he sat wid his head on his hand, and nobody could 'muse him or make him take any interest in anyting." They passed along in safety, and at length found themselves in the cars, approaching Suspension Bridge. The rest were very joyous and happy, but Joe sat silent and sad. Their fellow-passengers all seemed interested in and for them, and listened with tears, as Harriet and all their party lifted up their voices and sang:

>I'm on my way to Canada,
>That cold and dreary land;
>The sad effects of slavery,

I can't no longer stand.
I've served my master all my days,
Widout a dime's reward;
And now I'm forced to run away,
To flee the lash abroad.
Farewell, ole master, don't think hard of me,
I'll travel on to Canada, where all the slaves are free.

The hounds are baying on my track,
Ole master comes behind.
Resolved that he will bring me back,
Before I cross de line;
I'm now embarked for yonder shore,
There a man's a man by law;
The iron horse will bear me o'er,
To shake de lion's paw.
Oh, righteous Father, wilt thou not pity me,
And aid me on to Canada where all the slaves are free.

Oh, I heard Queen Victoria say,
That if we would forsake
Our native land of slavery,
And come across the lake;
That she was standin' on de shore,
Wid arms extended wide,
To give us all a peaceful home
Beyond de rolling tide.
Farewell, ole master, etc.

The cars began to cross the bridge. Harriet was very anxious to have her companions see the Falls. William, Peter, and Eliza came eagerly to look at the wonderful sight; but Joe sat still, with his head upon his hand.

"Joe, come look at de Falls! Joe, you fool you, come see de Falls! its your last chance." But Joe sat still and never raised his head. At length Harriet knew by the rise in the center of the bridge, and the descent on the other side, that they had crossed "the line." She sprang across to Joe's seat, shook him with all her might, and shouted, "Joe, you've shook de lion's paw!" Joe did not know what she meant. "Joe, you're free!" shouted Harriet. Then Joe's head went up, he raised his hands on high, and his face, streaming with tears, to heaven, and broke out in loud and thrilling tones:

> "Glory to God and Jesus too,
> One more soul is safe!
> Oh, go and carry de news,
> One more soul got safe."

"Joe, come and look at de Falls!" called Harriet.

> "Glory to God and Jesus too,
> One more soul got safe."

was all the answer. The cars stopped on the other side. Joe's feet were the first to touch British soil, after those of the conductor.

Loud roared the waters of Niagara, but louder still ascended the anthem of praise from the overflowing heart of the freeman. And can we doubt that the strain was taken up by angel voices, and that through the arches of Heaven echoed and reechoed the strain:

> Glory to God in the Highest,
> Glory to God and Jesus too,
> One more soul is safe.

"The ladies and gentlemen gathered round him," said Harriet, "till I couldn't see Joe for the crowd, only I heard 'Glory to God and Jesus too!' louder than ever." William went after him, and pulled him, saying, "Joe, stop your noise! you act like a fool!' Then Peter ran it, and jerked him mos' off his feet,--"Joe, stop your hollerin'! Folks 'll think you're crazy!" But Joe gave no heed. The ladies were crying, and the tears like rain ran down Joe's sable cheeks. A lady reached over her fine cambric handkerchief to him. Joe wiped his face, and then he spoke.

"Oh! if I'd felt like dis down South, it would hab taken nine men to take me; only one more journey for me now, and dat is to Hebben!" "Well, you ole fool you," said Harriet, with whom there seems but one step from the sublime to the ridiculous, "you might a' looked at de Falls fust, and den gone to Hebben afterwards." She has seen Joe several times since, a happy and industrious freeman in Canada.

When asked, as she often is, how it was possible that she was not afraid to go back, with that tremendous price upon her head, Harriet always answers, "Why, don't I tell you, Missus, t'wan't me, 'twas de Lord! I always tole him, 'I trust to you. I don't know where to go or what to do, but I expect you to lead me,' an' he always did." At one time she was going down, watched for everywhere, after there had been a meeting of slaveholders in the court-house of one of the large cities of Maryland, and an added reward had been put upon her head, with various threats of the different cruel devices by which she should be tortured and put to death; friends gathered round her, imploring her not to go on directly in the face of danger and death, and this was Harriet's answer to them:

"Now look yer! John saw the city, didn't he? Yes, John saw the city. Well, what did he see? He saw twelve gates--three of dose gates was on de north--three of 'em was on de east--and three of 'em was on de west --but dere was three of 'em on de South too; an' I reckon if dey kill me down dere, I'll git into one of dem gates, don't you?"

Whether Harriet's ideas of the geographical bearings of the gates of the Celestial City, as seen in the Apocalyptic vision, were correct or not, we cannot doubt that she was right in the deduction her faith drew from them; and that somewhere, whether north, south, east, or west, to our dim vision, there is a gate to be opened for

Harriet, where the welcome will be given, "Come in thou blessed of my Father."

Many of the stories told me by Harriet, in answer to questions, have been corroborated by letters, some of which will appear in this book. Of others, I have not been able to procure confirmation, owing to ignorance of the address of those conversant with the facts. I find among her papers, many of which are defaced by being carried about with her for years, portions of letters addressed to myself, by persons at the South, and speaking of the valuable assistance Harriet was rendering our soldiers in the hospital, and our armies in the field. At this time her manner of life, as related by herself, was this:

"Well, Missus, I'd go to de hospital, I would, early eb'ry mornin'. I'd get a big chunk of ice, I would, and put it in a basin, and fill it with water; den I'd take a sponge and begin. Fust man I'd come to, I'd thrash away de flies, an' dey'd rise, dey would, like bees roun' a hive. Den I'd begin to bathe der wounds, an' by de time I'd bathed off three or four, de fire and heat would have melted de ice and made de water warm, an' it would be as red as clar blood. Den I'd go an' git more ice, I would, an' by de time I got to de nex' ones, de flies would be roun' de fust ones, black an' thick as eber." In this way she worked, day after day, till late at night; then she went home to her little cabin, and made about fifty pies, a great quantity of ginger-bread, and two casks of root beer. These she would hire some contraband to sell for her through the camps, and thus she would provide her support for another day; for this woman never received pay or pension, and never drew for herself but twenty days' rations during the four years of her labors. At one time she was called away from Hilton Head, by one of our officers, to come to Fernandina, where the men were "dying off like sheep," from dysentery. Harriet had acquired quite a reputation for her skill in curing this disease, by a medicine which she prepared from roots which grew near the waters which gave the disease. Here she found thousands of sick soldiers and contrabands, and immediately gave up her time and attention to them. At another time, we find her nursing those who were down by hundreds with small-pox and malignant fevers. She had never had these diseases, but she seems to have no more fear of death in one form than another. "De Lord would take keer of her till her time came, an' den she was ready to go."

When our armies and gun-boats first appeared in any part of the South, many of the poor negroes were as much afraid of "de Yankee Buckra" as of their own masters. It was almost impossible to win their confidence, or to get information from them. But to Harriet they would tell anything; and so it became quite important that she should accompany expeditions going up the rivers, or into unexplored parts of the country, to control and get information from those whom they took with them as guides.

Gen. Hunter asked her at one time if she would go with several gunboats up the Combahee River, the object of the expedition being to take up the torpedoes placed by the rebels in the river, to destroy railroads and bridges, and to cut off supplies from the rebel troops. She said she would go if Col. Montgomery was to be appointed commander of the expedition. Col. Montgomery was one of John Brown's men, and was well known to Harriet. Accordingly, Col. Montgomery was appointed to the command, and Harriet, with several men under her, the principal of whom was J. Plowden, whose pass I have, accompanied the expedition. Harriet describes in the most graphic manner the appearance of the plantations as they passed up the river; the frightened negroes leaving their work and taking to the woods, at sight of the gun-boats; then coming to peer out like startled deer, and scudding away like the wind at the sound of the steam-whistle. "Well," said one old negro, "Mas'r said de Yankees had horns and tails, but I nebber beliebed it till now." But the word was passed along by the mysterious telegraphic communication existing among these simple people, that these were "Lincoln's gun-boats come to set them free." In vain, then, the drivers used their whips, in their efforts to hurry the poor creatures back to their quarters; they all turned and ran for the gun-boats. They came down every road, across every field, just as they had left their work and their cabins; women with children clinging around their necks, hanging to their dresses, running behind, all making at full speed for "Lincoln's gun-boats." Eight hundred poor wretches at one time crowded the banks, with their hands extended towards their deliverers, and they were all taken off upon the gunboats, and carried down to Beaufort.

"I nebber see such a sight," said Harriet; we laughed, an' laughed, an' laughed. Here you'd see a woman wid a pail on her head, rice a smokin' in it jus as she'd taken it from de fire, young one hangin' on behind, one han' roun' her forehead to hold on, 'tother han' diggin' into de rice-pot, eatin' wid all its might; hold of her dress two or three more; down her back a bag wid a pig in it. One woman brought two pigs, a white one, an' a black one; we took 'em all on board; named de white pig Beauregard, an' de black pig Jeff Davis. Sometimes de women would come wid twins hangin' roun' der necks; 'pears like I nebber see so many twins in my life; bags on der shoulders, baskets on der heads, and young ones taggin' behin', all loaded; pigs squealin', chickens screamin', young ones squallin'." And so they came pouring down to the gunboats. When they stood on the shore, and the small boats put out to take them off, they all wanted to get in at once. After the boats were crowded, they would hold on to them so that they could not leave the shore. The oarsmen would beat them on their hands, but they would not let go; they were afraid the gun-boats would go off and leave them, and all wanted to make sure of one of these arks of refuge. At length Col. Montgomery shouted from the upper deck, above the clamor of appealing tones, "Moses, you'll have to give 'em a song." Then Harriet lifted up her voice and sang:

"Of all the whole creation in the east or in the west,
The glorious Yankee nation is the greatest and the best.
Come along! Come along! don't be alarmed,
Uncle Sam is rich enough to give you all a farm."

At the end of every verse, the negroes in their enthusiasm would throw up their hands and shout "Glory," and the row-boats would take that opportunity to push off; and so at last they were all brought on board. The masters fled; houses and barns and railroad bridges were burned, tracks torn up, torpedoes destroyed, and the expedition was in all respects successful.

This fearless woman was often sent into the rebel lines as a spy, and brought back valuable information as to the position of armies and batteries; she has been in battle when the shot was falling like hail, and the bodies of dead and wounded men were dropping around her like leaves in autumn; but the thought of fear never seems to have had place for a moment in her mind. She had her duty to perform, and she expected to be taken care of till it was done.

Would that instead of taking them in this poor way at second-hand, my readers could hear this woman's graphic accounts of scenes she herself witnessed, could listen to her imitations of negro preachers in their own very peculiar dialect, her singing of camp-meeting hymns, her account of "experience meetings," her imitations of the dances, and the funeral ceremonies of these simple people. "Why, der language down dar in de far South is jus' as different from ours in Maryland, as you can think," said she. "Dey laughed when dey heard me talk, an' I could not understand dem, no how." She described a midnight funeral which she attended; for the slaves, never having been allowed to bury their dead in the day time, continued the custom of night funerals from habit.

The corpse was laid upon the ground, and the people all sat round, the group being lighted up by pine torches.

The old negro preacher began by giving out a hymn, which was sung by all. "An' oh! I wish you could hear 'em sing, Missus," said Harriet. "Der voices is so sweet, and dey can sing eberyting we sing, an' den dey can sing a great many hymns dat we can't nebber catch at all."

The old preacher began his sermon by pointing to the dead man, who lay in a rude box on the ground before him.

"Shum? Ded-a-de-dah! Shum, David? Ded-a-de-dah! Now I want you all to flec' for moment. Who ob all dis congregation is gwine next to lie ded-a-de-dah? You can't go nowheres, my frien's and bredren, but Deff 'll fin' you. You can't dig no hole so deep an' bury yourself dar, but God A'mighty's far-seein' eye 'll fine you, an' Deff 'll come arter you. You can't go into that big fort (pointing to Hilton Head), an' shut yourself up dar; dat fort dat Sesh Buckner said de debil couldn't take, but

Deff 'll fin' you dar. All your frien's may forget you, but Deff 'll nebber forget you. Now, my bredren, prepare to lie ded-a-de-dah!"

This was the burden of a very long sermon, after which the whole congregation went round in a sort of solemn dance, called the "spiritual shuffle," shaking hands with each other, and calling each other by name as they sang:

> My sis'r Mary's boun' to go;
> My sis'r Nanny's boun' to go;
> My brudder Tony's boun' to go;
> My brudder July's boun' to go.

This to the same tune, till every hand had been shaken by every one of the company. When they came to Harriet, who was a stranger, they sang:

> Eberybody's boun' to go!

The body was then placed in a Government wagon, and by the light of the pine torches, the strange, dark procession moved along, singing a rude funeral hymn, till they reached the place of burial.

Harriet's account of her interview with an old negro she met at Hilton Head, is amusing and interesting. He said "I'd been yere seventy-three years, workin' for my master widout even a dime wages. I'd worked rain-wet sun dry. I'd worked wid my mouf full of dust, but would not stop to get a drink of water. I'd been whipped, an' starved, an' I was always prayin', 'Oh! Lord, come an' delibber us!' All dat time de birds had been flyin', an' de rabens had been cryin', and de fish had been sunnin' in de waters. One day I look up, an' I see a big cloud; it didn't come up like as de clouds come out far yonder, but it 'peared to be right ober head. Der was tunders out of dat, an' der was lightnin's. Den I looked down on de water, an' I see, 'peared to me a big house in de water, an' out of de big house came great big eggs, and de good eggs went on trou' de air, an' fell into de fort; an' de bad eggs burst before dey got dar. Den de Sesh Buckra begin to run, an de neber stop running till de git to de swamp, an' de stick dar an' de die dar. Den I heard 'twas the Yankee ship[*]

[*] The Wabash.

firin' out de big eggs, an dey had come to set us free. Den I praise de Lord. He come an' put he little finger in de work, an' dey Sesh Buckra all go; and de birds stop flyin', and de rabens stop cryin', an' when I go to catch a fish to eat wid my rice, de 's no fish dar. De Lord A'mighty 'd come and frightened 'em all out of de waters. Oh! Praise de Lord! I 'd prayed seventy-three years, an' now he 's come an' we's all free."

The last time Harriet was returning from the war, with her pass as hospital nurse, she bought a half-fare ticket, as she was told she must do; and missing the other train, she got into an emigrant train on the Amboy Railroad. When the conductor looked at her ticket, he said, "Come, hustle out of here! We don't carry niggers for half-fare." Harriet explained to him that she was in the employ of Government, and was entitled to transportation as the soldiers were. But the conductor took her forcibly by the arm, and said, "I'll make you tired of trying to stay here." She resisted, and being very strong, she could probably have got the better of the conductor, had he not called three men to his assistance. The car was filled with emigrants, and no one seemed to take her part. The only word, she heard, accompanied with fearful oaths, were, "Pitch the nagur out!" They nearly wrenched her arm off, and at length threw her, with all their strength, into a baggage-car. She supposed her arm was broken, and in intense suffering she came on to New York. As she left the car, a delicate-looking young man came up to her, and, handing her a card, said, "You ought to sue that conductor, and if you want a witness, call on me." Harriet remained all winter under the care of a physician in New York; he advised her to sue the Railroad company, and said that he would willingly testify as to her injuries. But the card the young man had given her was only a visiting card, and she did not know where to find him, and so she let the matter go.

  The writer here finds it necessary to apologize for the very desultory and hasty manner in which this little book is written. Being herself pressed for time, in the expectation of soon leaving the country, she is obliged to pen down the material to be used in the short and interrupted interviews she can obtain with Harriet, and also to use such letters and accounts as may be sent her, as they come, without being able to work them in, in the order of time. A very material assistance is to be rendered her by the kind offer of an account of Harriet's services during the war, written by Mr. Charles P. Wood, of Auburn, and kindly copied by one of Harriet's most faithful and most efficient friends, Mrs. S. M. Hopkins, of that place.

It was a wise plan of our sagacious heroine to leave her old parents till the last to be brought away. They were pensioned off as too old to work, had a cabin, and a horse and cow, and were quite comfortable. If Harriet had taken them away before the young people, these last would have been sold into Southern slavery, to keep them out of her way. But at length Harriet heard that the old man had been betrayed by a slave whom he had assisted, but who had turned back, and when questioned by his wife, told her the story of his intended escape, and of the aid he had received from "Old Ben." This woman, hoping to curry favor with her master, revealed the whole to him, and "Old Ben" was arrested. He was to be tried the next week, when Harriet appeared upon the scene and, as she says, "saved dem de expense ob de trial,["] and removed her father to a higher court, by taking him off to Canada. The manner of their escape is detailed in the following letter from Thomas Garrett, the Wilmington Quaker:

WILMINGTON, 6th Mo., 1868.

MY FRIEND: Thy favor of the 12th reached me yesterday, requesting such reminiscences as I could give respecting the remarkable labors of Harriet Tubman, in aiding her colored friends from bondage. I may begin by saying, living as I have in a slave State, and the laws being very severe where my proof could be made of any one aiding slaves on their way to freedom, I have not felt at liberty to keep any written word of Harriet's or my own labors, except in numbering those whom I have aided. For that reason I cannot furnish so interesting an account of Harriet's labors as I otherwise could, and now would be glad to do; for in truth I never met with any person, of any color, who had more confidence in the voice of God, as spoken direct to her soul. She has frequently told me that she talked with God, and he talked with her every day of her life, and she has declared to me that she felt no more fear of being arrested by her former master, or any other person, when in his immediate neighborhood, than she did in the State of New York, or Canada, for she said she never ventured only where God sent her, and her faith in a Supreme Power truly was great.

I have now been confined to my room with indisposition more than four weeks, and cannot sit to write much; but I feel so much interested in Harriet that I will try to give some of the most remarkable incidents that now present themselves to my mind. The date of the commencement of her labors, I cannot certainly give; but I think it must have been about 1845; from that time till 1860, I think she must have brought from the neighborhood where she had been held as a slave, from 60 to 80 persons, from Maryland, some 80 miles from here. No slave who placed himself under her care, was ever arrested that I have heard of; she mostly had her regular stopping places on her route; but in one instance, when she had two stout men with her, some 30 miles below here, she said that God told her to stop, which she did; and then asked him what she must do. He told her to leave the road, and turn to the left; she obeyed, and soon came to a small stream of tide water; there was no boat, no bridge; she again inquired of her Guide what she was to do. She was told to go through. It was cold, in the month of March; but having confidence in her Guide, she went in; the water came up to her arm-pits; the men refused to follow till they saw her safe on the opposite shore. They then followed, and if I mistake not, she had soon to wade a second stream; soon after which she came to a cabin of colored people, who took them all in, put them to bed, and dried their clothes, ready to proceed next night on their journey. Harriet had run out of money, and gave them some of her underclothing to pay for their kindness. When she called on me two days after, she was so hoarse she could hardly speak, and was also suffering with violent toothache. The strange part of the story we found to be, that the master of these two men had put up the previous day, at the railroad station near where she left, an advertisement for them, offering a large reward for their apprehension; but they made a safe exit. She at one time brought as many as seven or eight, several of whom were women and children. She was well known here in Chester County and

Philadelphia, and respected by all true abolitionists. I had been in the habit of furnishing her and those that accompanied her, as she returned from her acts of mercy, with new shoes; and on one occasion when I had not seen her for three months, she came into my store. I said, "Harriet, I am glad to see thee! I suppose thee wants a pair of new shoes." Her reply was "I want more than that." I, in jest, said, "I have always been liberal with thee, and wish to be; but I am not rich, and cannot afford to give much." Her reply was: "God tells me you have money for me." I asked her "if God never deceived her?" She said, "No!" "Well! how much does thee want?" After studying a moment, she said: "About twenty-three dollars." I then gave her twenty-four dollars and some odd cents, the net proceeds of five pounds sterling, received through Eliza Wigham, of Scotland, for her. I had given some accounts of Harriet's labor to the Anti-Slavery Society of Edinburgh, of which Eliza Wigham was Secretary. On the reading of my letter, a gentleman present said he would send Harriet four pounds if he knew of any way to get it to her. Eliza Wigham offered to forward it to me for her, and that was the first money ever received by me for her. Some twelve months after, she called on me again, and said that God told her I had some money for her, but not so much as before. I had, a few days previous, received the net proceeds of one pound ten shillings from Europe for her. To say the least, there was something remarkable in these facts, whether clairvoyance, or the divine impression on her mind from the source of all power, I cannot tell; but certain it was she had a guide within herself other than the written word, for she never had any education. She brought away her aged parents in a singular manner. They started with an old horse, fitted out in primitive style with a straw collar, a pair of old chaise wheels, with a board on the axle to sit on, another board swung with ropes, fastened to the axle, to rest their feet on. She got her parents, who were both slaves belonging to different masters, on this rude vehicle to the railroad, put them in the cars, turned Jehu herself, and drove to town in a style that no human being ever did before or since; but she was happy at having arrived safe. Next day, I furnished her with money to take them all to Canada. I afterwards sold their horse, and sent them the balance of the proceeds. I believe that Harriet succeeded in freeing all her relatives but one sister and her three children. Etc., etc.

Thy friend,

THOS. GARRETT.

Friend Garrett probably refers here to those who passed through his hands. Harriet was obliged to come by many different routes on her different journeys, and though she never counted those whom she brought away with her, it would seem, by the computation of others, that there must have been somewhere near three hundred brought by her to the Northern States and Canada.

Extracts from a letter written by Mr. Sanborn, Secretary of the Massachusetts Board of State Charities.

My DEAR MADAME: Mr. Phillips has sent me your note, asking for reminiscences of Harriet Tubman, and testimonials to her extraordinary story, which all her New England friends will, I am sure, be glad to furnish.

I never had reason to doubt the truth of what Harriet said in regard to her own career, for I found her singularly truthful. Her imagination is warm and rich, and there is a whole region of the marvelous in her nature, which has manifested itself at times remarkably. Her dreams and visions, misgivings and forewarnings, ought not to be omitted in any life of her, particularly those relating to John Brown.

She was in his confidence in 1858-9, and he had a great regard for her, which he often expressed to me. She aided him in his plans, and expected to do so still further, when his career was closed by that wonderful campaign in Virginia. The first time she came to my house, in Concord, after that tragedy, she was shown into a room in the evening, where Brackett's bust of John Brown was standing. The sight of it, which was new to her, threw her into a sort of ecstacy of sorrow and admiration, and she went on in her rhapsodical way to pronounce his apotheosis.

She has often been in Concord, where she resided at the houses of Emerson, Alcott, the Whitneys, the

Brooks family, Mrs. Horace Mann, and other well known persons. They all admired and respected her, and nobody doubted the reality of her adventures. She was too real a person to be suspected. In 1862, I think it was, she went from Boston to Port Royal, under the advice and encouragement of Mr. Garrison, Governor Andrew, Dr. Howe, and other leading people. Her career in South Carolina is well known to some of our officers, and I think to Colonel Higginson, now of Newport, R. I., and Colonel James Montgomery, of Kansas, to both of whom she was useful as a spy and guide, if I mistake not. I regard her as, on the whole, the most extraordinary person of her race I have ever met. She is a negro of pure or almost pure blood, can neither read nor write, and has the characteristics of her race and condition. But she has done what can scarcely be credited on the best authority, and she has accomplished her purposes with a coolness, foresight, patience, and wisdom, which in a white man would have raised him to the highest pitch of reputation.

I am, dear Madame, very truly your servant,

F. B. SANBORN.

Of the "dreams and visions" mentioned in this letter, the writer might have given many wonderful instances; but it was thought best not to insert anything which, with any, might bring discredit upon the story. When these turns of somnolency come upon Harriet, she imagines that her "spirit" leaves her body, and visits other scenes and places, not only in this world, but in the world of spirits. And her ideas of these scenes show, to say the least of it, a vividness of imagination seldom equaled in the soarings of the most cultivated minds.

Not long since, the writer, on going into Harriet's room in the morning, sat down by her and began to read that wonderful and glorious description of the heavenly Jerusalem in the two last chapters of Revelations. When the reading was finished, Harriet burst into a rhapsody which perfectly amazed her hearer--telling of what she had seen in one of these visions, sights which no one could doubt had been real to her, and which no human imagination could have conceived, it would seem, unless in dream or vision. There was a wild poetry in these descriptions which seemed to border almost on inspiration, but by many they might be characterized as the ravings of insanity. All that can be said is, however, if this woman is insane, there has been a wonderful "method in her madness."

At one time, Harriet was much troubled in spirit about her three brothers, feeling sure that some great evil was impending over their heads. She wrote a letter, by the hand of a friend, to a man named Jacob Jackson, who lived near there. Jacob was a free negro, who could both read and write, and who was under suspicion at that time, as it was thought he had something to do with the disappearance of so many slaves. It was necessary, therefore, to be very cautious in writing to him. Jacob had an adopted son, William Henry Jackson, also free, who had come South; and so Harriet determined to sign her letter with his name, knowing that Jacob would be clever enough to understand, by her peculiar phraseology, what meaning she intended to convey to him. She, therefore, after speaking of indifferent matters, said, "Read my letter to the old folks, and give my love to them, and tell my brothers to be always watching unto prayer, and when the good old ship of Zion comes along, to be ready to step aboard."

The letter was signed "William Henry Jackson." Jacob was not allowed to have his letters till the self-elected inspectors had had the reading of them, and studied into their secret meaning. They, therefore, got together, wiped their glasses, and got them on, and proceeded to a careful perusal of this mysterious document. What it meant, they could not imagine; William Henry Jackson had no parents or brothers, and the letter was incomprehensible. White genius having exhausted itself, black genius was called in, and Jacob's letter was at last handed to him. Jacob saw at once what it meant, but tossed it down, saying, "Dat letter can't be meant for me, no how. I can't make head nor tail of it," and walked off and took immediate measures to let Harriet's brothers know secretly that she was coming, and they must be ready to start at a moment's notice for the North. When Harriet arrived there, it was the day before Christmas, and she found her three brothers, who had attempted to escape, were advertised to be sold on Christmas day to the highest bidder, to go down to the cotton and rice fields with the chain gang. Christmas came on Sunday, and therefore they were not to be sold till Monday. Harriet arrived on Saturday, and gave them secret notice to be ready to start Saturday night, immediately after dark, the first stopping-place to be their father's cabin, forty miles away. When they assembled, their brother John was missing; but when Harriet was ready, the word was "Forward!" and she "nebber waited for no one." Poor John was almost ready to start, when his wife was taken ill, and in an hour or two, another little inheritor of the blessings of slavery had come into the world. John must go off for a "Granny," and then he would not leave his wife in her present circumstances. But after the birth of the child, he began to think he must start; the North and Liberty, or the South and life-long Slavery--these were the alternatives, and this was his last chance. He tried again and again to steal out of the door, but a watchful eye was on him, and he was always arrested by the question, "Where you gwine John?" At length he told her he was going to try to see if he couldn't get hired out on Christmas to another man. His wife did not think that he was to be sold. He went out of the door, and stood by the corner of the house, near her bed, listening. At length, he heard her sobbing and crying, and not being able to endure it, he went back. "Oh! John," said his wife, "you's gwine to lebe me; but, wherebber you go, remember me an' de chillen." John went out and started at full speed for his father's cabin, forty miles away. At daybreak, he overtook the others in the "fodder house," near the cabin of their parents. Harriet had not seen her mother there for six years, but they did not dare to let the old woman know of their being in her neighborhood, or of their intentions, for she would have raised such an uproar in her efforts to detain them with her, that the whole plantation would have been alarmed. The poor old woman had been expecting the boys all day, to spend Christmas with her as usual. She had been hard at work, had killed a pig, and put it to all the various uses to which sinner's flesh is doomed, and had made all the preparations her circumstances admitted of, to give them a sumptuous entertainment, and there she sat watching. In the night, when Harriet and two of her brothers and two other men, who had escaped with them, arrived at the "fodder house," they were exhausted and famished. They sent the two strange men up to the house to try and speak to "Old Ben," their father, but not to let their mother know of their being in the neighborhood. The men succeeded in rousing old Ben, who came out, and as soon as he heard their story, he gathered together a quantity of provisions, and came down to the fodder house, and slipped them inside the door, taking care not to see his children. Up among the ears of corn they lay, and one of them he had not seen for six years. It rained very hard all that Sunday, and there they lay all day, for they could not start till night. At about daybreak, John joined them. There were wide chinks in the boards of the fodder house, and through them they could see their father's cabin; and all day long, every few minutes, they would see the old woman come out, and, shading her eyes with her hand, take a long look down the road to see if her children were coming, and then they could almost hear her sigh as she turned into the house, disappointed.

Two or three times, the old man came down, and pushed food inside the door, and after nightfall he came to accompany them part of the way upon their journey. When he reached the fodder house, he tied his handkerchief tight over his eyes, and two of his sons taking him by each arm, he accompanied them some miles upon their journey. They then bade him farewell, and left him standing blind-fold in the middle of the road. When he could no longer hear their footsteps, he took off the handkerchief, and turned back.

But before leaving, they had gone up to the cabin to take a silent farewell of the poor old mother. Through the little window of the cabin, they saw the old woman sitting by her fire with a pipe in her mouth, her head on her hand, rocking back and forth as she did when she was in trouble, and wondering what new evil had come to her children. With streaming eyes, they watched her for ten or fifteen minutes; but time was precious, and they must reach their next station before daybreak, and so they turned sadly away.

When the holidays were over, and the men came for the three brothers to sell them, they could not be found. The first place to search was of course the plantation where all their relatives and friends lived. They went to the "big house," and asked the "Doctor" if he had seen anything of them. The Doctor said, "No, they mostly came up there to see the other niggers when they came for Christmas, but they hadn't been round at all.["] "Have you been down to Old Ben's?" the Doctor asked. "Yes." "What does Old Rit say?" "Old Rit says not one of 'em came this Christmas. She was looking for 'em most all day, and most broke her heart about it." "What does Old Ben say?" "Old Ben says that he hasn't seen one of his children this Christmas." "Well, if Old Ben says that, they haven't been round." And so the man-hunters went off disappointed.

One of the other brothers, William Henry, had long been attached to a girl named Catherine, who lived with another master; but her master would not let her marry him. When William Henry made up his mind to start with Harriet, he determined to bring Catherine with him. And so he went to a tailor's, and bought a new suit of men's clothes, and threw them over the garden fence of Catherine's master. The garden ran down to a run, and Catherine had been notified where to find the clothes. When the time had come to get ready, Catherine went to the foot of the garden and dressed herself in the suit of men's clothes. She was soon missed, and all the girls in the house were set to looking for Catherine. Presently they saw coming up through the garden, as if from the river, a well-dressed little darkey, and they all stopped looking for Catherine to stare at him. He walked directly by them round the house, and went out of the gate, without the slightest suspicion being excited as to who he was. In a fortnight from that time, the whole party were safe in Canada.

William Henry died in Canada, but Catherine has been seen and talked with by the writer, at the house of the old people.

Of the many letters, testimonials, and passes, placed in the hands of the writer by Harriet, the following are selected for insertion in this book, and are quite sufficient to verify her statements.

A Letter from Gen. Saxton to a Lady of Auburn.

ATLANTA, GA., March 21, 1868.

MY DEAR MADAME: I have just received your letter informing me that Hon. Wm. H. Seward, Secretary of State, would present a petition to Congress for a pension to Harriet Tubman, for services rendered in the Union Army during the late war. I can bear witness to the value of her services in South Carolina and Florida. She was employed in the hospitals and as a spy. She made many a raid inside the enemy's lines, displaying remarkable courage, zeal, and fidelity. She was employed by General Hunter, and I think by Generals Stevens and Sherman, and is as deserving of a pension from the Government for her services as any other of its faithful servants.

I am very truly yours,

RUFUS SAXTON, Bvt. Brig.-Gen. U. S. A.

Letter from Hon. Wm. H. Seward.

WASHINGTON, July 25, 1868.

MAJ.-GEN. HUNTER--

My DEAR SIR: Harriet Tubman, a colored woman, has been nursing our soldiers during nearly all the war. She believes she has a claim for faithful services to the command in South Carolina with which you are connected, and she thinks that you would be disposed to see her claim justly settled.

I have known her long, and a nobler, higher spirit, or a truer, seldom dwells in the human form. I commend her, therefore, to your kind and best attentions.

Faithfully your friend,

WILLIAM H. SEWARD.

Letter from Col. James Montgomery.

ST. HELENA ISLAND, S. C., July 6, 1863.
HEADQUARTERS COLORED BRIGADE.

BRIG.-GEN. GILMAN, Commanding Department of the South--

GENERAL: I wish to commend to your attention, Mrs. Harriet Tubman, a most remarkable woman, and invaluable as a scout. I have been acquainted with her character and actions for several years.

Walter D. Plowden is a man of tried courage, and can be made highly useful.

I am, General, your most ob't servant,

JAMES MONTGOMERY, Col. Com. Brigade.

Letter from Mrs. Gen. A. Baird.

PETERBORO, Nov. 24, 1864.

The bearer of this, Harriet Tubman, a most excellent woman, who has rendered faithful and good services to our Union army, not only in the hospital, but in various capacities, having been employed under Government at Hilton Head, and in Florida; and I commend her to the protection of all officers in whose department she may happen to be.

She has been known and esteemed for years by the family of my uncle, Hon. Gerrit Smith, as a person of great rectitude and capabilities.

Mrs. GEN. A. BAIRD.

Letter from Hon. Gerrit Smith.

PETERBORO, N. Y., Nov. 4, 1867.

I have known Mrs. Harriet Tubman for many years. Seldom, if ever, have I met with a person more philanthropic, more self-denying, and of more bravery. Nor must I omit to say that she combines with her sublime spirit, remarkable discernment and judgment.

During the late war, Mrs. Tubman was eminently faithful and useful to the cause of our country. She is poor and has poor parents. Such a servant of the country should be well paid by the country. I hope that the Government will look into her case.

GERRIT SMITH.

Testimonial from Gerrit Smith.

PETERBORO, Nov. 22, 1864.

The bearer, Harriet Tubman, needs not any recommendation. Nearly all the nation over, she has been heard of for her wisdom, integrity, patriotism, and bravery. The cause of freedom owes her much. The country owes her much.

I have known Harriet for many years, and I hold her in my high esteem.

GERRIT SMITH.

Certificate from Henry K. Durrant, Acting Asst. Surgeon, U. S. A.

I certify that I have been acquainted with Harriet Tubman for nearly two years; and my position as Medical Officer in charge of "contrabands" in this town and in hospital, has given me frequent and ample opportunities to observe her general deportment; particularly her kindness and attention to the sick and suffering of her own race. I take much pleasure in testifying to the esteem in which she is generally held.

HENRY K. DURRANT,
Acting Assistant Surgeon, U. S. A. In charge "Contraband" Hospital.

Dated at Beaufort, S. C., the 3d day of May, 1864. I concur fully in the above.
R. SAXTON, Brig.-Gen. Vol.

The following are a few of the passes used by Harriet throughout the war. Many others are so defaced that it is impossible to decipher them.

HEADQUARTERS DEPARTMENT OF THE SOUTH, HILTON HEAD, PORT ROYAL, S. C., Feb. 19, 1863.

Pass the bearer, Harriet Tubman, to Beaufort and back to this place, and wherever she wishes to go; and give her free passage at all times, on all Government transports. Harriet was sent to me from Boston by Gov. Andrew of Mass., and is a valuable woman. She has permission, as a servant of the Government, to purchase such provisions from the Commissary as she may need.

D. HUNTER, Maj.-Gen. Com.

General Gillman, who succeeded General Hunter in command of the Department of the South, appends his signature to the same pass.

HEADQUARTERS OF THE DEPARTMENT OF THE SOUTH,
July 1, 1863.

Continued in force.

I. A. GILLMAN, Brig.-Gen. Com.

BEAUFORT, Aug. 28, 1862.

Will Capt. Warfield please let "Moses" have a little Bourbon whiskey for medicinal purposes.

HENRY K. DURRANT, Act. Ass. Surgeon.

WAR DEPARTINIENT, WASHINGTON, D. C.,
March 20, 1865.

Pass Mrs. Harriet Tubman (colored) to Hilton Head and Charleston, S. C., with free transportation on a Government transport.

By order of the Sec. of War.

> Louis H., Asst. Adj.-Gen., U. S. A.
> To Bvt. Brig.-Gen. Van Vliet, U. S. Q. M., N. Y.

Not transferable.

> WAR DEPARTMENT, WASHINGTON, D. C.,
> July 22, 1865.

Permit Harriet Tubman to proceed to Fortress Monroe, Va., on a Government transport. Transportation will be furnished free of cost.

By order of the Secretary of War.

> L. H., Asst. Adj.-Gen.

Not transferable.

Appointment as Nurse.

SIR:--I have the honor to inform you that the Medical Director Department of Virginia has been instructed to appoint Harriet Tubman nurse or matron at the Colored Hospital, Fort Monroe, Va.

Very respectfully, your obdt. servant,

V. K. BARNES, Surgeon-General.

Hon. WM. H. SEWARD,
Secretary of State, Washington, D. C.

Names of Harriet's Assistants, Scouts, or Pilots.

Scouts who are residents of Beaufort, and well acquainted with the main land: Peter Barns, Mott Blake, Sandy Selters, Solomon Gregory, Isaac Hayward, Gabriel Cohen, George Chrisholm.

Pilots who know the channels of the rivers in this vicinity, and who acted as such for Col. Montgomery up the Combahee River: Charles Simmons, Samuel Hayward.

App'd, R. SAXTON, Brig.-Gen.

At this point the following good and kind letter from Rev. Henry Fowler is received:

AUBURN, June 23, 1868.

MY DEAR FRIEND:--I wish to say to you how gratified I am that you are writing the biography of Harriet Tubman. I feel that her life forms part of the history of the country, and that it ought not to depend upon tradition to keep it in remembrance. Had not the pressure of professional claims prevented, I should have aspired to be her historian myself; but my disappointment in this regard is more than met by the satisfaction experienced in hearing that you are the chosen Miriam of this African "Moses;" the name by which she was known among her emancipated followers from the land of bondage. Blessed be God! a "Greater than Moses" has at last broken every bond.

As ever, with warm regard, your friend,

HENRY FOWLER.

The following account of the subject of this memoir is cut from the Boston Commonwealth of 1863, kindly sent the writer by Mr. Sanborn:

"It was said long ago that the true romance of America was not in the fortunes of the Indian, where Cooper sought it, nor in the New England character, where Judd found it, nor in the social contrasts of Virginia planters, as Thackeray imagined, but in the story of the fugitive slaves. The observation is as true now as it was before war, with swift, gigantic hand, sketched the vast shadows, and dashed in the high lights in which romance loves to lurk and flash forth. But the stage is enlarged on which those dramas are played, the whole world now sit as spectators, and the desperation or the magnanimity of a poor black woman has power to shake the nation that so long was deaf to her cries. We write of one of these heroines, of whom our slave annals are full,--a woman whose career is as extraordinary as the most famous of her sex can show.

"Araminta Ross, now known by her married name of Tubman, with her sounding Christian name changed to Harriet, is the grand-daughter of a slave imported from Africa, and has not a drop of white blood in her veins. Her parents were Benjamin Ross and Harriet Greene, both slaves, but married and faithful to each other. They still live in old age and poverty, but free, on a little property at Auburn, N. Y., which their daughter purchased for them from Mr. Seward, the Secretary of State. She was born, as near as she can remember, in 1820 or in 1821, in Dorchester County, on the Eastern shore of Maryland, and not far from the town of Cambridge. She had ten brothers and sisters, of whom three are now living, all at the North, and all rescued from slavery by Harriet, before the War. She went back just as the South was preparing to secede, to bring away a fourth, but before she could reach her, she was dead. Three years before, she had brought away her old father and mother, at great risk to herself.

"When Harriet was six years old, she was taken from her mother and carried ten miles to live with James Cook, whose wife was a weaver, to learn the trade of weaving. While still a mere child, Cook set her to watching his musk-rat traps, which compelled her to wade through the water. It happened that she was once sent when she was ill with the measles, and, taking cold from wading in the water in this condition, she grew very sick, and her mother persuaded her master to take her away from Cook's until she could get well.

"Another attempt was made to teach her weaving, but she would not learn, for she hated her mistress, and did not want to live at home, as she would have done as a weayer, for it was the custom then to weave the cloth for the family, or a part of it, in the house.

"Soon after she entered her teens she was hired out as a field hand, and it was while thus employed that she received a wound which nearly proved fatal, from the effects of which she still suffers. In the fall of the year, the slaves there work in the evening, cleaning up wheat, husking corn, etc. On this occasion, one of the slaves of a farmer named Barrett, left his work, and went to the village store in the evening. The overseer followed him, and so did Harriet. When the slave was found, the overseer swore he should be whipped, and called on Harriet, among others, to help tie him. She refused, and as the man ran away, she placed herself in the door to stop pursuit. The overseer caught up a two-pound weight from the counter and threw it at the fugitive, but it fell short and struck Harriet a stunning blow on the head. It was long before she recovered from this, and it has left her subject to a sort of stupor or lethargy at times; coming upon her in the midst of conversation, or whatever she may be doing, and throwing her into a deep slumber, from which she will presently rouse herself, and go on with her conversation or work.

"After this she lived for five or six years with John Stewart, where at first she worked in the house, but afterwards 'hired her time,' and Dr. Thompson, son of her master's guardian, 'stood for her,' that is, was her surety for the payment of what she owed. She employed the time thus hired in the rudest labors,--drove oxen, carted, plowed, and did all the work of a man,-- sometimes earning money enough in a year, beyond what she paid her master, 'to buy a pair of steers,' worth forty dollars. The amount exacted of a woman for her time was fifty or sixty dollars,--of a man, one hundred to one hundred and fifty dollars. Frequently Harriet worked for her father, who was a timber inspector, and superintended the cutting and hauling of great quantities of timber for the Baltimore shipyards. Stewart, his temporary master, was a builder, and for the work of Ross used to receive as much as five dollars a day sometimes, he being a superior workman. While engaged with her father, she would cut wood, haul logs, etc. Her usual 'stint' was half a cord of wood in a day.

"Harriet was married somewhere about 1844, to a free colored man named John Tubman, but she had no children. For the last two years of slavery she lived with Dr. Thompson, before mentioned, her own master not being yet of age, and Dr. T.'s father being his guardian, as well as the owner of her own father. In 1849 the young man died, and the slaves were to be sold, though previously set free by an old will. Harriet resolved not to be sold, and so, with no knowledge of the North --having only heard of Pennsylvania and New Jersey--she walked away one night alone. She found a friend in a white lady, who knew her story and helped her on her way. After many adventures, she reached Philadelphia, where she found work and earned a small stock of money. With this money in her purse, she traveled back to Maryland for her husband, but she found him married to another woman, and no longer caring to live with her. This, however, was not until two years after her escape, for she does not seem to have reached her old home in her first two expeditions. In December, 1850, she had visited Baltimore and brought away her sister and two children, who had come up from Cambridge in a boat, under charge of her sister's husband, a free black. A few months after she had brought away her brother and two other men, but it was not till the fall of 1851 that she found her husband and learned of his infidelity. She did not give way to rage or grief, but collected a part of fugitives and brought them safely to Philadelphia. In December of the same year, she returned, and led out a party of eleven, among them her brother and his wife. With these she journeyed to Canada, and there spent the winter, for this was after the enforcement of Mason's Fugitive Slave Bill in Philadelphia and Boston, and there was no safety except 'under the paw of the British Lion,' as she quaintly said. But the first winter was terribly severe for these poor runaways. They earned their bread by chopping wood in the snows of a Canadian forest; they were frost-bitten, hungry, and naked. Harriet was their good angel. She kept house for her brother, and the poor creatures boarded with her. She worked for them, begged for them, prayed for them, with the strange familiarity of communion with God which seems natural to these people, and carried them by the help of God through the hard winter.

"In the spring she returned to the States, and as usual earned money by working in hotels and families as a cook. From Cape May, in the fall of 1852, she went back once more to Maryland, and brought away nine more fugitives.

"Up to this time she had expended chiefly her own money in these expeditions--money which she had earned by hard work in the drudgery of the kitchen. Never did any one more exactly fulfill the sense of George Herbert--

"A servant with this clause
Makes drudgery divine."

"But it was not possible for such virtues long to remain hidden from the keen eyes of the Abolitionists. She became known to Thomas Garrett, the large-hearted Quaker of Wilmington, who has aided the escape of three thousand fugitives; she found warm friends in Philadelphia and New York, and wherever she went. These gave her money, which she never spent for her own use, but laid up for the help of her people, and especially for her journeys back to the 'land of Egypt,' as she called her old home. By reason of her frequent visits there, always carrying away some of the oppressed, she got among her people the name of 'Moses,' which it seems she still retains.

"Between 1852 and 1857, she made but two of these journeys, in consequence partly of the increased vigilance of the slaveholders, who had suffered so much by the loss of their property. A great reward was offered for her capture, and she several times was on the point of being taken, but always escaped by her quick wit, or by 'warnings' from Heaven--for it is time to notice one singular trait in her character. She is the most shrewd and practical person in the world, yet she is a firm believer in omens, dreams, and warnings. She declares that before her escape from slavery, she used to dream of flying over fields and towns, and rivers and mountains, looking down upon them 'like a bird,' and reaching at last a great fence, or sometimes a river, over which she would try to fly, 'but it 'peard like I wouldn't hab de strength, and jes as I was sinkin' down, dare would be ladies all drest in white ober dere, and dey would put out dere arms and pull me 'cross.' There is nothing strange in this, perhaps, but she declares that when she came North she remembered these very places as those she had seen in her dreams, and many of the ladies who befriended her were those she had been helped by in her visions.

"Then she says she always knows when there is danger near her,--she does not know how, exactly, but ' 'pears like my heart go flutter, flutter, and den dey may say "Peace, Peace," as much as dey likes, I know its gwine to be war!' She is very firm on this point, and ascribes to this her great impunity, in spite of the lethargy before mentioned, which would seem likely to throw her into the hands of her enemies. She says she inherited this power, that her father could always predict the weather, and that he foretold the Mexican war.

"In 1857 she made her most venturesome journey, for she brought with her to the North her old parents, who were no longer able to walk such distances as she must go by night. Consequently she must hire a wagon for them, and it required all her ingenuity to get them through Maryland and Delaware safe. She accomplished it, however, and by the aid of her friends she brought them safe to Canada, where they spent the winter. Her account of their sufferings there--of her mother's complaining and her own philosophy about it--is a lesson of trust in Providence better than many sermons. But she decided to bring them to a more comfortable place, and so she negotiated with Mr. Seward--then in the Senate--for a little patch of ground with a house on it, at Auburn, near his own home. To the credit of the Secretary of State it should be said, that he sold her the property on very favorable terms, and gave her some time for payment. To this house she removed her parents, and set herself to work to pay for her purchase. It was on this errand that she first visited Boston--we believe in the winter of 1858-9. She brought a few letters from her friends in New York, but she could herself neither read nor write, and she was obliged to trust to her wits that they were delivered to the right persons. One of them, as it happened, was to the present writer, who received it by another hand, and called to see her at her boarding-house. It was curious to see the caution with which she received her visitor until she felt assured that there was no mistake. One of her means of security was to carry with her the daguerreotypes of her friends, and show them to each new person. If they recognized the likeness, then it was all right.

"Pains were taken to secure her the attention to which her great services to humanity entitled her, and she left New England with a handsome sum of money towards the payment of her debt to Mr. Seward. Before she left, however, she had several interviews with Captain Brown, then in Boston. He is supposed to have communicated his plans to her, and to have been aided by her in obtaining recruits and money among her people. At any rate, he always spoke of her with the greatest respect, and declared that 'General Tubman,' as he styled her, was a better officer than most whom he had seen, and could command an army as successfully as she had led her small parties of fugitives.

"Her own veneration for Captain Brown has always been profound, and since his murder, has taken the form of a religion. She had often risked her own life for her people, and she thought nothing of that; but that a white man, and a man so noble and strong, should so take upon himself the burden of a despised race, she could not understand, and she took refuge from her perplexity in the mysteries of her fervid religion.

"Again, she laid great stress on a dream which she had just before she met Captain Brown in Canada. She thought she was in 'a wilderness sort of place, all full of rocks and bushes,' when she saw a serpent raise its head among the rocks, and as it did so, it became the head of an old man with a long white beard, gazing at her 'wishful like, jes as ef he war gwine to speak to me,' and then two other heads rose up beside him, younger than he,-- and as she stood looking at them, and wondering what they could want with her, a great crowd of men rushed in and struck down the younger heads, and then the head of the old man, still looking at her so 'wishful.' This dream she had again and again, and could not interpret it; but, when she met Captain Brown, shortly after, behold, he was the very image of the head she had seen. But still she could not make out what her dream signified, till the news came to her of the tragedy of Harper's Ferry, and then she knew the two other heads were his two sons. She was in New York at that time, and on the day of the affair at Harper's Ferry, she felt her usual warning that something was wrong--she could not tell what. Finally she told her hostess that it must be Captain Brown who was in trouble, and that they should soon hear bad news from him. The next day's newspaper brought tidings of what had happened.

"Her last visit to Maryland was made after this, in December, 1860; and in spite of the agitated condition of the country, and the greater watchfulness of the slaveholders, she brought away seven fugitives, one of them an infant, which must be drugged with opium to keep it from crying on the way, and so revealing the hiding place of the party. She brought these safely to New York, but there a new difficulty met her. It was the mad winter of compromises, when State after State, and politician after politician, went down on their knees to beg the South not to secede. The hunting of fugitive slaves began again. Mr. Seward went over to the side of compromise. He knew the history of this poor woman;

he had given his enemies a hold on him, by dealing with her; it was thought he would not scruple to betray her. The suspicion was an unworthy one, for though the Secretary could betray a cause, he could not surely have put her enemies on the track of a woman who was thus in his power, after such a career as hers had been. But so little confidence was then felt in Mr. Seward, by men who had voted for him and with him, that they hurried Harriet off to Canada, sorely against her will.

"She did not long remain there. The war broke out, for which she had been long looking, and she hastened to her New England friends to prepare for another expedition to Maryland, to bring away the last of her family.

"Before she could start, however, the news came of the capture of Port Royal. Instantly she conceived the idea of going there and working among her people on the islands and the mainland. Money was given her, a pass was secured through the agency of Governor Andrew, and she went to Beaufort. There she has made herself useful in many ways--has been employed as a spy by General Hunter, and finally has piloted Col. Montgomery on his most successful expedition. We gave some notice of this fact last week. Since then we have received the following letter, dictated by her, from which it appears that she needs some contributions for her work. We trust she will receive them, for none has better deserved it. She asks nothing for herself, except that her wardrobe may be replenished, and even this she will probably share with the first needy person she meets.

"'BEAUFORT, S. C., June 30, 1863.

* * * "'Last fall, when the people here became very much alarmed for fear of an invasion from the rebels, all my clothes were packed and sent with others to Hilton Head, and lost; and I have never been able to get any trace of them since. I was sick at the time, and unable to look after them myself. I want, among the rest, a bloomer dress, made of some coarse, strong material, to wear on expeditions. In our late expedition up the Combahee River, in coming on board the boat, I was carrying two pigs for a poor sick woman, who had a child to carry, and the order "double quick" was given, and I started to run, stepped on my dress, it being rather long, and fell and tore it almost off, so that when I got on board the boat, there was hardly anything left of it but shreds. I made up my mind then I would never wear a long dress on another expedition of the kind, but would have a bloomer as soon as I could get it. So please make this known to the ladies, if you will, for I expect to have use for it very soon, probably before they can get it to me.

"'You have, without doubt, seen a full account of the expedition I refer to. Don't you think we colored people are entitled to some credit for that exploit, under the lead of the brave Colonel Montgomery? We weakened the rebels somewhat on the Combahee River, by taking and bringing away seven hundred and fifty-six head of their most valuable live stock, known up in your region as "contrabands," and this, too, without the loss of a single life on our part, though we had good reason to believe that a number of rebels bit the dust. Of these seven hundred and fifty-six contrabands, nearly or quite all the able-bodied men have joined the colored regiments here.

"'I have now been absent two years almost, and have just got letters from my friends in Auburn, urging me to come home. My father and mother are old and in feeble health, and need my care and attention. I hope the good people there will not allow them to suffer, and I do not believe they will. But I do not see how I am to leave at present the very important work to be done here. Among other duties which I have, is that of looking after the hospital here for contrabands. Most of those coming from the mainland are very destitute, almost naked. I am trying to find places for those able to work, and provide for them as best I can, so as to lighten the burden on the Government as much as possible, while at the same time they learn to respect themselves by earning their own living.

"'Remember me very kindly to Mrs.--and her daughters; also, if you will, to my Boston friends, Mrs. C., Miss H., and especially to Mr. and Mrs. George L. Stearns, to whom I am under great obligations for their many kindnesses. I shall be sure to come and see you all if I live to go North. If you write, direct your letter to the care of C.'"

In the Spring of 1860, Harriet Tubman was requested by Mr. Gerrit Smith to go to Boston to attend a large Anti-Slavery meeting. On her way, she stopped at Troy to visit a cousin, and while there, the colored people were one day startled with the intelligence that a fugitive slave, by the name of Charles Nalle, had been followed by his master (who was his younger brother, and not one grain whiter than he), and that he was already in the hands of the officers, and was to be taken back to the South. The instant Harriet heard the news, she started for the office of the U. S. Commissioner, scattering the tidings as she went. An excited crowd were gathered about the office, through which Harriet forced her way, and rushed up stairs to the door of the room where the fugitive was detained. A wagon was already waiting before the door to carry off the man, but the crowd was even then so great, and in such a state of excitement, that the officers did not dare to bring the man down. On the opposite side of the street stood the colored people, watching the window where they could see Harriet's sun-bonnet, and feeling assured that so long as she stood there, the fugitive was still in the office. Time passed on, and he did not appear. "They've taken him out another way, depend upon that," said some of the colored people. "No," replied others, "there stands 'Moses' yet, and as long as she is there, he is safe." Harriet, now seeing the necessity for a tremendous effort for his rescue, sent out some little boys to cry fire. The bells rang, the crowd increased, till the whole street was a dense mass of people. Again and again, the officers came out to try and clear the stairs, and make a way to take their captive down; others were driven down, but Harriet stood her ground, her head bent down, and her arms folded. "Come, old woman, you must get out of this," said one of the officers; "I must have the way cleared; if you can't get down alone, someone will help you." Harriet, still putting on a greater appearance of decrepitude, twitched away from him, and kept her place. Offers were made to buy Charles from his master, who at first agreed to take twelve hundred dollars for him; but when that was subscribed, he immediately raised the price to fifteen hundred. The crowd grew more excited. A gentleman raised a window and called out, "Two hundred dollars for his rescue, but not one cent to his master!" This was responded to by a roar of satisfaction from the crowd below. At length the officers appeared, and announced to the crowd that if they would open a lane to the wagon, they would promise to bring the man down the front way.

The lane was opened, and the man was brought out--a tall, handsome, intelligent white man, with his wrists manacled together, walking between the U. S. Marshal and another officer, and behind him his brother and his master, so like him that one could hardly be told from the other. The moment they appeared, Harriet roused from her stooping posture, threw up a window, and cried to her friends: "Here he comes--take him!" and then darted down the stairs like a wild-cat. She seized one officer and pulled him down, then another, and tore him away from the man; and keeping her arms about the slave, she cried to her friends: "Drag us out! Drag him to the river! Drown him! but don't let them have him!" They were knocked down together, and while down she tore off her sunbonnet and tied it on the head of the fugitive. When he rose, only his head could be seen, and amid the surging mass of people, the slave was no longer recognized, while the master appeared like the slave. Again and again they were knocked down, the poor slave utterly helpless, with his manacled wrists streaming with blood. Harriet's outer clothes were torn from her, and even her stout shoes were all pulled from her feet, yet she never relinquished her hold of the man, till she had dragged him to the river, where he was tumbled into a boat, Harriet following in a ferryboat to the other side. But the telegraph was ahead of them, and as soon as they landed he was seized and hurried from her sight. After a time, some school children came hurrying along, and to her anxious inquiries they answered, "He is up in that house, in the third story." Harriet rushed up to the place. Some men were attempting to make their way up the stairs. The officers were firing down, and two men were lying on the stairs, who had been shot. Over their bodies our heroine rushed, and with the help of others burst open the door of the room, dragged out the fugitive, whom Harriet carried down stairs in her arms. A gentleman who was riding by with a fine horse, stopped to ask what the disturbance meant; and on hearing the story, his sympathies seemed to be thoroughly aroused; he sprang from his wagon, calling out, "That is a blood-horse, drive him till he drops." The poor man was hurried in; some of his friends jumped in after him, and drove at the most rapid rate to Schenectady.

This is the story Harriet told to the writer. By some persons, it seemed too wonderful for belief, and an attempt was made to corroborate it. Rev. Henry Fowler, who was at the time at Saratoga, kindly volunteered to go to Troy and ascertain the facts. His report was, that he had had a long interview with Mr. Townsend, who acted during the trial as counsel for the slave, that he had given him a "rich narration," which he would write out the next week for this little book. But before he was to begin his generous labor, and while engaged in some kind efforts for the prisoners at Auburn, he was stricken down by the heat of the sun, and is for a long time debarred from labor.

FUGITIVE SLAVE RESCUE IN TROY.
From the Troy Whig, April 28, 1859.

Yesterday afternoon, the streets of this city and West Troy were made the scenes of unexampled excitement. For the first time since the passage of the Fugitive Slave Law, an attempt was made here to carry its provisions into execution, and the result was a terrific encounter between the officers and the prisoner's friends, the triumph of mob law, and the final rescue of the fugitive. Our city was thrown into a grand state of turmoil, and for a time every other topic was forgotten, to give place to this new excitement. People did not think last evening to ask who was nominated at Charleston, or whether the news of the Heenan and Sayers battle had arrived--everything was merged into the fugitive slave case, of which it seems the end is not yet.

Charles Nalle, the fugitive, who was the cause of all this excitement, was a slave on the plantation of B. W. Hansborough, in Culpepper County, Virginia, till the 19th of October, 1858, when he made his escape, and went to live in Columbia, Pennsylvania. A wife and five children are residing there now. Not long since he came to Sandlake, in this county, and resided in the family of Mr. Crosby until about three weeks ago. Since that time, he has been employed as coachman by Uri Gilbert, Esq., of this city. He is about thirty years of age, tall, quite light-complexioned, and good-looking. He is said to have been an excellent and faithful servant.

At Sandlake, we understand that Nalle was often seen by one H. F. Averill, formerly connected with one of the papers of this city, who communicated with his reputed owner in Virginia, and gave the information that led to a knowledge of the whereabouts of the fugitive. Averill wrote letters for him, and thus obtained an acquaintance with his history. Mr. Hansborough sent on an agent, Henry J. Wall, by whom the necessary papers were got out to arrest the fugitive.

Yesterday morning about 11 o'clock, Charles Nalle was sent to procure some bread for the family by whom he was employed. He failed to return. At the baker's, he was arrested by Deputy United States Marshal J. W. Holmes, and immediately taken before United States Commissioner Miles Beach. The son of Mr. Gilbert, thinking it strange that he did not come back, sent to the house of William Henry, on Division Street, where he boarded, and his whereabouts was discovered.

The examination before Commissioner Beach was quite brief. The evidence of Averill and the agent was taken, and the Commissioner decided to remand Nalle to Virginia. The necessary papers were made out and given to the Marshal.

By this time it was two o'clock, and the fact began to be noised abroad that there was a fugitive slave in Mr. Beach's office, corner of State and First Streets. People in knots of ten or twelve collected near the entrance, looking at Nalle, who could be seen at an upper window.

William Henry, a colored man, with whom Nalle boarded, commenced talking from the curbstone in a loud voice to the crowd. He uttered such sentences as, "There is a fugitive slave in that office--pretty soon you will see him come forth. He is going to be taken down South, and you will have a chance to see him. He is to be taken to the depot, to go to Virginia in the first train. Keep watch of those stairs, and you will have a sight." A number of women kept shouting, crying, and by loud appeals excited, the colored persons assembled.

Still the crowd grew in numbers. Wagons halted in front of the locality, and were soon piled with spectators. An alarm of fire was sounded, and hose carriages dashed through the ranks of men, women, and boys; but they closed again, and kept looking with expectant eyes at the window where the negro was visible. Meanwhile, angry discussions commenced. Some persons agitated a rescue, and others favored law and order. Mr. Brockway, a lawyer, had his coat torn for expressing his sentiments, and other melees kept the interest alive.

All at once there was a wild hulloa, and every eye was turned up to see the legs and part of the body of the prisoner protruding from the second-story window, at which he was endeavoring to escape. Then arose a shout! "Drop him!" "Catch him!" "Hurrah!" But the attempt was a fruitless one, for somebody in the office pulled Nalle back again, amid the shouts of a hundred pair of lungs. The crowd at this time numbered nearly a thousand persons. Many of them were black, and a good share were of the female sex. They blocked up State Street from First Street to the alley, and kept surging to and fro.

Martin I. Townsend, Esq., who acted as counsel for the fugitive, did not arrive in the Commissioner's office until a decision had been rendered. He immediately went before Judge Gould, of the Supreme Court, and procured a writ of habeas corpus in the usual form, returnable immediately. This was given Deputy Sheriff Nathaniel Upham, who at once proceeded to Commissioner Beach's office, and served it on Holmes. Very injudiciously, the officers proceeded at once to Judge Gould's office, although it was evident they would have to pass through an excited, unreasonable crowd. As soon as the officers and their prisoner emerged from the door, an old negro, who had been standing at the bottom of the stairs, shouted, "Here they come," and the crowd made a terrific rush at the party.

From the office of Commissioner Beach, in the Mutual Building, to that of Judge Gould, in Congress Street, is less than two blocks, but it was made a regular battle-field. The moment the prisoner emerged from the doorway, in custody of Deputy-Sheriff Upham, Chief of Police Quin, Officers Cleveland and Holmes, the crowd made one grand charge, and those nearest the prisoner seized him violently, with the intention of pulling him away from the officers, but they were foiled; and down First to Congress Street, and up the latter in front of Judge Gould's chambers, went the surging mass. Exactly what did go on in the crowd, it is impossible to say, but the pulling, hauling, mauling, and shouting, gave evidences of frantic efforts on the part of the rescuers, and a stern resistance from the conservators of the law. In front of Judge Gould's office the combat was at its height. No stones or other missiles were used; the battle was fist to fist. We believe an order was given to take the prisoner the other way, and there was a grand rush towards the West, past First and River Streets, as far as Dock Street. All this time there was a continual melee. Many of the officers were hurt-- among them Mr. Upham, whose object was solely to do his duty by taking Nalle before Judge Gould in accordance with the writ of habeas corpus. A number in the crowd were more or less hurt, and it is a wonder that these were not badly injured, as pistols were drawn and chisels used.

The battle had raged as far as the corner of Dock and Congress Streets, and the victory remained with the rescuers at last. The officers were completely worn out with their exertions, and it was impossible to continue their hold upon him any longer. Nalle was at liberty. His friends rushed him down Dock Street to the lower ferry, where there was a skiff lying ready to start. The fugitive was put in, the ferryman rowed off, and amid the shouts of hundreds who fined the banks of the river, Nalle was carried into Albany County.

As the skiff landed in West Troy, a negro sympathizer waded up to the waist, and pulled Nalle out of the boat. He went up the hill alone, however, and there who should he meet but Constable Becker? The latter official seeing a man with manacles on, considered it his duty to arrest him. He did so, and took him in a wagon to the office of Justice Stewart, on the second floor of the corner building near the ferry. The Justice was absent.

When the crowd on the Troy bank had seen Nalle safely landed, it was suggested that he might be recaptured. Then there was another rush made for the steam ferry-boat, which carried over about 400 persons, and left as many more--a few of the latter being soused in their efforts to get on the boat. On landing in West Troy, there, sure enough, was the prisoner, locked up in a strong office, protected by Officers Becker, Brown and Morrison, and the door barricaded.

Not a moment was lost. Upstairs went a score or more of resolute men--the rest "piling in" promiscuously, shouting and execrating the officers. Soon a stone flew against the door--then another--and bang, bang! went off a couple of pistols, but the officers who fired them took good care to aim pretty high. The assailants were forced to retreat for a moment. "They 've got pistols," said one. "Who cares?" was the reply; "they can only kill a dozen of us--come on." More stones and more pistol-shots ensued. At last the door was pulled open by an immense negro, and in a moment he was felled by a hatchet in the hands of Deputy Sheriff Morrison; but the body of the fallen man blocked up the door so that it could not be shut, and a friend of the prisoner pulled him out. Poor fellow! he might well say, "Save me from my friends." Amid the pulling and hauling, the iron had cut his arms, which were bleeding profusely, and he could hardly walk, owing to fatigue.

He has since arrived safely in Canada.

Statements made by Martin I. Townsend, Esq., of Troy, who was counsel for the fugitive, Charles Nalle.

Nalle is an octoroon; his wife has the same infusion of Caucasian blood. She was the daughter of her master, and had, with her sister, been bred by him in his family, as his own child. When the father died, both of these daughters were married and had large families of children. Under the highly Christian national laws of "Old Virginny," these children were the slaves of their grandfather. The old man died, leaving a will, whereby he manumitted his daughters and their children, and provided for the purchase of the freedom of their husbands. The manumission of the children and grandchildren took effect; but the estate was insufficient to purchase the husbands of his daughters, and the father of his grandchildren. The manumitted, by another Christian, "conservative," and "national" provision of law, were forced to leave the State, while the slave husbands remained in slavery. Nalle and his brother-in-law were allowed for a while to visit their families outside Virginia about once a year, but were at length ordered to provide themselves with new wives, as they would be allowed to visit their former ones no more. It was after this that Nalle and his brother-in-law started for the land of freedom, guided by the steady light of the north star. Thank God, neither family now need fear any earthly master or the bay of the blood-hound dogging their fugitive steps.

Nalle returned to Troy with his family about July, 1860, and resided with them there for more than seven years. They are all now residents of the city of Washington, D. C. Nalle and his family are persons of refined manners, and of the highest respectability. Several of his children are red-haired, and a stranger would discover no trace of African blood in their complexions or features. It was the head of this family whom H. F. Averill proposed to doom to returnless exile and lifelong slavery.

When Nalle was brought from Commissioner Beach's office into the street, Harriet Tubman, who had been standing with the excited crowd, rushed amongst the foremost to Nalle, and running one of her arms around his manacled arm, held on to him without ever loosening her hold through the more than half-hour's struggle to Judge Gould's office, and from Judge Gould's office to the dock, where Nalle's liberation was accomplished. In the melee, she was repeatedly beaten over the head with policemen's clubs, but she never for a moment released her hold, but cheered Nalle and his friends with her voice, and struggled with the officers until they were literally worn out with their exertions, and Nalle was separated from them.

True, she had strong and earnest helpers in her struggle, some of whom had white faces as well as human hearts, and are now in Heaven. But she exposed herself to the fury of the sympathizers with slavery, without fear, and suffered their blows without flinching.

Harriet crossed the river with the crowd, in the ferryboat, and when the men who led the assault upon the door of Judge Stewart's office, were stricken down, Harriet and a number of other colored women rushed over their bodies, brought Nalle out, and putting him in the first wagon passing, started him for the West.

A livery team, driven by a colored man, was immediately sent on to relieve the other, and Nalle was seen about Troy no more until he returned a free man by purchase from his master. Harriet also disappeared, and the crowd dispersed. How she came to be in Troy that day, is entirely unknown to our citizens; and where she hid herself after the rescue, is equally a mystery. But her struggle was in the sight of a thousand, perhaps of five thousand spectators.

This woman of whom you have been reading is poor, and partially disabled from her injuries; yet she supports cheerfully and uncomplainingly herself and her old parents, and always has several poor children in her house, who are dependent entirely upon her exertions. At present she has three of these children for whom she is providing, while their parents are working to pay back money borrowed to bring them on. She also maintains by her exertions among the good people of Auburn, two schools of freedmen at the South, providing them teachers and sending them clothes and books. She never asks for anything for herself, but she does ask the charity of the public for "her people."

> For them her tears will fall,
> For them her prayers ascend;
> To them her toils and cares be given,
> Till toils and cares will end.

If any persons are disposed to aid her in her benevolent efforts, they may send donations to Rev. S. M. Hopkins, Professor in the Auburn Theological Seminary, who will make such disposition of the funds sent as may be designated by the donors.

APPENDIX.

A few circumstances having come out in conversation with Harriet, they are added here, as they may be of interest to the reader.

On asking Harriet particularly as to the age of her mother, she answered, "Well, I'll tell you, Missis. Twenty-three years ago, in Maryland, I paid a lawyer $5 to look up the will of my mother's first master. He looked back sixty years, and said it was time to give up. I told him to go back furder.["] He went back sixty-five years, and there he found the will--giving the girl Ritty to his grand-daughter (Mary Patterson), to serve her and her offspring till she was forty-five years of age. This grand-daughter died soon after, unmarried; and as there was no provision for Ritty, in case of her death, she was actually emancipated at that time. But no one informed her of the fact, and she and her dear children remained in bondage till emancipated by the courage and determination of this heroic daughter and sister. The old woman must then, it seems, be ninety-eight years of age, and the old man has probably numbered as many years. And yet these old people, living out beyond the toll-gate, on the South Street road, Auburn, come in every Sunday--more than a mile--to the Central Church. To be sure, deep slumbers settle down upon them as soon as they are seated, which continue undisturbed till the congregation is dismissed; but they have done their best, and who can doubt that they receive a blessing. Immediately after this they go to class-meeting at the

Methodist Church. Then they wait for a third service, and after that start out home again.

On asking Harriet where they got anything to eat on Sunday, she said, in her quiet way, "Oh! de ole folks nebber eats anyting on Sunday, Missis! We nebber has no food to get for dem on Sunday. Dey always fasts; and dey nebber eats anyting on Fridays. Good Friday, an' five Fridays hand gwine from Good Friday, my fader nebber eats or drinks, all day--fasting for de five bleeding wounds ob Jesus. All the oder Fridays ob de year he nebber eats till de sun goes down; den he takes a little tea an' a piece ob bread." "But is he a Roman Catholic, Harriet?" "Oh no, Misses; he does it for conscience; we was taught to do so down South. He says if he denies himself for the sufferings of his Lord an' Master, Jesus will sustain him."

It has been mentioned that Harriet never asks anything for herself, but whenever her people were in trouble, or she felt impelled to go South to guide to freedom friend or brother, or father and mother, if she had not time to work for the money, she was persistent till she got it from somebody. When she received one of her intimations that the old people were in trouble, and it was time for her to go to them, she asked the Lord where she should go for the money. She was in some way, as she supposed, directed to the office of a certain gentleman in New York. When she left the house of her friends to go there, she said, "I'm gwine to Mr.--'s office, an' I ain't gwine to lebe there, an' I ain't gwine to eat or drink till I git enough money to take me down after the ole people."

She went into this gentleman's office.

"What do you want, Harriet?" was the first greeting.

"I want some money, sir."

"You do? How much do you want?"

"I want twenty dollars, sir."

"Twenty dollars? Who told you to come here for twenty dollars?"

"De Lord tole me, sir."

"Well, I guess the Lord's mistaken this time."

"I guess he isn't, sir. Anyhow I'm gwine to sit here till I git it."

So she sat down and went to sleep. All the morning and all the afternoon she sat there still, sleeping and rousing up--sometimes finding the office full of gentlemen--sometimes finding herself alone. Many fugitives were passing through Now York at that time, and those who came in supposed that she was one of them, tired out and resting. Sometimes she would be roused up with the words, "Come, Harriet, you had better go. There's no money for you here." "No, sir. I'm not gwine till I git my twenty dollars."

    She does not know all that happened, for deep sleep fell upon her; but probably her story was whispered about, and she roused at last to find herself the happy possessor of sixty dollars, which had been raised among those who came into the office. She went on her way rejoicing, to bring her old parents from the land of bondage. She found that her father was to be tried the next Monday, for helping off slaves; so, as she says, she "removed his trial to a higher court," and hurried him off to Canada. One more little incident, which, it is hoped, may not be offensive to the young lady to whom it alludes, may be mentioned here, showing Harriet's extreme delicacy in asking anything for herself. Last winter ('67 and '68), as we all know, the snow was very deep for months, and Harriet and the old people were completely snowed-in in their little home. The old man was laid up with rheumatism, and Harriet could not leave home for a long time to procure supplies of corn, if she could have made her way into the city. At length, stern necessity compelled her to plunge through the drifts to the city, and she appeared at the house of one of her firm and fast friends, and was directed to the room of one of the young ladies. She began to walk up and down, as she always does when in trouble. At length she said, "Miss Annie?" "What, Harriet?" A long pause; then again, "Miss Annie?" "Well, what is it, Harriet?" This was repeated four times, when the young lady, looking up, saw her eyes filled with tears. She then insisted on knowing what she wanted. And with a great effort, she said, "Miss Annie, could you lend me a quarter till Monday? I never asked it before." Kind friends immediately supplied all the wants of the family, but on Monday Harriet appeared with the quarter she had borrowed.

But though so timid for herself, she is bold enough when the wants of her race are concerned. Even now, while friends are trying to raise the means to publish this little book for her, she is going around with the greatest zeal and interest to raise a subscription for her Freedmen's Fair. She called on Hon. Wm. H. Seward, the other day, for a subscription to this object. He said, "Harriet, you have worked for others long enough. It is time you should think of yourself. If you ask for a donation for yourself, I will give it to you; but I will not help you to rob yourself for others."

Harriet's charity for all the human race is unbounded. It embraces even the slaveholder--it sympathizes even with Jeff. Davis, and rejoices at his departure to other lands, with some prospect of peace for the future. She says, "I tink dar's many a slaveholder 'll git to Heaven. Dey don't know no better. Dey acts up to de light dey hab. You take dat sweet little child (pointing to a lonely baby)--'pears more like an angel dan anyting else--take her down dere, let her nebber know nothing 'bout niggers but they was made to be whipped, an' she 'll grow up to use the whip on 'em jus' like de rest. No, Missus, its because dey don't know no better." May God give the people to whom the story of this woman shall come, a like charity, so that through their kindness the last days of her stormy and troubled life may be calm and peaceful.

ESSAY ON WOMAN-WHIPPING.

THE subject of the preceding memoir appears to have retained all her life a feeling recollection of the effects of the whip in the hands of her youthful mistress. Considering the vigor and frequency of the application, this is not strange. Infinite cuffs and thwacks, more or less, pass into oblivion; but a flogging with a raw-hide is not easily forgotten. A slave's experience of the whip, however, was not confined to his or to her early days. A slave race must be controlled by fear and pain: and the discipline, it was naturally thought, could not begin too early. From childhood to old age they were liable to stripes, for any reason or for no reason. If the slave was guilty of no fault, he might be whipped, as appears from the preceding narrative, merely to impress him with a salutary sense of the master's right and disposition to whip.

A Northern man, born and bred under the influences of freedom and the protection of law, and made acquainted with slavery in its old palmy days, can never forget his sensations at his first sight of a slave-whipping. The utmost he has ever seen in the way of corporal punishment has been the switching of some obstreperous child by competent authority; a discipline administered with prudence and moderation; drawing no blood and leaving no scar. He now sees an adult person stripped to the skin, his arms tied at their utmost stretch above his head, or across some object, which binds, him into a posture the best adapted to feel the full force of each blow. The instrument of suffering is not a birch twig or a ferule, but a twisted rawhide, or heavy "black snake;" either of them highly effective weapons in the hands of a stout executioner. Our Northern novice stands horror-stricken and paralyzed for a moment; but at the second or third blow, and the piteous scream of Oh Lord! Massa! which follows, he digs his fingers into his ears, and rushes to the furthest corner of his tent or dwelling, to escape the scene. Even if he could have endured the sight and sound a while longer, he dared not. The horror in his face, and perhaps the irrepressible word or act of interference was too sure to bring upon himself the vengeance due to a "d--d Abolitionist." The little knot of Southern habituès look on with critical inspection, squirting tobacco-juice, with their hands in their pockets.

If the subject is a woman, the interest rises higher, and the crowd would be greater. There is a refinement of cruelty in the whipping of a woman which used to stimulate agreeably the dull sensibilities of a Southern mob. A dish of torture had to be peppered very high to please the palates of those epicures in brutality. The helplessness and terror of the victim, the exposure of her person, the opportunity for coarse jests at her expense, all combined to make it a scene of rare enjoyment. How the "chivalric" mind can endure the loss of such gratifications it is difficult to conceive. The Romans were weaned from crucifixions and gladiatorial combats very gradually. The process of ameliorating criminal law and humanizing public sentiment went on for more than two centuries. It was full four hundred years after the epoch of our redemption when the monk Telemachus threw himself between the hired swordsmen, whom a Christian audience was applauding, and laid down his own life to wind up the spectacle. But the bloody morsel has been snatched from the mouths of the "chivalry" at one clutch. No wonder their mortification vents itself in weeping and wailing, and knashing of teeth, and in such miscellaneous atrocities as their "Ku-Klux-Klan's" can venture to inflict on helpless freedmen and radicals.*

It is curiously illustrative of the mixed childishness and ferocity which characterizes the Southern civilization, that this secret association of ruffians, organized to terrorize the loyal South, styles itself by an absurd, misspelled name, and goes about on its nightly work of murder in harlequin costume, with one of its leaders acting the part of ghost, to frighten the superstitious blacks. Some more courageous freedman occasionally makes a bona fide ghost of this masquerade.

A recent Southern paper (the Virginia Advertiser) finds a providential provision for the enslavement of the negro race in the thickness of their skulls, enabling them to bear without injury the blows inflicted in sudden rage by their masters; a suggestive confession, by the way, of the influence of slavery on the tempers of the slaveholders. The whole race must be prepared, it seems, for blows on the head with whatever weapon came to hand! But admitting the thickness of the skulls, it appears from an incident in the preceding pages, as well as from other known instances, that the inventive genius of the slave-whipping chivalry contrived to baffle the humane designs of Providence--a negro skull well-padded with wool might bear without injury the blow of a boot-jack or a hammer, and yet prove insufficient to resist the impact or a musket-ball or a ten-pound weight. It is of no avail to plate a vessel with six inches of iron, if she is to be pounded with bolts that can mash an eight-inch armor. Apparently, Divine Providence stopped short of the necessary security for the predestined slave race. It should have arranged for a progressive thickening of the negro cranium to meet the increase of violence on the part of the master; until at length slavery might be encountered with a difficulty like that which besets naval gunnery, viz., what would be the result if an infrangible African skull should be beaten by an irresistible Caucasian club?

But even this Virginia laudator temporis acti, this melancholy mourner at the tomb of defunct slavery, does not allege any such Providential thickening of the negro cuticle as to amount to a satisfactory anæsthesis against whipping. It has never been proven that a Virginia paddle or a Georgia raw-hide well applied did not make the blood spin as freely through a black skin as through a white one; nor has any Southern savant of the Nott and Gliddon school shown that there was not the same relative delicacy of organization in the slave woman as in the free. A black woman was, relatively to the black man, the more delicate subject for the whip; something more sensitive to the shame of stripping, more liable to terror, and of rather softer fiber; so that the lash went deeper both into soul and sense than in the case of her sable brother.

And this fact made the black woman a very suitable subject for the whip in the hands of the Southern lady. To succeed in slave whipping as in any other fine art, the Horatian canon must be regarded, which requires us to take a subject suited to our strength. It would have been unreasonable, in ordinary cases, to expect a "dark-eyed daughter of the South" to flog handsomely a stalwart negro man; she sometimes did it, after he had been well tied up. But the slave girl was exactly suited to her flagellating capacities. A good many women, North as well as South, manifest a tendency to become tyrants in their own households, and love to bully their servants. But this is an evil of a mitigated nature in Northern society. The stupidest "help" in the kitchen knows she is safe from any other lash than her mistress' tongue, and is commonly an adept at the business of answering back again.

But the Southern mistress was a domestic devil with horns and claws; selfish, insolent, accustomed to be waited on for everything. She grew up with the instinct of tyranny--to punish violently the least neglect or disobedience in her servants. The variable temper of girlhood, not ugly unless thwarted, became in the "Southern matron" a chronic fury. She was her own "overseer," and, like that out-door functionary, had her own scepter, which she did not bear in vain. The rawhide lay upon the shelf within easy reach, and her arm was vigorous with exercise. The breaking of a plate, the spilling of a cup, the misplacing of a pin in her dress, or any other misadventure in the chapter of accidents, was promptly illustrated with numerous cuts. The lash well laid on the shoulders of a black femme-de-chambre, or screaming child, was an agreeable titillation of the nervous sensibilities of the languid creole; a headache, or a heartache, transferred itself through the medium of the rawhide to the back of Phillis or Araminta. They no doubt whipped sometimes, like Mr. Squeers, for the mere fun of the thing. It is an exquisite pleasure to a cowardly nature to have some creature to torment; and there is this nemesis about cruelty that it engenders an appetite, which, like that for alcoholic stimulants, forever demands increased indulgence. It was the vindictive woman's nature in the South that protracted and gave added ferocity to the rebellion. These woman-whipping wives and mothers it was who hounded on the masculine chivalry to the work of exterminating the "accursed Yankees," and thus made their own punishment so much sorer than it need have been.

The mention of these amiable Southern characteristics cannot fail to recall that highly suggestive scene of the Malebolge, with the illustration of Gustave Doré, in which the tempters and destroyers of women are seen scourged with whips, in the hands of demons; especially when we remember that the whipping of slave women to make them consent to their own dishonor, was one of the usages of the patriarchal chivalry. There is not a scene in which the imaginings of Dante have been better seconded by the pencil of the great French artist: the flying wretches hurrying in opposite directions, as the crowds in the Jubilee year trampled each other, going and returning across the St. Angelo Bridge; among them the bat-winged fiends with whips, lashing right and left! In the throng are female figures: women who in life tortured and corrupted other women. What terror in face an attitude! How desperately they grapple with the rocks to lift themselves out of reach of the scourge! And these two demons in the foreground! What an absolute idealization of muscular ferocity! Every sinewy line in their cantour displays the force of a fallen demi-god; their very tails curl with delight in their ministry of vengeance.

> Ah! come facen levar le berze,
> Alle prime percosse, e gia nessuno,
> Le second aspettava ne le terze!

Ah! how they make them skip! There is Legree and Tom Gordon, and Madame de Schlangenbad, from Louisiana, and Mrs. Crawley (née Sharp) from South Carolina, squirming under the torture! A very instructive, if not agreeable exhibition!

But this fury in celestial Southern bosoms was merely institutional. Dip the gentlest nature into the element of irresponsible power, and it becomes in time covered over with a foul incrustation of cruelty. Those beastly Roman ladies of Juvenal's time, who could order a slave woman to be whipped to death without condeseending to give any other reason than their sic volo, sic jubeo, were not naturally worse than others. Take any Roman or Southern girl of ten years of age, put a whip in her hands, and a helpless slave child at her mercy; let her see nothing but brutality to inferiors all around her, and by the time she is ready to be married, she can hold up her thumb to the standing gladiator in the arena, or beg her lover to bring her back from Bull Run a ring from the bones of some Yankee soldier. It is a publicly known private fact, illustrative of the influence of slavery on the female character, that when a certain Northern clergyman applied to her father for the hand of a celebrated Maryland heiress, the reply was, "You are quite welcome to her! but I think it only fair to tell you that if I were going to storm hell, I should put her in the advance."

There is every reason to hope, therefore, that the Southern character, both male and female, will become gradually ameliorated by the changed condition under which it will hereafter be formed. It is a common error, one in which the Southern people themselves share, that there is something in their climate to nurse and to justify their "high spirit," anqlicé their quarrelsomeness and brutality of temper. It is very pleasant to lay off upon Nature or Providence what belongs only to will or institutions. A man indulges in violent passions with little restraint or remorse, so long as he can persuade himself he is merely what certain positive natural laws make him. What an opiate for a conscience defiled with lust and blood, to think that this is only natural to the "sunny South." But in fact, the people of warm, temperate, and tropical regions are most commonly gentle of mood; the climate acts as an anodyne, and soothes them into a peaceful equilibrium of the passions. The negroes of the Southern States are not passionate or vindictive--well for their late masters and present persecutors that they are not! What they may become from the treatment they are experiencing from those preternatural and predestinated fools, is another question.

The only reason the "chivalry" are bad-tempered and quarrelsome, is found in that despotism in which they have been nursed, and which associates the idea of personal dignity with an instant resort to violence at any contradiction. But for slavery, the people of Mississippi would have been no more addicted to street fights, dueling, midnight assassinations, etc., than the people of Massachusetts. That the former have any advantage in respect to courage, has been sufficiently disproved by the rebellion. Whether the ex-Confederate ladies may or may not be able to "fire the Southern heart" for another attempt to overthrow the Government, it will at least never be done under the persuasion that one Southerner is equal to five or any other number above unity, of Yankees.

The traditions of slavery, indeed, will remain to keep alive among the late slaveholding caste, the insolent and unchristian temper on which they have prided themselves. But having no more helpless pendants to storm at and abuse, their valor will needs submit to gradual modifications. Some degree of self-government will become a necessity. It may require several generations; but institutions ceasing to corrupt them, the loss of wealth, the necessity of work and a new Gospel of peace, better than their old slaveholding Christianity, will gradually educate them into a law-abiding, orderly, and virtuous people.

The Southern woman will of course share early in this beneficent change--no longer perverted into a she-devil by the possession of unrestrained power, and paying just wages to servants, who, if not suited with their work, can leave without having to run off; her gentler virtues will have a chance to assert themselves. Her striking qualities will subside into a charming vivacity of temper. She will become a gracious and pious mater-familias; she will perhaps in time learn to apply to her own children a portion of that discipline of which her slaves enjoyed a monopoly. In short, there neither is nor ever was any reason, slavery excepted, why the Southern whites should not possess a character for industry, peacefulness, and religion, equal to that of the rural districts of New York and New England.

Thank God that we have lived to see such awful barbarisms extinct! In fifty years the last woman-whipper at the South will be as dead as Cleopatra; as dead as the pre-Adamite brute organizations. History will be ashamed to record their doings. The fictions in which they are enbalmed will be lost in the better coming era of morals and letters. By the time the South has been overflowed and regenerated by a beneficent inundation of Northern "carpet-baggers," with Yankee capital and enterprise, it will be forgotten that a race capable of the crimes referred to in the preceding story, ever existed.

LIST OF SUBSCRIBERS TO THE PUBLISHING FUND.

- GERRIT SMITH, ... Peterboro, N. Y $25 00
- WENDELL PHILLIPS, ... Boston, Mass 25 00
- J. S. SEYMOUR, ... Auburn, N. Y., ... 25 00
- D. M. OSBORNE, ... " " 25 00
- CHAS. P. WOOD, ... " " 25 00
- WM. H. SEWARD, JR., ... " " 25 00
- J. N. KNAPP, ... " " 25 00
- RUFUS SARGENT, ... " " 25 00
- H. IVISON, ... New York 25 00
- TIMOTHY L. BARKER, ... San Francisco, Cal., ... 20 00
- WM. G. WISE, ... Auburn, N. Y., ... 10 00
- G. I. LETCHWORTH, ... " " 10 00
- S. L. BRADLEY, ... " " 10 00
- I F. TERRILL, ... " " 10 00
- ABIJAH FITCH, ... " " 10 00
- T. M. POMEROY, M. C., ... " " 10 00
- F. L. GRISWOLD, ... " " 10 00
- CYRENUS WHEELER, ... " " 10 00
- JOHN CHEDELL, ... " " 10 00
- DAVID WRIGHT, ... " " 10 00
- JO IAH BARBER, ... " " 10 00
- GEO. E. BARBER, ... " " 10 0
- S. WILLARD, M. D, ... " " 10 00

- RICHARD STEEL, ... Auburn, N. Y $5 00
- C. H. MERRIMAN, ... " " 5 00
- J. LEWIS GRANT, ... " " 5 00
- A. H. GOSS, ... " " 5 00
- CHRISTOPHER MORGAN, ... " " 5 00
- J. M. HURD, ... " " 5 00
- W. J. SUTTON, ... " " 5 00
- WM. A. KIRBY, ... " " 5 00
- THOS. MCCREA, ... " " 5 00
- J. N. STARIN, ... " " 5 00
- C. P. FORD, ... " " 5 00

SUPERWOMEN

SUPERWOMEN

BOOK TWO

Narrative of Sojourner Truth

Sojourner Truth

Narrative of Sojourner Truth:
a Bondswoman of Olden Time, Emancipated by the New York Legislature
in the Early Part of the Present Century;
with a History of Her Labors and Correspondence,
Drawn from Her "Book of Life"
(1875)

By

Sojourner Truth

Olive Gilbert

Franccs W. Titus

SUPERWOMEN

SOJOURNER TRUTH,
"THE LIBYAN SIBYL."

SUPERWOMEN

NARRATIVE OF SOJOURNER TRUTH:

A Bondswoman of Olden Time, EMANCIPATED BY THE NEW YORK LEGISLATURE IN THE EARLY PART OF THE PRESENT CENTURY; WITH A HISTORY OF HER Labors and Correspondence, DRAWN FROM HER "BOOK OF LIFE."

By
Sojourner Truth
Olive Gilbert
Frances W. Titus

BOSTON:
PUBLISHED FOR THE AUTHOR.
1875.

SUPERWOMEN

Entered, according to Act of Congress, in the year 1875, BY MRS. FRANCES W. TITUS, In the Office of the Librarian of Congress, at Washington.

TO THE READER.

THE first 128 pages of this work are reprinted from stereotype plates, made in 1850. This will account for the style of the Preface, and portions of the Narrative, which were especially adapted to those dark days of oppression.

An extract on page 134 represents Sojourner as the mother of thirteen children. It should read five children.

Lines in the middle of page 186 should be transposed so as to read thus: "Street cars are designed for poor white and colored folks, and will take them two or three miles for sixpence. Then ask for a nigger car!! Carriages are for ladies and gentlemen."

SUPERWOMEN

PREFACE.

THE following is the unpretending narrative of the life of a remarkable and meritorious woman--a life which has been checkered by strange vicissitudes, severe hardships, and singular adventures. Born a slave, and held in that brutal condition until the entire abolition of slavery in the State of New York in 1827, she has known what it is to drink to the dregs the bitterest cup of human degradation. That one thus placed on a level with cattle and swine, and for so many years subjected to the most demoralizing influences, should have retained her moral integrity to such an extent, and cherished so successfully the religious sentiment in her soul, shows a mind of no common order, while it heightens the detestation that is felt in every humane bosom, of that system of oppression which seeks to cripple the intellect, impair the understanding, and deprave the hearts of its victims--a system which has subjected to its own foul purposes, in the United States, all that is wealthy, talented, influential, and reputedly pious, in an overwhelming measure!

O the 'fantastic tricks' which the American people are 'playing before high Heaven!' O their profane use of the sacred name of Liberty! O their impious appeals to the God of the oppressed, for his divine benediction, while they are making merchandise of his image! Do they not blush? Nay, they glory in their shame! Once a year they take special pains to exhibit themselves to the world, in all their republican deformity and Christian barbarity, insanely supposing that they thus excite the envy, admiration and applause of mankind. The nations are looking at the dreadful spectacle with disgust and amazement. However sunken and degraded they may be, they are too elevated, too virtuous, too humane to be guilty of such conduct. Their voice is heard, saying-- 'Americans! we hear your boasts of liberty, your shouts of independence, your declarations of hostility to every form of tyranny, your assertions that all men are created free and equal, and endowed by their Creator with an inalienable right to liberty, the merry peal of your bells, and the deafening roar of your artillery; but, mingling with all these, and rising above them all, we also hear the clanking of chains! the shrieks and wailings of millions of your own countrymen, whom you wickedly hold in a state of slavery as much more frightful than the oppression which your fathers resisted unto blood, as the tortures of the Inquisition surpass the stings of an insect! We see your banner floating proudly in the breeze from every flag-staff and mast-head in the land; but its blood-red stripes are emblematical of your own slave-driving cruelty, as you apply the lash to the flesh of your guiltless victim, even the flesh of a wife and mother, shrieking for the restoration of the babe of her bosom, sold to the remorseless slave speculator! We catch the gleam of your illuminated hills, everywhere blazing with bonfires; we mark your gay processions; we note the number of your orators; we listen to the recital of your revolutionary achievements: we see you kneeling at the shrine of Freedom, as her best, her truest, her sincerest worshippers! Hypocrites! liars! adulterers! tyrants! menstealers! atheists! Professing to believe in the natural equality of the human race--yet dooming a sixth portion of your immense population to beastly servitude, and ranking them among your goods and chattels! Professing to believe in the existence of a God--yet trading in his image, and selling those in the shambles for whose redemption the Son of God laid down his life! Professing to be Christians--yet withholding the Bible, the means of religious instruction, even the knowledge of the alphabet, from a benighted multitude, under terrible penalties! Boasting of your democracy--yet determining the rights of men by the texture of their hair and the color of their skin! Assuming to be 'the land of the free and the home of the brave,' yet keeping in chains more slaves than any other nation, not excepting slave-cursed Brazil! Prating of your morality and honesty--yet denying the rites of marriage to three millions of human beings, and plundering them of all their hard earnings! Affecting to be horror-struck in view of the foreign slave-trade--yet eagerly pursuing a domestic traffic equally cruel and unnatural, and reducing to slavery not less than seventy thousand new victims annually! Vaunting of your freedom of speech and of the press--your matchless Constitution and your glorious Union--yet denouncing as traitors, and treating as outlaws, those who have the courage and fidelity to plead for immediate, untrammelled, universal emancipation! Monsters that ye are! how can ye expect to escape the scorn of the world, and the wrath of Heaven? Emancipate your slaves, if you would redeem your tarnished character--if you would obtain forgiveness here, and salvation hereafter! Until you do so, "there will be a stain upon your national escutcheon, which all the waters of the Atlantic cannot wash out!" '

It is thus that, as a people, we are justly subjected to the reproach, the execration, the derision of mankind, and are made a proverb and a hissing among the nations. We cannot plead not guilty; every accusation that is registered against us is true; the act of violence is in our hands; the stolen property is in our possession; our fingers are stained with blood; the cup of our iniquity is full.

> 'Just God! and shall we calmly rest,
> The Christian's scorn--the Heathen's mirth--
> Content to live the lingering jest
> And by-word of a mocking earth?
> Shall our own glorious land retain
> That curse which Europe scorns to bear?
> Shall our own brethren drag the chain,
> Which not even Russia's menials wear?'

It is useless, it is dreadful, it is impious for this nation longer to contend with the Almighty. All his attributes are against us, and on the side of the oppressed. Is it not a fearful thing to fall into the hands of the living God? Who may abide the day of his coming, and who shall stand when he appeareth as 'a swift witness against the adulterers, and against false swearers, and against those that oppress the hireling in his wages, the widow, and the fatherless, and that turn aside the stranger from his right?' Woe to this bloody land! it is all full of lies and robbery--the prey departeth not, and the sound of a whip is heard continually. 'Judgment is turned away backward, and justice standeth afar off: for truth is fallen in the street, and equity cannot enter. Yea, truth faileth; and he that departeth from evil, maketh himself a prey.' The Lord sees it, and is displeased that there is no judgment; and he hath put on the garments of vengeance for clothing, and is clad with zeal as a cloak,--and, unless we repent by immediately undoing the heavy burdens and letting the oppressed go free, according to our deeds, accordingly he will repay, fury to his adversaries, recompense to his enemies. 'The Lord executeth righteousness and judgment for all that are oppressed.' 'O give thanks unto the Lord; for he is good: for his mercy endureth for ever. To him that smote Egypt in their first-born: for his mercy endureth for ever. And overthrew Pharaoh and his hosts in the Red sea: for his mercy endureth for ever.' 'Sing unto the Lord, for he hath triumphed gloriously: the horse and his rider hath he thrown into the sea. Thou didst blow with thy wind, the sea covered them: they sank as lead in the mighty waters.' 'Even so, Lord God Almighty, for so it seemeth good in thy sight.' 'Who is like unto thee, O Lord, among the gods? who is like thee, glorious in holiness, fearful in praises, doing wonders?'

In this great contest of Right against Wrong, of Liberty against Slavery, who are the wicked, if they be not those, who, like vultures and vampyres, are gorging themselves with human blood? if they be not the plunderers of the poor, the spoilers of the defenceless, the traffickers in 'slaves and the souls of men?' Who are the cowards, if not those who shrink from manly argumentation, the light of truth, the concussion of mind, and a fair field? if not those whose prowess, stimulated by whisky potations, or the spirit of murder, grows rampant as the darkness of night approaches; whose shouts and yells are savage and fiend-like; who furiously exclaim, 'Down with free discussion! down with the liberty of the press! down with the right of petition! down with constitutional law!'--who rifle mail-bags, throw types and printing-presses into the river, burn public halls dedicated to 'Virtue, Liberty and Independence,' and assassinate the defenders of inalienable human rights? And who are the righteous, in this case, if they be not those who will 'have no fellowship with the unfruitful works of darkness, but rather reprove them;' who maintain that the laborer is worthy of his hire, that the marriage institution is sacred, that slavery is a system accursed of God, that tyrants are the enemies of mankind, and that immediate emancipation should be given to all who are pining in bondage! Who are the truly brave, if not those who demand for truth and error alike, free speech, a free press, an open arena, the right of petition, AND NO QUARTERS? if not those, who, instead of skulking from the light, stand forth in the noontide blaze of day, and challenge their opponents to emerge from their wolf-like dens, that, by a rigid examination, it may be seen who has stolen the wedge of gold, in whose pocket are the thirty pieces of silver, and whose garments are stained with the blood of innocence?

It is hoped that the perusal of the following Narrative may increase the sympathy that is felt for the suffering colored population of this country, and inspire to renewed efforts for the liberation of all who are pining in bondage on the American soil.

WM. LLOYD GARRISON.

NARRATIVE OF SOJOURNER TRUTH.

HER BIRTH AND PARENTAGE.

THE subject of this biography, SOJOURNER TRUTH, as she now calls herself--but whose name, originally, was Isabella--was born, as near as she can now calculate, between the years 1797 and 1800. She was the daughter of James and Betsey, slaves of one Colonel Ardinburgh, Hurley, Ulster County, New York.

Colonel Ardinburgh belonged to that class of people called Low Dutch.

Of her first master, she can give no account, as she must have been a mere infant when he died; and she, with her parents and some ten or twelve other fellow human chattels, became the legal property of his son, Charles Ardinburgh. She distinctly remembers hearing her father and mother say, that their lot was a fortunate one, as Master Charles was the best of the family,--being, comparatively speaking, a kind master to his slaves.

James and Betsey having, by their faithfulness, docility, and respectful behavior, won his particular regard, received from him particular favors--among which was a lot of land, lying back on the slope of a mountain, where, by improving the pleasant evenings and Sundays, they managed to raise a little tobacco, corn, or flax; which they exchanged for extras, in the articles of food or clothing for themselves and children. She has no remembrance that Saturday afternoon was ever added to their own time, as it is by some masters in the Southern States.

ACCOMMODATIONS.

Among Isabella's earliest recollections was the removal of her master, Charles Ardinburgh, into his new house, which he had built for a hotel, soon after the decease of his father. A cellar, under this hotel, was assigned to his slaves, as their sleeping apartment,--all the slaves he possessed, of both sexes, sleeping (as is quite common in a state of slavery) in the same room. She carries in her mind, to this day, a vivid picture of this dismal chamber; its only lights consisting of a few panes of glass, through which she thinks the sun never shone, but with thrice reflected rays; and the space between the loose boards of the floor, and the uneven earth below, was often filled with mud and water, the uncomfortable splashings of which were as annoying as its noxious vapors must have been chilling and fatal to health. She shudders, even now, as she goes back in memory, and revisits this cellar, and sees its inmates, of both sexes and all ages, sleeping on those damp boards, like the horse, with a little straw and a blanket; and she wonders not at the rheumatisms, and fever-sores, and palsies, that distorted the limbs and racked the bodies of those fellow-slaves in after-life. Still, she does not attribute this cruelty--for cruelty it certainly is, to be so unmindful of the health and comfort of any being, leaving entirely out of sight his more important part, his everlasting interests,--so much to any innate or constitutional cruelty of the master, as to that gigantic inconsistency, that inherited habit among slave-holders, of expecting a willing and intelligent obedience from the slave, because he is a MAN--at the same time everything belonging to the soul-harrowing system does its best to crush the last vestige of a man within him; and when it is crushed, and often before, he is denied the comforts of life, on the plea that he knows neither the want nor the use of them, and because he is considered to be little more or little less than a beast.

HER BROTHERS AND SISTERS.

Isabella's father was very tall and straight, when young, which gave him the name of 'Bomefree'--low Dutch for tree--at least, this is SOJOURNER'S pronunciation of it--and by this name he usually went. The most familiar appellation of her mother was 'Mau-mau Bett.' She was the mother of some ten or twelve children; though Sojourner is far from knowing the exact number of her brothers and sisters; she being the youngest, save one, and all older than herself having been sold before her remembrance. She was privileged to behold six of them while she remained a slave.

Of the two that immediately preceded her in age, a boy of five years, and a girl of three, who were sold when she was an infant, she heard much; and she wishes that all who would fain believe that slave parents have not natural affection for their offspring could have listened as she did, while Bomefree and Mau-mau Bett,--their dark cellar lighted by a blazing pine-knot,--would sit for hours, recalling and recounting every endearing, as well as harrowing circumstance that taxed memory could supply, from the histories of those dear departed ones, of whom they had been robbed, and for whom their hearts still bled. Among the rest, they would relate how the little boy, on the last morning he was with them, arose with the birds, kindled a fire, calling for his Mau-mau to 'come, for all was now ready for her'--little dreaming of the dreadful separation which was so near at hand, but of which his parents had an uncertain, but all the more cruel foreboding. There was snow on the ground, at the time of which we are speaking; and a large old-fashioned sleigh was seen to drive up to the door of the late Col. Ardinburgh. This event was noticed with childish pleasure by the unsuspicious boy; but when he was taken and put into the sleigh, and saw his little sister actually shut and locked into the sleigh box, his eyes were at once opened to their intentions; and, like a frightened deer he sprang from the sleigh, and running into the house, concealed himself under a bed. But this availed him little. He was re-conveyed to the sleigh, and separated forever from those whom God had constituted his natural guardians and protectors, and who should have found him, in return, a stay and a staff to them in their declining years. But I make no comments on facts like these, knowing that the heart of every slave parent will make its own comments, involuntarily and correctly, as soon as each heart shall make the case its own. Those who are not parents will draw their conclusions from the promptings of humanity and philanthropy:--these, enlightened by reason and revelation, are also unerring.

HER RELIGIOUS INSTRUCTION.

Isabella and Peter, her youngest brother, remained with their parents, the legal property of Charles Ardinburgh till his decease, which took place when Isabella was near nine years old.

After this event, she was often surprised to find her mother in tears; and when, in her simplicity, she inquired 'Mau-mau, what makes you cry?' she would answer, 'Oh my child, I am thinking of your brothers and sisters that have been sold away from me.' And she would proceed to detail many circumstances respecting them. But Isabella long since concluded that it was the impending fate of her only remaining children, which her mother but too well understood, even then, that called up those memories from the past, and made them crucify her heart afresh.

In the evening, when her mother's work was done, she would sit down under the sparkling vault of heaven, and calling her children to her, would talk to them of the only Being that could effectually aid or protect them. Her teachings were delivered in Low Dutch, her only language, and, translated into English, ran nearly as follows:--

'My children, there is a God, who hears and sees you.' 'A God, mau-mau! Where does he live?' asked the children. 'He lives in the sky,' she replied; 'and when you are beaten, or cruelly treated, or fall into any trouble, you must ask help of him, and he will always hear and help you.' She taught them to kneel and say the Lord's prayer. She entreated them to refrain from lying and stealing, and to strive to obey their masters.

At times, a groan would escape her, and she would break cut in the language of the Psalmist--'Oh Lord, how long?' 'Oh Lord, how long?' And in reply to Isabella's question--'What ails you, mau-mau?' her only answer was, 'Oh, a good deal ails me'--'Enough ails me.' Then again, she would point them to the stars, and say, in her peculiar language, 'Those are the same stars, and that is the same moon, that look down upon your brothers and sisters, and which they see as they look up to them, though they are ever so far away from us, and each other.'

Thus, in her humble way, did she endeavor to show them their Heavenly Father, as the only being who could protect them in their perilous condition; at the same time, she would strengthen and brighten the chain of family affection, which she trusted extended itself sufficiently to connect the widely scattered members of her precious flock. These instructions of the mother were treasured up and held sacred by Isabella, as our future narrative will show.

THE AUCTION.

At length, the never-to be-forgotten day of the terrible auction arrived, when the 'slaves, horses, and other cattle' of Charles Ardinburgh, deceased, were to be put under the hammer, and again change masters. Not only Isabella and Peter, but their mother, was now destined to the auction block, and would have been struck off with the rest to the highest bidder, but for the following circumstance: A question arose among the heirs, 'Who shall be burdened with Bomefree, when we have sent away his faithful Mau-mau Bett?' He was becoming weak and infirm; his limbs were painfully rheumatic and distorted-- more from exposure and hardship than from old age, though he was several years older than Mau-mau Bett: he was no longer considered of value, but must soon be a burden and care to some one. After some contention on the point at issue, none being willing to be burdened with him, it was finally agreed, as most expedient for the heirs, that the price of Mau-mau Bett should be sacrificed, and she receive her freedom, on condition that she take care of and support her faithful James,--faithful, not only to her as a husband, but proverbially faithful as a slave to those who would not willingly sacrifice a dollar for his comfort, now that he had commenced his descent into the dark vale of decrepitude and suffering. This important decision was received as joyful news indeed to our ancient couple, who were the objects of it, and who were trying to prepare their hearts for a severe struggle, and one altogether new to them, as they had never before been separated; for, though ignorant, helpless, crushed in spirit, and weighed down with hardship and cruel bereavement, they were still human, and their human hearts beat within them with as true an affection as ever caused a human heart to beat. And their anticipated separation now, in the decline of life, after the last child had been torn from them, must have been truly appalling. Another privilege was granted them--that of remaining occupants of the same dark, humid cellar I have before described: otherwise, they were to support themselves as they best could. And as her mother was still able to do considerable work, and her father a little, they got on for some time very comfortably. The strangers who rented the house were humane people, and very kind to them; they were not rich, and owned no slaves. How long this state of things continued, we are unable to say, as Isabella had not then sufficiently cultivated her organ of time to calculate years, or even weeks or hours. But she thinks her mother must have lived several years after the death of Master Charles. She remembers going to visit her parents some three or four times before the death of her mother, and a good deal of time seemed to her to intervene between each visit.

At length her mother's health began to decline--a fever-sore made its ravages on one of her limbs, and the palsy began to shake her frame; still, she and James tottered about, picking up a little here and there, which, added to the mites contributed by their kind neighbors, sufficed to sustain life, and drive famine from the door.

DEATH OF MAU-MAU BETT.

One morning, in early autumn, (from the reason above mentioned, we cannot tell what year,) Mau-mau Bett told James she would make him a leaf of rye-bread, and get Mrs. Simmons, their kind neighbor, to bake it for them, as she would bake that forenoon. James told her he had engaged to rake after the cart for his neighbors that morning; but before he commenced, he would pole off some apples from a tree near, which they were allowed to gather; and if she could get some of them baked with the bread, it would give it a nice relish for their dinner. He beat off the apples, and soon after, saw Mau-mau Bett come out and gather them up.

At the blowing of the horn for dinner, he groped his way into his cellar, anticipating his humble, but warm and nourishing meal; when, lo! instead of being cheered by the sight and odor of fresh-baked bread and the savory apples, his cellar seemed more cheerless than usual, and at first neither sight nor sound met eye or ear. But, on groping his way through the room, his staff, which he used as a pioneer to go before, and warn him of danger, seemed to be impeded in its progress, and a low, gurgling, choking sound proceeded from the object before him, giving him the first intimation of the truth as it was, that Mau-mau Bett, his bosom companion, the only remaining member of his large family, had fallen in a fit of the palsy, and lay helpless and senseless on the earth! Who among us, located in pleasant homes, surrounded with every comfort, and so many kind and sympathizing friends, can picture to ourselves the dark and desolate state of poor old James--penniless, weak, lame, and nearly blind, as he was at the moment he found his companion was removed from him, and he was left alone in the world, with no one to aid, comfort, or console him? for she never revived again, and lived only a few hours after being discovered senseless by her poor bereaved James.

LAST DAYS OF BOMEFREE.

    Isabella and Peter were permitted to see the remains of their mother laid in their last narrow dwelling, and to make their bereaved father a little visit, ere they returned to their servitude. And most piteous were the lamentations of the poor old man, when, at last, they also were obliged to bid him "Farewell!" Juan Fernandes, on his desolate island, was not so pitiable an object as this poor lame man. Blind and crippled, he was too superannuated to think for a moment of taking care of himself, and he greatly feared no persons would interest themselves in his behalf. 'Oh,' he would exclaim, 'I had thought God would take me first,--Mau-mau was so much smarter than I, and could get about and take care of herself;--and I am so old, and so helpless. What is to become of me? I can't do anything more--my children are all gone, and here I am left helpless and alone.' 'And then, as I was taking leave of him,' said his daughter, in relating it, 'he raised his voice, and cried aloud like a child--Oh, how he DID cry! I HEAR it now--and remember it as well as if it were but yesterday--poor old man!!! He thought God had done it all--and my heart bled within me at the sight of his misery. He begged me to get permission to come and see him sometimes, which I readily and heartily promised him.' But when all had left him, the Ardinburghs, having some feeling left for their faithful and favorite slave, 'took turns about' in keeping him--permitting him to stay a few weeks at one house, and then a while at another, and so around. If, when he made a removal, the place where he was going was not too far off, he took up his line of march, staff in hand, and asked for no assistance. If it was twelve or twenty miles, they gave him a ride. While he was living in this way, Isabella was twice permitted to visit him. Another time she walked twelve miles, and carried her infant in her arms to see him, but when she reached the place where she hoped to find him, he had just left for a place some twenty miles distant, and she never saw him more. The last time she did see him, she found him seated on a rock, by the-road side, alone, and far from any house. He was then migrating from the house of one Ardinburgh to that of another, several miles distant. His hair was white like wool--he was almost blind--and his gait was more a creep than a walk--but the weather was warm and pleasant, and he did not dislike the journey. When Isabella addressed him, he recognized her voice, and was exceeding glad to see her. He was assisted to mount the wagon, was carried back to the famous cellar of which we have spoken, and there they held their last earthly conversation. He again, as usual, bewailed his loneliness,--spoke in tones of anguish of his many children, saying "They are all taken away from me! I have now not one to give me a cup of cold water--why should I live and not die?" Isabella, whose heart yearned over her father, and who would have made any sacrifice to have been able to be with, and take care of him, tried to comfort, by telling him that 'she had heard the white folks say, that all the slaves in the State would be freed in ten years, and that then she would come and take care of him.' 'I would take just as good care of you as Mau-mau would, if she was here'--continued Isabel. 'Oh, my child,' replied he, 'I cannot live the long.' 'Oh do, daddy, do live, and I will take such good care of you,' was her rejoinder. She now says, 'Why, I thought then, in my ignorance, that he could live, if he would. I just as much thought so, as I ever thought any thing in my life--and I insisted on his living: but he shook his head, and insisted he could not.'

But before Bomefree's good constitution would yield either to age, exposure, or a strong desire to die, the Ardinburghs again tired of him, and offered freedom to two old slaves--Cæsar, brother of Mau-mau Bett, and his wife Betsey--on condition that they should take care of James. (I was about to say, 'their brother-in-law'--but as slaves are neither husbands nor wives in law, the idea of their being brothers-in-law is truly ludicrous.) And although they were too old and infirm to take care of themselves, (Cæsar having been afflicted for a long time with fever-sores, and his wife with the jaundice) they eagerly accepted the boon of freedom, which had been the life-long desire of their souls--though at a time when emancipation was to them little more than destitution, and was a freedom more to be desired by the master than the slave. Sojourner declares of the slaves in their ignorance, that 'their thoughts are no longer than her finger.'

DEATH OF BOMEFREE.

A rude cabin, in a lone wood, far from any neighbors, was granted to our freed friends, as the only assistance they were now to expect. Bomefree, from this time, found his poor needs hardly supplied, as his new providers were scarce able to administer to their own wants. However, the time drew near when things were to be decidedly worse rather than better; for they had not been together long, before Betty died, and shortly after, Cæsar followed her to 'that bourne front whence no traveller returns'--leaving poor James again desolate, and more helpless than ever before; as, this time, there was no kind family in the house, and the Ardinburghs no longer invited him to their homes. Yet, lone, blind and helpless as he was, James for a time lived on. One day, an aged colored woman, named Soan, called at his shanty, and James besought her, in the most moving manner, even with tears, to tarry awhile and wash and mend him up, so that he might once more be decent and comfortable; for he was suffering dreadfully with the filth and vermin that had collected upon him.

Soan was herself an emancipated slave, old and weak, with no one to care for her; and she lacked the courage to undertake a job of such seeming magnitude, fearing she might herself get sick, and perish there without assistance; and with great reluctance, and a heart swelling with pity, as she afterwards declared, she felt obliged to leave him in his wretchedness and filth. And shortly after her visit, this faithful slave, this deserted wreck of humanity, was found on his miserable pallet, frozen and stiff in death. The kind angel had come at last, and relieved him of the many miseries that his fellow-man had heaped upon him. Yes, he had died, chilled and starved, with none to speak a kindly word, or do a kindly deed for him, in that last dread hour of need!

The news of his death reached the ears of John Ardinburgh, a grandson of the old Colonel; and he declared that 'Bomefree, who had ever been a kind and faithful slave, should now have a good funeral.' And now, gentle reader, what think you constituted a good funeral? Answer--some black paint for the coffin, and--a jug of ardent spirits! What a compensation for a life of toil, of patient submission to repeated robberies of the most aggravated kind, and, also, far more than murderous neglect!! Mankind often vainly attempt to atone for unkindness or cruelty to the living, by honoring the same after death; but John Ardinburgh undoubtedly meant his pot of paint and jug of whisky should act as an opiate on his slaves, rather than on his own seared conscience.

COMMENCEMENT OF ISABELLA'S TRIALS IN LIFE.

Having seen the sad end of her parents, so far as it relates to this earthly life, we will return with Isabella to that memorable auction which threatened to separate her father and mother. A slave auction is a terrible affair to its victims, and its incidents and consequences are graven on their hearts as with a pen of burning steel.

At this memorable time, Isabella was struck off, for the sum of one hundred dollars, to one John Nealy, of Ulster County, New York; and she has an impression that in this sale she was connected with a lot of sheep. She was now nine years of age, and her trials in life may be dated from this period. She says, with emphasis, 'Now the war begun.' She could only talk Dutch--and the Nealys could only talk English. Mr. Nealy could understand Dutch, but Isabel and her mistress could neither of them understand the language of the other--and this, of itself, was a formidable obstacle in the way of a good understanding between them, and for some time was a fruitful source of dissatisfaction to the mistress, and of punishment and suffering to Isabella. She says, 'If they sent me for a frying-pan, not knowing what they meant, perhaps I carried them the pot-hooks and trammels. Then, oh! how angry mistress would be with me!' Then she suffered 'terribly--terribly,' with the cold. During the winter her feet were badly frozen, for want of proper covering. They gave her a plenty to eat, and also a plenty of whippings. One Sunday morning, in particular, she was told to go to the barn; on going there, she found her master with a bundle of rods, prepared in the embers, and bound together with cords. When he had tied her hands together before her, he gave her the most cruel whipping she was ever tortured with. He whipped her till the flesh was deeply lacerated, and the blood streamed from her wounds--and the scars remain to the present day, to testify to the fact. 'And now,' she says, 'when I hear 'em tell of whipping women on the bare flesh, it makes my flesh crawl, and my very hair rise on my head! Oh! my God!' she continues, 'what a way is this of treating human beings?' In these hours of her extremity, she did not forget the instructions of her mother, to go to God in all her trials, and every affliction; and she not only remembered, but obeyed: going to him, 'and telling him all--and asking Him if He thought it was right,' and begging him to protect and shield her from her persecutors.

She always asked with an unwavering faith that she should receive just what she plead for,--'And now,' she says, 'though it seems curious, I do not remember ever asking for anything but what I got it. And I always received it as an answer to my prayers. When I got beaten, I never knew it long enough beforehand to pray; and I always thought if I only had had time to pray to God for help, I should have escaped the beating.' She had no idea God had any knowledge of her thoughts, save what she told him; or heard her prayers, unless they were spoken audibly. And consequently, she could not pray unless she had time and opportunity to go by herself, where she could talk to God without being overheard.

TRIALS CONTINUED.

When she had been at Mr. Nealy's several months, she began to beg God most earnestly to send her father to her, and as soon as she commenced to pray, she began as confidently to look for his coming, and, ere it was long to her great joy, he came. She had no opportunity to speak to him of the troubles that weighed so heavily on her spirit, while he remained; but when he left, she followed him to the gate, and unburdened her heart to him, inquiring if he could not do something to get her a new and better place. In this way the slaves often assist each other, by ascertaining who are kind to their slaves, comparatively; and then using their influence to get such an one to hire or buy their friends; and masters, often from policy, as well as from latent humanity, allow those they are about to sell or let, to choose their own places, if the persons they happen to select for masters are considered safe pay. He promised to do all he could, and they parted. But, every day, as long as the snow lasted, (for there was snow on the ground at the time,) she returned to the spot where they separated, and walking in the tracks her father had made in the snow, repeated her prayer that 'God would help her father get her a new and better place.'

A long time had not elapsed, when a fisherman by the name of Scriver appeared at Mr. Nealy's, and inquired of Isabel 'if she would like to go and live with him.' She eagerly answered 'Yes,' nothing doubting but he was sent in answer to her prayer; and she soon started off with him, walking while he rode; for he had bought her at the suggestion of her father, paying one hundred and five dollars for her. He also lived in Ulster County, but some five or six miles from Mr. Nealy's.

Scriver, besides being a fisherman, kept a tavern for the accommodation of people of his own class--for his was a rude, uneducated family, exceedingly profane in their language, but, on the whole, an honest, kind and well-disposed people.

They owned a large farm, but left it wholly unimproved; attending mainly to their vocations of fishing and inn-keeping. Isabella declares she can ill describe the life she led with them. It was a wild, out-of-door kind of lief. She was expected to carry fish, to hoe corn, to bring roots and herbs from the wood for beers, go to the Strand for a gallon of molasses or liquor as the case might require, and 'browse around,' as she expresses it. It was a life that suited her well for the time--being as devoid of hardship or terror as it was of improvement; a need which had not yet become a want. Instead of improving at this place, morally, she retrograded, as their example taught her to curse; and it was here that she took her first oath. After living with them about a year and a half, she was sold to one John J. Dumont, for the sum of seventy pounds. This was in 1810. Mr. Dumont lived in the same county as her former masters, in the town of New Paltz, and she remained with him till a short time previous to her emancipation by the State, in 1828.

HER STANDING WITH HER NEW MASTER AND MISTRESS.

Had Mrs. Dumont possessed that vein of kindness and consideration for the slaves, so perceptible in her husband's character, Isabella would have been as comfortable here, as one had best be, if one must be a slave. Mr. Dumont had been nursed in the very lap of slavery, and being naturally a man of kind feelings, treated his slaves with all the consideration he did his other animals, and more, perhaps. But Mrs. Dumont, who had been born and educated in a non-slaveholding family, and, like many others, used only to work-people, who, under the most stimulating of human motives, were willing to put forth their every energy, could not have patience with the creeping gait, the dull understanding, or see any cause for the listless manners and careless, slovenly habits of the poor down-trodden outcast-- entirely forgetting that every high and efficient motive had been removed far from him; and that, had not his very intellect been crushed out of him, the slave would find little ground for aught but hopeless despondency. From this source arose a long series of trials in the life of our heroine, which we must pass over in silence; some from motives of delicacy, and others, because the relation of them might inflict undeserved pain on some now living, whom Isabel remembers only with esteem and love; therefore, the reader will not be surprised if our narrative appear somewhat tame at this point, and may rest assured that it is not for want of facts, as the most thrilling incidents of this portion of her life are from various motives suppressed.

One comparatively trifling incident she wishes related, as it made a deep impression on her mind at the time--showing, as she thinks, how God shields the innocent, and causes them to triumph over their enemies, and also how she stood between master and mistress. In her family, Mrs. Dumont employed two white girls, one of whom, named Kate, evinced a disposition to 'lord it over' Isabel, and, in her emphatic language, 'to grind her down.' Her master often shielded her from the attacks and accusations of others, praising her for her readiness and ability to work, and these praises seemed to foster a spirit of hostility to her, in the minds of Mrs. Dumont and her white servant, the latter of whom took every opportunity to cry up her faults, lessen her in the esteem of her master and increase against her the displeasure of her mistress, which was already more than sufficient for Isabel's comfort. Her master insisted that she could do as much work as half a dozen common people, and do it well, too; whilst her mistress insisted that the first was true, only because it ever came from her hand but half performed. A good deal of feeling arose from this difference of opinion, which was getting to rather an uncomfortable height, when, all at once, the potatoes that Isabel cooked for breakfast assumed a dingy, dirty look. Her mistress blamed her severely, asking her master to observe 'a fine specimen of Bell's work!'--adding, 'it is the way all her work is done.' Her master scolded also this time, and commanded her to be more careful in future. Kate joined with zest in the censures, and was very hard upon her. Isabella thought that she had done all she well could to have them nice; and became quite distressed at these appearances, and wondered what she should do to avoid them. In this dilemma, Gertrude Dumont, (Mr. D.'s eldest child, a good, kind-hearted girl of ten years, who pitied Isabel sincerely,) when she heard them all blame her so unsparingly, came forward, offering her sympathy and assistance; and when about to retire to bed, on the night of Isabella's humiliation, she advanced to Isabel, and told her, if she would wake her early next morning, she would get up and attend to her potatoes for her, while she (Isabella) went to milking, and they would see if they could not have them nice, and not have 'Poppee,' her word for father, and 'Matty,' her word for mother, and all of 'em, scolding so terribly.

Isabella gladly availed herself of this kindness, which touched her to the heart, amid so much of an opposite spirit. When Isabella had put the potatoes over to boil. Getty told her she would herself tend the fire, while Isabel milked. She had not long been seated by the fire, in performance of her promise, when Kate entered, and requested Gertrude to go out of the room and do something for her, which she refused, still keeping her place in the corner. While there, Kate came sweeping about the fire, caught up a chip, lifted some ashes with it, and dashed them into the kettle. Now the mystery was solved, the plot discovered! Kate was working a little too fast at making her mistress's words good, at showing that

Mrs. Dumont and herself were on the right side of the dispute, and consequently at gaining power over Isabella. Yes, she was quite too fast, inasmuch as she had overlooked the little figure of justice, which sat in the corner, with scales nicely balanced, waiting to give all their dues.

But the time had come when she was to be overlooked no longer. It was Getty's turn to speak now. 'Oh, Poppee! oh, Poppee!' said she, 'Kate has been putting ashes in among the potatoes! I saw her do it! Look at those that fell on the outside of the kettle! You can now see what made the potatoes so dingy every morning, though Bell washed them clean!' And she repeated her story to every new comer, till the fraud was made as public as the censure of Isabella had been. Her mistress looked blank, and remained dumb--her master muttered something which sounded very like an oath-- and poor Kate was so chop-fallen, she looked like a convicted criminal, who would gladly have hid herself, (now that the baseness was out,) to conceal her mortified pride and deep chagrin.

It was a fine triumph for Isabella and her master, and she became more ambitious than ever to please him; and he stimulated her ambition by his commendation, and by boasting of her to his friends, telling them that 'tha wench' (pointing to Isabel) 'is better to me than a man--for she will do a good family's washing in the night, and be ready in the morning to go into the field, where she will do as much at raking and binding as my best hands.' Her ambition and desire to please were so great, that she often worked several nights in succession, sleeping only short snatches, as she sat in her chair; and some nights she would not allow herself to take any sleep, save what she could get resting herself against the wall, fearing that if she sat down, she would sleep too long. These extra exertions to please, and the praises consequent upon them, brought upon her head the envy of her fellow-slaves, and they taunted her with being the 'white folks' nigger.' On the other hand, she received a larger share of the confidence of her master, and many small favors that were by them unattainable. I asked her if her master, Dumont, ever whipped her? She answered, 'Oh yes, he sometimes whipped me soundly, though never cruelly. And the most severe whipping he ever give me was because I was cruel to a cat.' At this time she looked upon her master as a God; and believed that he knew of and could see her at all times, even as God himself. And she used sometimes to confess her delinquencies, from the conviction that he already knew them, and that she should fare better if she confessed voluntarily: and if any one talked to her of the injustice of her being a slave, she answered them with contempt and immediately told her master. She then firmly believed that slavery was right and honorable. Yet she now sees very clearly the false position they were all in, both masters and slaves; and she looks back, with utter astonishment, at the absurdity of the claims so arrogantly set up by the masters, over beings designed by God to be as free as kings; and at the perfect stupidity of the slave, in admitting for one moment the validity of these claims.

In obedience to her mother's instructions, she had educated herself to such a sense of honesty, that, when she had become a mother, she would sometimes whip her child when it cried to her for bread, rather than give it a piece secretly, lest it should learn to take what was not its own! And the writer of this knows, from personal observation, that the slaveholders of the South feel it to be a religious duty to teach their slaves to be honest, and never to take what is not their own! Oh consistency, art thou not a jewel? Yet Isabella glories in the fact that she was faithful and true to her master; she says, 'It made me true to my God'--meaning, that it helped to form in her a character that loved truth, and hated a lie, and had saved her from the bitter pains and fears that are sure to follow in the wake of insincerity and hypocrisy.

As she advanced in years, an attachment sprung up between herself and a slave named Robert. But his master, an Englishman by the name of Catlin, anxious that no one's property but his own should be enhanced by the increase of his slaves, forbade Robert's visits to Isabella, and commanded him to take a wife among his fellow-servants. Notwithstanding this interdiction, Robert, following the bent of his inclinations, continued his visits to Isabel, though very stealthily, and, as he believed, without exciting the suspicion of his master; but one Saturday afternoon, hearing that Bell was ill, he took the liberty to go and see her. The first intimation she had of his visit was the appearance of her master, inquiring if she had seen Bob.' On her answering in the negative, he said to her, 'If you see him, tell him to take care of himself, for the Catlins are after him.' Almost at that instant, Bob made his appearance; and the first people he met were his old and his young masters. They were terribly enraged at finding him there, and the eldest began cursing, and calling upon his son to 'Knock down the d--d black rascal;' at the same time, they both fell upon him like tigers, beating him with the heavy ends of their canes, bruising and mangling his head and face in the most awful manner, and causing the blood, which streamed from his wounds, to cover him like a slaughtered beast, constituting him a most shocking spectacle. Mr. Dumont interposed at this point, telling the ruffians they could no longer thus spill human blood on his premises--he would have 'no niggers killed there.' The Catlins then took a rope they had taken with them for the purpose, and tied Bob's hands behind him in such a manner, that Mr. Dumont insisted on loosening the cord, declaring that no brute should be tied in that manner, where he was. And as they led him away, like the greatest of criminals, the more humane Dumont followed them to their homes, as Robert's protector; and when he returned, he kindly went to Bell, as he called her, telling her he did not think they would strike him any more, as their wrath had greatly cooled before he left them. Isabella had witnessed this scene from her window, and was greatly shocked at the murderous treatment of poor Robert, whom she truly loved, and whose only crime, in the eye of his persecutors, was his affection for her. This beating, and we know not what after treatment, completely subdued the spirit of its victim, for Robert ventured no more to visit Isabella, but like an obedient and faithful chattel, took himself a wife from the house of his master. Robert did not live many years after his last visit to Isabel, but took his departure to that country, where 'they neither marry nor are given in marriage,' and where the oppressor cannot molest.

SUPERWOMEN

ISABELLA'S MARRIAGE.

Subsequently, Isabella was married to a fellow slave, named Thomas, who had previously had two wives, one of whom, if not both, had been torn from him and sold far away. And it is more than probable, that he was not only allowed but encouraged to take another at each successive sale. I say it is probable, because the writer of this knows from personal observation, that such is the custom among slaveholders at the present day; and that in a twenty months' residence among them, we never knew anyone to open the lip against the practice; and when we severely censured it, the slaveholder had nothing to say; and the slave pleaded that, under existing circumstances, he could do no better.

Such an abominable state of things is silently tolerated, to say the least, by slaveholders--deny it who may. And what is that religion that sanctions, even by its silence all that is embraced in the 'Peculiar Institution?' If there can be anything more diametrically opposed to the religion of Jesus, than the working of this soul-killing system--which is as truly sanctioned by the religion of America as are her ministers and churches--we wish to be shown where it can be found.

We have said, Isabella was married to Thomas--she was, after the fashion of slavery, one of the slaves performing the ceremony for them; as no true minister of Christ can perform, as in the presence of God, what he knows to be a mere farce, a mock marriage, unrecognized by any civil law, and liable to be annulled any moment, when the interest or caprice of the master should dictate.

With what feelings must slaveholders expect us to listen to their horror of amalgamation in prospect, while they are well aware that we know how calmly and quietly they contemplate the present state of licentiousness their own wicked laws have created, not only as it regards the slave, but as it regards the more privileged portion of the population of the South?

Slaveholders appear to me to take the same notice of the vices of the slave, as one does of the vicious disposition of his horse. They are often an inconvenience; further than that, they care not to trouble themselves about the matter.

MARRIAGE OF A COLORED SOLDIER AT VICKSBURG BY CHAPLAIN WARREN OF THE FREEDMEN'S BUREAU.

ISABELLA AS A MOTHER.

In process of time, Isabella found herself the mother of five children, and she rejoiced in being permitted to be the instrument of increasing the property of her oppressors! Think, dear reader, without a blush, if you can, for one moment, of a mother thus willingly, and with pride, laying her own children, the 'flesh of her flesh,' on the altar of slavery--a sacrifice to the bloody Moloch! But we must remember that beings capable of such sacrifices are not mothers; they are only 'things,' 'chattels,' 'property.'

But since that time, the subject of this narrative has made some advances from a state of chattelism towards that of a woman and a mother; and she now looks back upon her thoughts and feelings there, in her state of ignorance and degradation, as one does on the dark imagery of a fitful dream. One moment it seems but a frightful illusion; again it appears a terrible reality. I would to God it were but a dreamy myth, and not, as it now stands, a horrid reality to some three millions of chattelized human beings.

I have already alluded to her care not to teach her children to steal, by her example; and she says, with groanings that cannot be written, 'The Lord only knows how many times I let my children go hungry, rather than take secretly the bread I liked not to ask for.' All parents who annul their preceptive teachings by their daily practices would do well to profit by her example.

Another proof of her master's kindness of heart is found in the following fact. If her master came into the house and found her infant crying, (as she could not always attend to its wants and the commands of her mistress at the same time,) he would turn to his wife with a look of reproof, and ask her why she did not see the child taken care of; saying, most earnestly, 'I will not hear this crying; I can't bear it, and I will not hear any child cry so. Here, Bell, take care of this child, if no more work is done for a week.' And he would linger to see if his orders were obeyed, and not countermanded.

When Isabella went to the field to work, she used to put her infant in a basket, tying a rope to each handle, and suspending the basket to a branch of a tree, set another small child to swing it. It was thus secure from reptiles, and was easily administered to, and even lulled to sleep, by a child too young for other labors. I was quite struck with the ingenuity of such a baby-tender, as I have sometimes been with the swinging hammock the native mother prepares for her sick infant--apparently so much easier than aught we have in our more civilized homes; easier for the child, because it gets the motion without the least jar; and easier for the nurse, because the hammock is strung so high as to supersede the necessity of stooping.

SLAVEHOLDER'S PROMISES.

After emancipation had been decreed by the State, some years before the time fixed for its consummation, Isabella's master told her if she would do well, and be faithful, he would give her 'free papers,' one year before she was legally free by statute. In the year 1826, she had a badly diseased hand, which greatly diminished her usefulness; but on the arrival of July 4, 1827, the time specified for her receiving her 'free papers,' she claimed the fulfillment of her master's promise; but he refused granting it, on account (as he alleged) of the loss he had sustained by her hand. She plead that she had worked all the time, and done many things she was not wholly able to do, although she knew she had been less useful than formerly; but her master remained inflexible. Her very faithfulness probably operated against her now, and he found it less easy than he thought to give up the profits of his faithful Bell, who had so long done him efficient service.

But Isabella inwardly determined that she would remain quietly with him only until she had spun his wool--about one hundred pounds--and then she would leave him, taking the rest of the time to herself. 'Ah!' she says, with emphasis that cannot be written, 'the slaveholders are TERRIBLE for promising to give you this or that, or such and such a privilege, if you will do thus and so; and when the time of fulfillment comes, and one claims the promise, they, forsooth, recollect nothing of the kind; and you are, like as not, taunted with being a

LIAR; or, at best, the slave is accused of not having performed his part or condition of the contract.' 'Oh!' said she, 'I have felt as if I could not live through the operation sometimes. Just think of us! so eager for our pleasures, and just foolish enough to keep feeding and feeding ourselves up with the idea that we should get what had been thus fairly promised; and when we think it is almost in our hands, find ourselves flatly denied! Just think! how could we bear it? Why, there was Charles Brodhead promised his slave Ned, that when harvesting was over, he might go and see his wife, who lived some twenty or thirty miles off. So Ned worked early and late, and as soon as the harvest was all in, he claimed the promised boon. His master said, he had merely told him he 'would see if he could go, when the harvest was over; but now he saw that he could not go.' But Ned, who still claimed a positive promise, on which he had fully depended, went on cleaning his shoes. His master asked him if he intended going, and on his replying 'yes,' took up a sled-stick that lay near him, and gave him such a blow on the head as broke his skull, killing him dead on the spot. The poor colored people all felt struck down by the blow.' Ah! and well they might. Yet it was but one of a long series of bloody, and other most effectual blows, struck against their liberty and their lives.*

* Yet no official notice was taken of his more than brutal murder.

But to return from our digression.

The subject of this narrative as to have been free July 4, 1827, but she continued with her master till the wool was spun, and the heaviest of the 'fall's work' closed up, when she concluded to take her freedom into her own hands, and seek her fortune in some other place.

HER ESCAPE.

The question in her mind, and one not easily solved, now was, 'How can I get away?' So, as was her usual custom, she 'told God she was afraid to go in the night, and in the day everybody would see her.' At length, the thought came to her that she could leave just before the day dawned, and get out of the neighborhood where she was known before the people were much astir. 'Yes,' said she, fervently, 'that's a good thought! Thank you, God, for that thought!' So, receiving it as coming direct from God, she acted upon it, and one fine morning, a little before day-break, she might have been seen stepping stealthily away from the rear of Master Dumont's house, her infant on one arm and her wardrobe on the other; the bulk and weight of which, probably, she never found so convenient as on the present occasion, a cotton handkerchief containing both her clothes and her provisions.

As she gained the summit of a high hill, a considerable distance from her master's, the sun offended her by coming forth in all his pristine splendor. She thought it never was so light before; indeed, she thought it much too light. She stopped to look about her, and ascertain if her pursuers were yet in sight. No one appeared, and, for the first time, the question came up for settlement, 'Where, and to whom, shall I go?' In all her thoughts of getting away, she had not once asked herself whither she should direct her steps. She sat down, fed her infant, and again turning her thoughts to

God, her only help, she prayed him to direct her to some safe asylum. And soon it occurred to her, that there was a man living somewhere in the direction she had been pursuing, by the name of Levi Rowe, whom she had known, and who, she thought, would be likely to befriend her. She accordingly pursued her way to his house, where she found him ready to entertain and assist her, though he was then on his death-bed. He bade her partake of the hospitalities of his house, said he knew of two good places where she might get in, and requested his wife to show her where they were to be found. As soon as she came in sight of the first house, she recollected having seen it and its inhabitants before, and instantly exclaimed, 'That's the place for me; I shall stop there.' She went there, and found the good people of the house, Mr. and Mrs. Van Wagener, absent, but was kindly received and hospitably entertained by their excellent mother, till the return of her children. When they arrived, she made her case known to them. They listened to her story, assuring her they never turned the needy away, and willingly gave her employment.

She had not been there long before her old master, Dumont, appeared, as she had anticipated; for when she took French leave of him, she resolved not to go too far from him, and not put him to as much trouble in looking her up--for the latter he was sure to do--as Tom and Jack had done when they ran away from him, a short time before. This was very considerate in her, to say the least, and a proof that 'like begets like.' He had often considered her feelings, though not always, and she was equally considerate.

When her master saw her, he said, 'Well, Bell, so you've run away from me.' 'No, I did not run away; I walked away by day-light, and all because you had promised me a year of my time.' His reply was, 'You must go back with me.' Her decisive answer was, 'No, I won't go back with you.' He said, 'Well, I shall take the child.' This also was as stoutly negative.

Mr. Isaac S. Van Wagener then interposed, saying, he had never been in the practice of buying and selling slaves; he did not believe in slavery; but, rather than have Isabella taken back by force, he would buy her services for the balance of the year--for which her master charged twenty dollars, and five in addition for the child. The sum was paid, and her master Dumont departed; but not till he had heard Mr. Van Wagener tell her not to call him master,--adding, 'there is but one master; and he who is your master is my master.' Isabella inquired what she should call him? He answered, 'Call me Isaac Van Wagener, and my wife is Maria Van Wagener.' Isabella could not understand this, and thought it a mighty change, as it most truly was from a master whose word was law, to simple Isaac S. Van Wagener, who was master to no one. With these noble people, who, though they could not be the masters of slaves, were undoubtedly a portion of God's nobility, she resided one year, and from them she derived the name of Van Wagener; he being her last master in the eye of the law, and a slave's surname is ever the same as his master; that is, if he is allowed to have any other name than Tom, Jack, or Guffin. Slaves have sometimes been severely punished for adding their master's name to their own. But when they have no particular title to it, it is no particular offence.

ILLEGAL SALE OF HER SON.

A little previous to Isabel's leaving her old master, he had sold her child, a boy of five years, to a Dr. Gedney, who took him with him as far as New York city, on his way to England; but finding the boy too small for his service, he sent him back to his brother, Solomon Gedney. This man disposed of him to his sister's husband, a wealthy planter, by the name of Fowler, who took him to his own home in Alabama.

This illegal and fraudulent transaction had been perpetrated some months before Isabella knew of it, as she was now living at Mr. Van Wagener's. The law expressly prohibited the sale of any slave out of the State,--and all minors were to be free at twenty-one years of age; and Mr. Dumont had sold Peter with the express under-standing, that he was soon to return to the State of New York, and be emancipated at the specified time.

When Isabel heard that her son had been sold South, she immediately started on foot and alone, to find the man who had thus dared, in the face of all law, human and divine, to sell her child out of the State; and if possible, to bring him to account for the deed.

Arriving at New Paltz, she went directly to her former mistress, Dumont, complaining bitterly of the removal of her son. Her mistress heard her through, and then replied--'Ugh! a fine fuss to make about a little nigger! Why, have n't you as many of 'em left as you can see to and take care of? A pity 'tis, the niggers are not all in Guinea!! Making such a halloo-balloo about the neighborhood; and all for a paltry nigger!!!' Isabella heard her through, and after a moment's hesitation, answered, in tons of deep determination--'I'll have my child again.' 'Have your child again!' repeated her mistress--her tones big with contempt, and scorning the absurd idea of her getting him. 'How can you get him? And what have you to support him with, if you could? Have you any money?' 'No,' answered Bell, 'I have no money, but God has enough, or what's better! And I'll have my child again.' These words were pronounced in the most slow, solemn and determined measure and manner. And in speaking of it, she says, 'Oh, my God! I know'd I'd have him agin. I was sure God would help me to get him. Why, I felt so tall within--I felt as if the power of a nation was with me!'

The impressions made by Isabella on her auditors, when moved by lofty or deep feeling, can never be transmitted to paper, (to use the words of another,) till by some Daguerrian art, we are enabled to transfer the look, the gesture, the tones of voice, in connection with the quaint, yet fit expressions used, and the spirit-stirring animation that, at such a time, pervades all she says.

After leaving her mistress, she called on Mrs. Gedney, mother of him who had sold her boy; who, after listening to her lamentations, her grief being mingled with indignation at the sale of her son, and her declaration that she would have him again--said, 'Dear me! What a disturbance to make about your child! What, is your child better than my child? My child is gone out there, and yours is gone to live with her, to have enough of everything, and to be treated like a gentleman!' And here she laughed at Isabel's absurd fears, as she would represent them to be. 'Yes,' said Isabel, 'your child has gone there, but she is married and my boy has gone as a slave, and he is too little to go so far from his mother. Oh, I must have my child.' And here the continued laugh of Mrs. G. seemed to Isabel, in this time of anguish and distress, almost demoniacal. And well it was for Mrs. Gedney, that, at that time, she could not even dream of the awful fate awaiting her own beloved daughter, at the hands of him whom she had chosen as worthy the wealth of her love and confidence, and in whose society her young heart had calculated on a happiness, purer and more elevated than was ever conferred by a kingly crown. But, alas! she was doomed to disappointment, as we shall relate by and by. At this point, Isabella earnestly begged of God that he would show to those about her that He was her helper; and she adds, in narrating, 'And He did; or, if He did not show them, he did me.'

IT IS OFTEN DARKEST JUST BEFORE DAWN.

This homely proverb was illustrated in the case of our sufferer; for, at the period at which we have arrived in our narrative, to her the darkness seemed palpable, and the waters of affliction covered her soul; yet light was about to break in upon her.

Soon after the scenes related in our last chapter, which had harrowed up her very soul to agony, she met a man, (we would like to tell you who, dear reader, but it would be doing him no kindness, even at the present day, to do so,) who evidently sympathized with her, and counseled her to go to the Quakers, telling her they were already feeling very indignant at the fraudulent sale of her son, and assuring her that they would readily assist her, and direct her what to do. He pointed out to her two houses, where lived some of those people, who formerly, more than any other sect, perhaps, lived out the principles of the gospel of Christ. She wended her way to their dwellings, was listened to, unknown as she personally was to them, with patience, and soon gained their sympathies and active co-operation.

They gave her lodgings for the night; and it is very amusing to hear her tell of the 'nice, high, clean, white, beautiful bed' assigned her to sleep in, which contrasted so strangely with her former pallets, that she sat down and contemplated it, perfectly absorbed in wonder that such a bed should have been appropriated to one like herself. For some time she thought that she would lie down beneath it, on her usual bedstead, the floor. 'I did, indeed,' says she, laughing heartily at her former self. However, she finally concluded to make use of the bed, for fear that not to do so might injure the feelings of her good hostess. In the morning, the Quaker saw that she was taken and set down near Kingston, with directions to go to the Court House, and enter complaint to the Grand Jury.

By a little inquiry, she found which was the building she sought, went into the door, and taking the first man she saw of imposing appearance for the grand jury, she commenced her complaint. But he very civilly informed her there was no Grand Jury there; she must go up stairs. When she had with some difficulty ascended the flight through the crowd that filled them, she again turned to the 'grandest' looking man she could select, telling him she had come to enter a complaint to the Grand Jury. For his own amusement, he inquired what her complaint was; but, when he saw it was a serious matter, he said to her, 'This is no place to enter a complaint--go in there, pointing in a particular direction.

She then went in, where she found the Grand Jurors indeed sitting, and again commenced to relate her injuries. After holding some conversation among themselves, one of them rose, and bidding her follow him, led the way to a side office, where he heard her story, and asked her 'if she could swear that the child she spoke of was her son?' 'Yes,' she answered, 'I swear it's my son.' 'Stop, stop!' said the lawyer, 'you must swear by this book'--giving her a book, which she thinks must have been the Bible. She took it, and putting it to her lips, began again to swear it was her child. The clerks, unable to preserve their gravity any longer, burst into an uproarious laugh; and one of them inquired of lawyer Chip of what use it could be to make her swear. 'It will answer the law,' replied the officer. He then made her comprehend just what he wished her to do, and she took a lawful oath, as far as the outward ceremony could make it one. All can judge how far she understood its spirit and meaning.

He now gave her a writ, directing her to take it to the constable of New Paltz, and have him serve it on Solomon Gedney. She obeyed, walking, or rather trotting, in her haste, some eight or nine miles.

But while the constable, through mistake, served the writ on a brother of the real culprit, Solomon Gedney slipped into a boat, and was nearly across the North River, on whose banks they were standing, before the dull Dutch constable was aware of his mistake. Solomon Gedney, meanwhile, consulted a lawyer, who advised him to go to Alabama and bring back the boy, otherwise it might cost him fourteen years' imprisonment, and a thousand dollars in cash. By this time, it is hoped he began to feel that selling slaves unlawfully was not so good a business as he had wished to find it. He secreted himself till due preparations could be made, and soon set sail for Alabama. Steamboats and railroads had not then annihilated distance to the extent they now have, and although he left in the fall of the year, spring came ere he returned, bringing the boy with him--but holding on to him as his property. It had ever been Isabella's prayer, not only that her son might be returned, but that he should be delivered from bondage, and into her own hands, lest he should be punished out of mere spite to her, who was so greatly annoying and irritating to her oppressors; and if her suit was gained, her very triumph would add vastly to their irritation.

She again sought advice of Esquire Chip, whose counsel was, that the aforesaid constable serve the before-mentioned writ upon the right person. This being done, soon brought Solomon Gedney up to Kingston, where he gave bonds for his appearance at court, in the sum of $600.

Esquire Chip next informed his client, that her case must now lie over till the next session of the court, some months in the future. 'The law must take its course,' said he.

'What! wait another court! wait months?' said the persevering mother. 'Why, long before that time, he can go clear off, and take my child with him--no one knows where. I cannot wait; I must have him now, whilst he is to be had.' 'Well,' said the lawyer, very coolly, 'if he puts the boy out of the way, he must pay the $600--one half of which will be yours;' supposing, perhaps, that $300 would pay for a 'heap of children,' in the eye of a slave who never, in all her life, called a dollar her own. But in this instance, he was mistaken in his reckoning. She assured him, that she had not been seeking money, neither would money satisfy her; it was her son, and her son alone she wanted, and her son she must have. Neither could she wait court, not she. The lawyer used his every argument to convince her, that she ought to be very thankful for what they had done for her; that it was a great deal, and it was but reasonable that she should now wait patiently the time of the court.

Yet she never felt, for a moment, like being influenced by these suggestions. She felt confident she was to receive a full and literal answer to her prayer, the burden of which had been--'O Lord, give my son into my hands, and that speedily! Let not the spoilers have him any longer.' Notwithstanding, she very distinctly saw that those who had thus far helped her on so kindly were wearied of her, and she feared God was wearied also. She had a short time previous learned that Jesus was a Savior, and an intercessor; and she thought that if Jesus could but be induced to plead for her in the present trial, God would listen to him, though he were wearied of her importunities. To him, of course, she applied. As she was walking about, scarcely knowing whither she went, asking within herself, 'Who will show me any good, and lend a helping hand in this matter,' she was accosted by a perfect stranger, and one whose name she has never learned, in the following terms: 'Halloo, there; how do you get along with your boy? do they give him up to you?' She told him all, adding that now everybody was tired, and she had none to help her. He said, 'Look here!

I'll tell you what you'd better do. Do you see that stone house yonder?' pointing in a particular direction. 'Well, lawyer Demain lives there, and do you go to him, and lay your case before him; I think he'll help you. Stick to him. Don't give him peace till he does. I feel sure if you press him, he'll do it for you.' She needed no further urging, but trotted off at her peculiar gait in the direction of his house, as fast as possible,--and she was not encumbered with stockings, shoes, or any other heavy article of dress. When she had told him her story, in her impassioned manner, he looked at her a few moments, as if to ascertain if he were contemplating a new variety of the genus homo, and then told her, if she would give him five dollars, he would get her son for her, in twenty-four hours. 'Why,' she replied, 'I have no money, and never had a dollar in my life!' Said he, 'If you will go to those Quakers in Poppletown, who carried you to court, they will help you to five dollars in cash, I have no doubt; and you shall have your son in twenty-four hours, from the time you bring me that sum.' She performed the journey to Poppletown, a distance of some ten miles, very expeditiously; collected considerable more than the sum specified by the barrister; then, shutting the money tightly in her hand, she trotted back, and paid the lawyer a larger fee than he had demanded. When inquired of by people what she had done with the overplus, she answered, 'Oh, I got it for lawyer Demain, and I gave it to him.' They assured her she was a fool to do so; that she should have kept all over five dollars, and purchased herself shoes with it. 'Oh, I do not want money or clothes now, I only want my son; and if five dollars will get him, more will surely get him.' And if the lawyer had returned it to her, she avers she would not have accepted it. She was perfectly willing he should have every coin she could raise, if he would but restore her lost son to her. Moreover, the five dollars he required were for the remuneration of him who should go after her son and his master, and not for his own services.

The lawyer now renewed his promise, that she should have her son in twenty-four hours. But Isabella, having no idea of this space of time, went several times in a day, to ascertain if her son had come. Once, when the servant opened the door and saw her, she said, in a tone expressive of much surprise, 'Why, this woman's come again!' She then wondered if she went too often. When the lawyer appeared, he told her the twenty-four hours would not expire till the next morning; if she would call then, she would see her son. The next morning saw Isabel at the lawyer's door, while he was yet in his bed. He now assured her it was morning till noon; and that before noon her son would be there, for he had sent the famous 'Matty Styles' after him, who would not fail to have the boy and his master on hand in due season, either dead or alive; of that he was sure. Telling her she need not come again; he would himself inform her of their arrival.

After dinner, he appeared at Mr. Rutzer's, (a place the lawyer had procured for her, while she awaited the arrival of her boy,) assuring her, her son had come; but that he stoutly denied having any mother, or any relatives in that place; and said, 'she must go over and identify him.' She went to the office, but at sight of her the boy cried aloud, and regarded her as some terrible being, who was about to take him away from a kind and loving friend. He knelt, even, and begged them, with tears, not to take him away from his dear master, who had brought him from the dreadful South, and been so kind to him.

When he was questioned relative to the bad scar on his forehead, he said, 'Fowler's horse hove him.' And of the one on his cheek, 'That was done by running against the carriage.' In answering these questions he looked imploringly at his master, as much as to say, 'If they are falsehoods, you bade me say them; may they be satisfactory to you, at least.'

The justice, noting his appearance, bade him forget his master and attend only to him. But the boy persisted in denying his mother, and clinging to his master, saying his mother did not live in such a place as that. However, they allowed the mother to identify her son; and Esquire Demain pleaded that he claimed the boy for her, on the ground that he had been sold out of the State, contrary to the laws in such cases made and provided--spoke of the penalties annexed to said crime, and of the sum of money the delinquent was to pay, in case any one chose to prosecute him for the offence he had committed. Isabella, who was sitting in a corner, scarcely daring to breathe, thought within herself, 'If I can but get the boy, the $200 may remain for whoever else chooses to prosecute--I have done enough to make myself enemies already'--and she trembled at the thought of the formidable enemies she had probably arrayed against herself--helpless and despised as she was. When the pleading was at an end, Isabella understood the Judge to declare, as the sentence of the Court, that the 'boy be delivered into the hands of the mother--having no other master, no other controller, no other conductor, but his mother.' This sentence was obeyed; he was delivered into her hands, the boy meanwhile begging, most piteously, not to be taken from his dear master, saying she was not his mother, and that his mother did not live in such a place as that. And it was some time before lawyer Demain, the clerks, and Isabella, could collectively succeed in calming the child's fears, and in convincing him that Isabella was not some terrible monster, as he had for the last months, probably, been trained to believe; and who, in taking him away from his master, was taking him from all good, and consigning him to all evil.

When at last kind words and bon bons had quieted his fears, and he could listen to their explanations, he said to Isabella--'Well, you do look like my mother used to;' and she was soon able to make him comprehend some of the obligations he was under, and the relation he stood in, both to herself and his master. She commenced as soon as practicable to examine the boy, and found, to her utter astonishment, that from the crown of his head to the sole of his foot, the callosities and indurations on his entire body were most frightful to behold. His back she described as being like her fingers, as she laid them side by side.

'Heavens! what is all this?' said Isabel. He answered, 'It is where Fowler whipped, kicked, and beat me.' She exclaimed, 'Oh, Lord Jesus, look! see my poor child! Oh Lord, "render unto them double" for all this! Oh my God! Pete, how did you bear it?'

'Oh, this is nothing, mammy--if you should see Phillis, I guess you'd scare! She had a little baby, and Fowler cut her till the milk as well as blood ran down her body. You would scare to see Phillis, mammy.'

When Isabella inquired, 'What did Miss Eliza*

* Meaning Mrs. Eliza Fowler.

say, Pete, when you were treated so badly?' he replied, 'Oh, mammy, she said she wished I was with Bell. Sometimes I crawled under the stoop, mammy, the blood running all about me, and my back would stick to the boards; and sometimes Miss Eliza would come and grease my sores, when all were abed and asleep.'

DEATH OF MRS. ELIZA FOWLER.

As soon as possible, she procured a place for Peter, as tender of locks, at a place called Wahkendall, near Green-kills. After he was thus disposed of, she visited her sister Sophia, who resided at Newburg, and spent the winter in several different families where she was acquainted. She remained sometime in the family of a Mr. Latin, who was a visiting relative of Solomon Gedney; and the latter, when he found Isabel with his cousin, used all his influence to persuade him she was a great mischief-maker and a very troublesome person,-- that she had put him to some hundreds of dollars expense, by fabricating lies about him, and especially his sister and her family, concerning her boy, when the latter was living so like a gentleman with them; and, for his part, he would not advise his friends to harbor or encourage her. However, his cousins, the Latins, could not see with the eyes of his feelings, and consequently his words fell powerless on them, and they retained her in their service as long as they had aught for her to do.

She then went to visit her former master, Dumont. She had scarcely arrived there, when Mr. Fred. Waring entered, and seeing Isabel, pleasantly accosted her, and asked her 'what she was driving at now-a-days.' On her answering 'nothing particular,' he requested her to go over to his place, and assist his folks, as some of them were sick, and they needed an extra hand. She very gladly assented. When Mr. W. retired, her master wanted to know why she wished to help people, that called her the 'worst of devils,' as Mr. Waring had done in the court-house--for he was the uncle of Solomon Gedney, and attended the trial we have described--and declared 'that she was a fool to; he wouldn't do it.' 'Oh,' she told him, 'she would not mind that, but was very glad to have people forget their anger towards her.' She went over, but too happy to feel that their resentment was passed, and commenced her work with a light heart and a strong will. She had not worked long in this frame of mind, before a young daughter of Mr. Waring rushed into the room, exclaiming, with uplifted hands--'Heavens and earth, Isabella! Fowler's murdered Cousin Eliza!' 'Ho,' said Isabel, 'that's nothing--he liked to have killed my child; nothing saved him but God.' Meaning, that she was not at all surprised at it, for a man whose heart was sufficiently hardened to treat a mere child as hers had been treated, was, in her opinion, more fiend than human, and prepared for the commission of any crime that his passions might prompt him to. The child further informed her, that a letter had arrived by mail bringing the news.

Immediately after this announcement, Solomon Gedney and his mother came in, going direct to Mrs. Waring's room, where she soon heard tones as of someone reading. She thought something said to her inwardly, 'Go up stairs and hear.' At first she hesitated, but it seemed to press her the more--'Go up and hear!' She went up, unusual as it is for slaves to leave their work and enter unbidden their mistress's room, for the sole purpose of seeing or hearing what may be seen or heard there. But on this occasion, Isabella says, she walked in at the door, shut it, placed her back against it, and listened. She saw them and heard them read--'He knocked her down with his fist, jumped on her with his knees, broke her collar bone, and tore out her wind-pipe! He then attempted his escape, but was pursued and arrested, and put in an iron bank for safe-keeping!' And the friends were requested to go down and take away the poor innocent children who had thus been made in one short day more than orphans.

If this narrative should ever meet the eye of those innocent sufferers for another's guilt, let them not be too deeply affected by the relation; but, placing their confidence in Him who sees the end from the beginning, and controls the results, rest secure in the faith, that, although they may physically suffer for the sins of others, if they remain but true to themselves, their highest and more enduring interests can never suffer from such a cause. This relation should be suppressed for their sakes, were it not even now so often denied, that slavery is fast undermining all true regard for human life. We know this one instance is not a demonstration to the contrary; but, adding this to the lists of tragedies that weekly come up to us through the Southern mails, may we not admit them as proofs irrefragable? The newspapers confirm this account of the terrible affair.

When Isabella had heard the letter, all being too much absorbed in their own feelings to take note of her, she returned to her work, her heart swelling with conflicting emotions. She was awed at the dreadful deed; she mourned the fate of the loved Eliza, who had in such an undeserved and barbarous manner been put away from her labors and watchings as a tender mother; and, 'last though not least,' in the development of her character and spirit, her heart bled for the afflicted relatives; even those of them who 'laughed at her calamity, and mocked when her fear came.' Her thoughts dwelt long and intently on the subject, and the wonderful chain of events that had conspired to bring her that day to that house, to listen to that piece of intelligence--to that house, where she never was before or afterwards in her life, and invited there by people who had so lately been hotly incensed against her. It all seemed very remarkable to her, and she viewed it as flowing from a special providence of God. She thought she saw clearly, that their unnatural bereavement was a blow dealt in retributive justice: but she found it not in her heart to exult or rejoice over them. She felt as if God had more than answered her petition, when she ejaculated, in her anguish of mind, 'Oh, Lord, render unto them double!' She said, 'I dared not find fault with God, exactly; but the language of my heart was, 'Oh, my God! that's too much--I did not mean quite so much, God!' It was a terrible blow to the friends of the deceased; and her selfish mother (who, said Isabella, made such a 'to-do about her boy, not from affection, 'but to have her own will and way') went deranged, and walking to and fro in her delirium, called aloud for her poor murdered daughter--'Eliza! Eliza!'

The derangement of Mrs. G. was a matter of hearsay, as Isabella saw her not after the trial; but she has no reason to doubt the truth of what she heard. Isabel could never learn the subsequent fate of Fowler, but heard in the spring of '49 that his children had been seen in Kingston--one of whom was spoken of as a fine, interesting girl, albeit a halo of sadness fell like a veil about her.

ISABELLA'S RELIGIOUS EXPERIENCE.

We will now turn from the outward and temporal to the inward and spiritual life of our subject. It is ever both interesting and instructive to trace the exercises of a human mind, through the trials and mysteries of life; and especially a naturally powerful mind, left as hers was almost entirely to its own workings, and the chance influences it met on its way; and especially to note its reception of that divine 'light, that lighteth every man that cometh into the world.'

We see, as knowledge dawns upon it, truth and error strangely commingled; here, a bright spot illuminated by truth--and there, one darkened and distorted by error; and the state of such a soul may be compared to a landscape at early dawn, where the sun is seen superbly gilding some objects, and causing others to send forth their lengthened, distorted, and sometimes hideous shadows.

Her mother, as we have already said, talked to her of God. From these conversations, her incipient mind drew the conclusion, that God was 'a great man;' greatly superior to other men in power; and being located 'high in the sky,' could see all that transpired on the earth. She believed he not only saw, but noted down all her actions in a great book, even as her master kept a record of whatever he wished not to forget. But she had no idea that God knew a thought of hers till she had uttered it aloud.

As we have before mentioned, she had ever been mindful of her mother's injunctions, spreading out in detail all her troubles before God, imploring and firmly trusting him to send her deliverance from them. Whilst yet a child, she listened to a story of a wounded soldier, left alone in the trail of a flying army, helpless and starving, who hardened the very ground about him with kneeling in his supplications to God for relief, until it arrived. From this narrative, she was deeply impressed with the idea, that if she also were to present her petitions under the open canopy of heaven, speaking very loud, she should the more readily be heard; consequently, she sought a fitting spot for this, her rural sanctuary. The place she selected, in which to offer up her daily orisons, was a small island in a small stream, covered with large willow shrubbery, beneath which the sheep had made their pleasant winding paths; and sheltering themselves from the scorching rays of a noon-tide sun, luxuriated in the cool shadows of the graceful willows, as they listened to the tiny falls of the silver waters. It was a lonely spot, and chosen by her for its beauty, its retirement, and because she thought that there, in the noise of those waters, she could speak louder to God, without being overheard by any who might pass that way. When she had made choice of her sanctum, at a point of the island where the stream met, after having been separated, she improved it by pulling away the branches of the shrubs from the centre, and weaving them together for a wall on the outside, forming a circular arched alcove, made entirely of the graceful willow. To this place she resorted daily, and in pressing times much more frequently.

At this time, her prayers, or, more appropriately, 'talks with God,' were perfectly original and unique, and would be well worth preserving, were it possible to give the tones and manner with the words; but no adequate idea of them can be written while the tones and manner remain inexpressible.

She would sometimes repeat, 'Our Father in heaven,' in her Low Dutch, as taught her by her mother, after that, all was from the suggestions of her own rude mind. She related to God, in minute detail, all her troubles and sufferings, inquiring, as she proceeded, 'Do you think that's right, God?' and closed by begging to be delivered from the evil, whatever it might be.

She talked to God as familiarly as if he had been a creature like herself; and a thousand times more so, than if she had been in the presence of some earthly potentate. She demanded, with little expenditure of reverence or fear, a supply of all her more pressing wants, and at times her demands approached very near to commands. She felt as if God was under obligation to her, much more than she was to him. He seemed to her benighted vision in some manner bound to do her bidding.

Her heart recoils now, with very dread, when she recalls these shocking, almost blasphemous conversations with the great Jehovah. And well for herself did she deem it, that, unlike earthly potentates, his infinite character combined the tender father with the omniscient and omnipotent Creator of the universe.

She at first commenced promising God, that if he would help her out of all her difficulties, she would pay him by being very good; and this goodness she intended as a remuneration to God. She could think of no benefit that was to accrue to herself or her fellow-creatures, from her leading a life of purity and generous self-sacrifice for the good of others; as far as any but God was concerned, she saw nothing in it but heart-trying penance, sustained by the sternest exertion; and this she soon found much more easily promised than performed.

Days wore away--new trials came--God's aid was invoked, and the same promises repeated; and every successive night found her part of the contract unfulfilled. She now began to excuse herself, by telling God she could not be good in her present circumstances; but if he would give her a new place, and a good master and mistress, she could and would be good; and she expressly stipulated, that she would be good one day to show God how good she would be all of the time, when he should surround her with the right influences, and she should be delivered from the temptations that then so sorely beset her. But, alas! when night came, and she became conscious that she had yielded to all her temptations, and entirely failed of keeping her word with God, having prayed and promised one hour, and fallen into the sins of anger and profanity the next, the mortifying reflection weighed on her mind, and blunted her enjoyment. Still, she did not lay it deeply to heart, but continued to repeat her demands for aid, and her promises of pay, with full purpose of heart, at each particular time, that that day she would not fail to keep her plighted word.

Thus perished the inward spark, like a flame just igniting, when one waits to see whether it will burn on or die out, till the long desired change came, and she found herself in a new place, with a good mistress, and one who never instigated an otherwise kind master to be unkind to her; in short, a place where she had literally nothing to complain of, and where, for a time, she was more happy than she could well express. 'Oh, everything there was so pleasant, and kind, and good, and all so comfortable; enough of everything; indeed, it was beautiful!' she exclaimed.

Here, at Mr. Van Wagener's,--as the reader will readily perceive she must have been,--she was so happy and satisfied, that God was entirely forgotten. Why should her thoughts turn to Him, who was only known to her as a help in trouble? She had no trouble now; her every prayer had been answered in every minute particular. She had been delivered from her persecutors and temptations, her youngest child had been given her, and the others she knew she had no means of sustaining if she had them with her, and was content to leave them behind. Their father, who was much older than Isabel, and who preferred serving his time out in slavery, to the trouble and dangers of the course she pursued, remained with and could keep an eye on them--though it is comparatively little that they can do for each other while they remain in slavery; and this little the slave, like persons in every other situation of life, is not always disposed to perform. There are slaves, who, copying the selfishness of their superiors in power, in their conduct towards their fellows who may be thrown upon their mercy, by infirmity or illness, allow them to suffer for want of that kindness and care which it is fully in their power to render them.

    The slaves in this country have ever been allowed to celebrate the principal, if not some of the lesser festivals observed by the Catholics and Church of England; many of them not being required to do the least service for several days, and at Christmas they have almost universally an entire week to themselves, except, perhaps, the attending to a few duties, which are absolutely required for the comfort of the families they belong to. If much service is desired, they are hired to do it, and paid for it as if they were free. The more sober portion of them spend these holidays in earning a little money. Most of them visit and attend parties and balls, and not a few of them spend it in the lowest dissipation. This respite from toil is granted them by all religionists, of whatever persuasion, and probably originated from the fact that many of the first slaveholders were members of the Church of England.

Frederick Douglass, who has devoted his great heart and noble talents entirely to the furtherance of the cause of his down-trodden race, has said--'From what I know of the effect of their holidays upon the slave, I believe them to be among the most effective means, in the hands of the slaveholder, in keeping down the spirit of insurrection. Were the slaveholders at once to abandon this practice, I have not the slightest doubt it would lead to an immediate insurrection among the slaves. These holidays serve as conductors, or safety valves, to carry off the rebellious spirit of enslaved humanity. But for these, the slave would be forced up to the wildest desperation; and woe betide the slaveholder, the day he ventures to remove or hinder the operation of those conductors! I warn him that, in such an event, a spirit will go forth in their midst, more to be dreaded than the most appalling earthquake.'

When Isabella had been at Mr. Van Wagener's a few months, she saw in prospect one of the festivals approaching. She knows it by none but the Dutch name, Pingster, as she calls it--but I think it must have been Whitsuntide, in English. She says she 'looked back into Egypt,' and everything looked 'so pleasant there,' as she saw retrospectively all her former companions enjoying their freedom for at least a little space, as well as their wonted convivialities, and in her heart she longed to be with them. With this picture before her mind's eye, she contrasted the quiet, peaceful life she was living with the excellent people of Wahkendall, and it seemed so dull and void of incident, that the very contrast served but to heighten her desire to return, that, at least, she might enjoy with them, once more, the coming festivities. These feelings had occupied a secret corner of her breast for some time, when, one morning, she told Mrs. Van Wagener that her old master Dumont would come that day, and that she should go home with him on his return. They expressed some surprise, and asked her where she obtained her information. She replied, that no one had told her, but she felt that he would come.

It seemed to have been one of those 'events that cast their shadows before;' for, before night, Mr. Dumont made his appearance. She informed him of her intention to accompany him home. He answered, with a smile, 'I shall not take you back again; you ran away from me.' Thinking his manner contradicted his words, she did not feel repulsed, but made herself and child ready; and when her former master had seated himself in the open dearborn, she walked towards it, intending to place herself and child in the rear, and go with him. But, ere she reached the vehicle, she says that God revealed himself to her, with all the suddenness of a flash of lightning, showing her, 'in the twinkling of an eye, that he was all over'--that he pervaded the universe--'and that there was no place where God was not.' She became instantly conscious of her great sin in forgetting her almighty Friend and 'ever-present help in time of trouble.' All her unfulfilled promises arose before her, like a vexed sea whose waves run mountains high; and her soul, which seemed but one mass of lies, shrunk back aghast from the 'awful look' of Him whom she had formerly talked to, as if he had been a being like herself; and she would now fain have hid herself in the bowels of the earth, to have escaped his dread presence. But she plainly saw there was no place, not even in hell, where he was not: and where could she flee? Another such 'a look,' as she expressed it, and she felt that she must be extinguished forever, even as one, with the breath of his mouth, 'blows out a lamp,' so that no spark remains.

A dire dread of annihilation now seized her, and she waited to see if, by 'another look,' she was to be stricken from existence,--swallowed up, even as the fire licketh up the oil with which it comes in contact.

When at last the second look came not, and her attention was once more called to outward things, she observed her master had left, and exclaiming aloud, 'Oh, God, I did not know you were so big,' walked into the house, and made an effort to resume her work. But the workings of the inward man were too absorbing to admit of much attention to her avocations. She desired to talk to God, but her vileness utterly forbade it, and she was not able to prefer a petition. 'What!' said she, 'shall I lie again to God? I have told him nothing but lies; and shall I speak again, and tell another lie to God?' She could not; and now she began to wish for someone to speak to God for her. Then a space seemed opening between her and God, and she felt that if someone, who was worthy in the sight of heaven, would but plead for her in their own name, and not let God know it came from her, who was so unworthy, God might grant it. At length a friend appeared to stand between herself and an insulted Deity; and she felt as sensibly refreshed as when, on a hot day, an umbrella had been interposed between her scorching head and a burning sun. But who was this friend? became the next inquiry. Was it Deencia, who had so often befriended her? She looked at her with her new power of sight--and, lo! she, too, seemed all 'bruises and putrifying sores,' like herself. No, it was someone very different from Deencia.

'Who are you?' she exclaimed, as the vision brightened into a form distinct, beaming with the beauty of holiness, and radiant with love. She then said, audibly addressing the mysterious visitant--'I know you, and I don't know you.' Meaning, 'You seem perfectly familiar; I feel that you not only love me, but that you always have loved me--yet I know you not--I cannot call you by name.' When she said, 'I know you,' the subject of the vision remained distinct and quiet. When she said, 'I don't know you,' it moved restlessly about, like agitated waters. So while she repeated, without intermission, 'I know you, I know you,' that the vision might remain-- 'Who are you?' was the cry of her heart, and her whole soul was in one deep prayer that this heavenly personage might be revealed to her, and remain with her. At length, after bending both soul and body with the intensity of this desire, till breath and strength seemed failing, and she could maintain her position no longer, an answer came to her, saying distinctly, 'It is Jesus.' 'Yes,' she responded, 'it is Jesus.'

Previous to these exercises of mind, she heard Jesus mentioned in reading or speaking, but had received from what she heard no impression that he was any other than an eminent man, like a Washington or a Lafayette. Now he appeared to her delighted mental vision as so mild, so good, and so every way lovely, and he loved her so much! And, how strange that he had always loved her, and she had never known it! And how great a blessing he conferred, in that he should stand between her and God! And God was no longer a terror and a dread to her.

She stopped not to argue the point, even in her own mind, whether he had reconciled her to God, or God to herself, (though she thinks the former now,) being but too happy that God was no longer to her as a consuming fire, and Jesus was 'altogether lovely.' Her heart was now full of joy and gladness, as it had been of terror, and at one time of despair. In the light of her great happiness, the world was clad in new beauty, the very air sparkled as with diamonds, and was redolent of heaven. She contemplated the unapproachable barriers that existed between herself and the great of this world, as the world calls greatness, and made surprising comparisons between them, and the union existing between herself and Jesus,--Jesus, the transcendently lovely as well as great and powerful; for so he appeared to her, though he seemed but human; and she watched for his bodily appearance, feeling that she should know him, if she saw him; and when he came, she should go and dwell with him, as with a dear friend.

It was not given her to see that he loved any other; and she thought if others came to know and love him, as she did, she should be thrust aside and forgotten, being herself but a poor ignorant slave, with little to recommend her to his notice. And when she heard him spoken of, she said mentally--'What! others know Jesus! I thought no one knew Jesus but me!' and she felt a sort of jealousy, lest she should be robbed of her newly found treasure.

She conceived, one day, as she listened to reading, that she heard an intimation that Jesus was married, and hastily inquired if Jesus had a wife. 'What!' said the reader, 'God have a wife?' 'Is Jesus God?' inquired Isabella. 'Yes, to be sure he is,' was the answer returned. From this time, her conceptions of Jesus became more elevated and spiritual; and she sometimes spoke of him as God, in accordance with the teaching she had received.

But when she was simply told, that the Christian world was much divided on the subject of Christ's nature--some believing him to be coequal with the Father--to be God in and of himself, 'very God, of very God;'--some, that he is the 'well-beloved,' 'only begotten Son of God;'--and others, that he is, or was, rather, but a mere man--she said, 'Of that I only know as I saw. I did not see him to be God; else, how could he stand between me and God? I saw him as a friend, standing between me and God, through whom, love flowed as from a fountain.' Now, so far from expressing her views of

Christ's character and office in accordance with any system of theology extant, she says she believes Jesus is the same spirit that was in our first parents, Adam and Eve, in the beginning, when they came from the hand of their Creator. When they sinned through disobedience, this pure spirit forsook them, and fled to heaven; that there it remained, until it returned again in the person of Jesus; and that, previous to a personal union with him, man is but a brute, possessing only the spirit of an animal.

She avers that, in her darkest hours, she had no fear of any worse hell than the one she then carried in her bosom; though it had ever been pictured to her in its deepest colors, and threatened her as a reward for all her misdemeanors. Her vileness and God's holiness and all-pervading presence, which filled immensity, and threatened her with instant annihilation, composed the burden of her vision of terror. Her faith in prayer is equal to her faith in the love of Jesus. Her language is, 'Let others say what they will of the efficacy of prayer, I believe in it, and I shall pray. Thank God! Yes, I shall always pray,' she exclaims, putting her hands together with the greatest enthusiasm.

For some time subsequent to the happy change we have spoken of, Isabella's prayers partook largely of their former character; and while, in deep affliction, she labored for the recovery of her son, she prayed with constancy and fervor; and the following may be taken as a specimen:--'Oh, God, you know how much I am distressed, for I have told you again and again. Now, God, help me get my son. If you were in trouble, as I am, and I could help you, as you can me, think I would n't do it? Yes, God, you know I would do it.' 'Oh, God, you know I have no money, but you can make the people do for me, and you must make the people do for me. I will never give you peace till you do, God.' 'Oh, God, make the people hear me--don't let them turn me off, without hearing and helping me.' And she has not a particle of doubt, that God heard her, and especially disposed the hearts of thoughtless clerks, eminent lawyers, and grave judges and others--between whom and herself there seemed to her almost an infinite remove--to listen to her suit with patient and respectful attention, backing it up with all needed aid. The sense of her nothingness, in the eyes of those with whom she contended for her rights, sometimes fell on her like a heavy weight, which nothing but her unwavering confidence in an arm which she believed to be stronger than all others combined could have raised from her sinking spirit. 'Oh! how little I did feel,' she repeated, with a powerful emphasis. 'Neither would you wonder, if you could have seen me, in my ignorance and destitution, trotting about the streets, meanly clad, bare-headed, and bare-footed! Oh, God only could have made such people hear me; and he did it in answer to my prayers.' And this perfect trust, based on the rock of Deity, was a soul-protecting fortress, which, raising her above the battlements of fear, and shielding her from the machinations of the enemy, impelled her onward in the struggle, till the foe was vanquished, and the victory gained.

We have now seen Isabella, her youngest daughter, and her only son, in possession of, at least, their nominal freedom. It has been said that the freedom of the most free of the colored people of this country is but nominal; but stinted and limited as it is, at best, it is an immense remove from chattel slavery. This fact is disputed, I know; but I have no confidence in the honesty of such questionings. If they are made in sincerity, I honor not the judgment that thus decides.

Her husband, quite advanced in age, and infirm of health, was emancipated, with the balance of the adult slaves of the State, according to law, the following summer, July 4, 1828.

For a few years after this event, he was able to earn a scanty living, and when he failed to do that, he was dependent on the 'world's cold charity,' and died in a poor-house. Isabella had herself and two children to provide for; her wages were trifling, for at that time the wages of females were at a small advance from nothing; and she doubtless had to learn the first elements of economy--for what slaves, that were never allowed to make any stipulations or calculations for themselves, ever possessed an adequate idea of the true value of time, or, in fact, of any material thing in the universe? To such, 'prudent using' is meanness--and 'saving' is a word to be sneered at. Of course, it was not in her power to make to herself a home, around whose sacred hearthstone she could collect her family, as they gradually emerged from their prison-house of bondage; a home, where she could cultivate their affection, administer to their wants, and instil into the opening minds of her children those principles of virtue, and that love of purity, truth and benevolence, which must ever form the foundation of a life of usefulness and happiness. No--all this was far beyond her power or means, in more senses than one; and it should be taken into the account, whenever a comparison is instituted between the progress made by her children in virtue and goodness, and the progress of those who have been nurtured in the genial warmth of a sunny home, where good influences cluster, and bad ones are carefully excluded--where 'line upon line, and precept upon precept,' are daily brought to their quotidian tasks--and where, in short, every appliance is brought in requisition, that self-denying parents can bring to bear on one of the dearest objects of a parent's life, the promotion of the welfare of their children. But God forbid that this suggestion should be wrested from its original intent, and made to shield any one from merited rebuke! Isabella's children are now of an age to know good from evil, and may easily inform themselves on any point where they may yet be in doubt; and if they now suffer themselves to be drawn by temptation into the paths of the destrover, or forget what is due to the mother who has done and suffered so much for them, and who, now that she is descending into the vale of years, and feels her health and strength declining, will turn her expecting eyes to them for aid and comfort, just as instinctively as the child turns its confiding eye to its fond parent, when it seeks for succor or for sympathy--(for it is now their turn to do the work, and bear the burdens of life, as all must bear them in turn, as the wheel of life rolls on)--if, I say, they forget this, their duty and their happiness, and pursue an opposite course of sin and folly, they must lose the respect of the wise and good, and find, when too late, that 'the way of the transgressor is hard.'

NEW TRIALS.

The reader will pardon this passing homily, while we return to our narrative.

We were saying that the day-dreams of Isabella and her husband--the plan they drew of what they would do, and the comforts they thought to have, when they should obtain their freedom, and a little home of their own--had all turned to 'thin air,' by the postponement of their freedom to so late a day. These delusive hopes were never to be realized, and a new set of trials was gradually to open before her. These were the heart-wasting trials of watching over her children, scattered, and imminently exposed to the temptations of the adversary, with few, if any, fixed principles to sustain them.

'Oh,' she says, 'how little did I know myself of the best way to instruct and counsel them! Yet I did the best I then knew, when with them. I took them to the religious meetings; I talked to, and prayed for and with them; when they did wrong, I scolded at and whipped them.'

Isabella and her son had been free about a year, when they went to reside in the city of New York; a place which she would doubtless have avoided, could she have seen what was there in store for her; for this view into the future would have taught her what she only learned by bitter experience, that the baneful influences going up from such a city were not the best helps to education, commenced as the education of her children had been.

Her son Peter was, at the time of which we are speaking, just at that age when no lad should be subjected to the temptations of such a place, unprotected as he was, save by the feeble arm of a mother, herself a servant there. He was growing up to be a tall, well-formed, active lad, of quick perceptions, mild and cheerful in his disposition, with much that was open, generous and winning about him, but with little power to withstand temptation, and a ready ingenuity to provide himself with ways and means to carry out his plans, and conceal from his mother and her friends, all such as he knew would not meet their approbation. As will be readily believed, he was soon drawn into a circle of associates who did not improve either his habits or his morals.

Two years passed before Isabella knew what character Peter was establishing for himself among his low and worthless comrades--passing under the assumed name of Peter Williams; and she began to feel a parent's pride in the promising appearance of her only son. But, alas! this pride and pleasure were shortly dissipated, as distressing facts relative to him came one by one to her astonished ear. A friend of Isabella's, a lady, who was much pleased with the good humor, ingenuity, and open confessions of Peter, when driven into a corner, and who, she said, 'was so smart, he ought to have an education, if any one ought,'--paid ten dollars, as tuition fee, for him to attend a navigation school. But Peter, little inclined to spend his leisure hours in study, when he might be enjoying himself in the dance, or otherwise, with his boon companions, went regularly and made some plausible excuses to the teacher, who received them as genuine, along with the ten dollars of Mrs.--, and while his mother and her friend believed him improving at school, he was, to their latent sorrow, improving in a very different place or places, and on entirely opposite principles. They also procured him an excellent place as a coachman. But, wanting money, he sold his livery, and other things belonging to his master; who, having conceived a kind regard for him, considered his youth, and prevented the law from falling, with all its rigor, upon his head. Still he continued to abuse his privileges, and to involve himself in repeated difficulties, from which his mother as often extricated him. At each time, she talked much, and reasoned and remonstrated with him; and he would, with such perfect frankness, lay open his whole soul to her, telling her he had never intended doing harm,--how he had been led along, little by little, till, before he was aware, he found himself in trouble--how he had tried to be good--and how, when he would have been so, 'evil was present with him,'--indeed he knew not how it was.

    His mother, beginning to feel that the city was no place for him, urged his going to sea, and would have shipped him on board a man-of-war; but Peter was not disposed to consent to that proposition, while the city and its pleasures were accessible to him. Isabella now became a prey to distressing fears, dreading lest the next day or hour come fraught with the report of some dreadful crime, committed or abetted by her son. She thanks the Lord for sparing her that giant sorrow, as all his wrong doings never ranked higher, in the eye of the law, than misdemeanors. But as she could see no improvement in Peter, as a last resort, she resolved to leave him, for a time, unassisted, to bear the penalty of his conduct, and see what effect that would have on him. In the trial hour, she remained firm in her resolution. Peter again fell into the hands of the police, and sent for his mother, as usual; but she went not to his relief. In his extremity, he sent for Peter Williams, a respectable colored barber, whose name he had been wearing, and who sometimes helped young culprits out of their troubles, and sent them from city dangers, by shipping them on board of whaling vessels.

The curiosity of this man was awakened by the culprit's bearing his own name. He went to the Tombs and inquired into his case, but could not believe what Peter told him respecting his mother and family. Yet he redeemed him, and Peter promised to leave New York in a vessel that was to sail in the course of a week. He went to see his mother, and informed her of what had happened to him. She listened incredulously, as to an idle tale. He asked her to go with him and see for herself. She went, giving no credence to his story till she found herself in the presence of Mr. Williams, and heard him saying to her, 'I am very glad I have assisted your son; he stood in great need of sympathy and assistance; but I could not think he had such a mother here, although he assured me he had.'

Isabella's great trouble now was, a fear lest her son should deceive his benefactor, and be missing when the vessel sailed; but he begged her earnestly to trust him, for he said he had resolved to do better, and meant to abide by the resolve. Isabella's heart gave her no peace till the time of sailing, when Peter sent Mr. Williams and another messenger whom she knew, to tell her he had sailed. But for a month afterwards, she looked to see him emerging from some by-place in the city, and appearing before her; so afraid was she that he was still unfaithful, and doing wrong. But he did not appear, and at length she believed him really gone. He left in the summer of 1839, and his friends heard nothing further from him till his mother received the following letter, dated 'October 17, 1840':--

MY DEAR AND BELOVED MOTHER:

'I take this opportunity to write to you and inform you that I am well, and in hopes for to find you the same. I am got on board the same unlucky ship Done, of Nantucket. I am sorry for to say, that I have been punished once severely, by shoving my head in the fire for other folks. We have had bad luck, but in hopes to have better. We have about 230 on board, but in hopes, if don't kave good luck, that my parents will receive me with thanks. I would like to know how my sisters are. Does my cousins live in New York yet? Have you got my letter? If not, inquire to Mr. Pierce Whiting's. I wish you would write me an answer as soon as possible. I am your only son, that is so far from your home, in the wide, briny ocean. I have seen more of the world than ever I expected, and if I ever should return home safe, I will tell you all my troubles and hardships. Mother, I hope you do not forget me, your dear and only son. I should like to know how Sophia, and Betsey, and Hannah, come on. I hope you all will forgive me for all that I have done.

'Your son,

PETER VAN WAGENER.'

Another letter reads as follows, dated 'March 22, 1841':--

'MY DEAR MOTHER:

'I take this opportunity to write to you, and inform you that I have been well and in good health. I have wrote you a letter before, but have received no answer from you, and was very anxious to see you. I hope to see you in a short time. I have had very hard luck, but are in hopes to have better in time to come. I should like if my sisters are well, and all the people round the neighborhood. I expect to be home in twenty-two months or thereabouts. I have seen Samuel Laterett. Beware! There has happened very bad news to tell you, that Peter Jackson is dead. He died within two days' sail of Otaheite, one of the Society Islands. The Peter Jackson that used to live at Laterett's; he died on board the ship Done, of Nantucket, Captain Miller, in the latitude 15 53, and longitude 148 30 W. I have no more to say at present, but write as soon as possible.

'Your only son,

'PETER VAN WAGENER.'

Another, containing the last intelligence she has had from her son, reads as follows, and was dated 'Sept. 19, 1841':--

'DEAR MOTHER:

'I take this opportunity to write to you and inform you that I am well and in good health, and in hopes to find you in the same. This is the fifth letter that I have wrote to you, and have received no answer, and it makes me very uneasy. So pray write as quick as you can, and tell me how all the people is about the neighborhood. We are out from home twenty-three months, and in hopes to be home in fifteen months. I have not much to say; but tell me if you have been up home since I left or not. I want to know what sort of a time is at home. We had very bad luck when we first came out, but since we have had very good; so I am in hopes to do well yet; but if I do n't do well, you need not expect me home these five years. So write as quick as you can, won't you? So now I am going to put an end to my writing, at present. Notice--when this you see, remember me, and place me in your mind.

     Get me to my home, that's in the far distant west,
     To the scenes of my childhood, that I like the best;
     There the tall cedars grow, and the bright waters flow,
     Where my parents will greet me, white man, let me go!

     Let me go to the spot where the cateract plays,
     Where oft I have sported in my boyish days;
     And there is my poor mother, whose heart ever flows,
     At the sight of her poor child, to her let me go, let me go!

'Your only son,

          'PETER VAN WAGENER.'

Since the date of the last letter, Isabella has heard no tidings from her long-absent son, though ardently does her mother's heart long for such tidings, as her thoughts follow him around the world, in his perilous vocation, saying within herself--'He is good now, I have no doubt; I feel sure that he has persevered, and kept the resolve he made before he left home;--he seemed so different before he went, so determined to do better.' His letters are inserted here for preservation, in case they prove the last she ever hears from him in this world.

FINDING A BROTHER AND SISTER.

When Isabella had obtained the freedom of her son, she remained in Kingston, where she had been drawn by the judicial process, about a year, during which time she became a member of the Methodist Church there: and when she went to New York, she took a letter missive from that church to the Methodist Church in John street Afterwards, she withdrew her connection with that church, and joined Zion's Church, in Church street, composed entirely of colored people. With the latter church she remained until she went to reside with Mr. Pierson, after which, she was gradually drawn into the 'kingdom' set up by the prophet Matthias, in the name of God the Father; for he said the spirit of God the Father dwelt in him.

While Isabella was in New York, her sister Sophia came from Newburg to reside in the former place. Isabel had been favored with occasional interviews with this sister, although at one time she lost sight of her for the space of seventeen years--almost the entire period of of her being at Mr. Dumont's--and when she appeared before her again, handsomely dressed, she did not recognize her, till informed who she was. Sophia informed her that her brother Michael--a brother she had never seen--was in the city; and when she introduced him to Isabella, he informed her that their sister Nancy had been living in the city, and had deceased a few months before. He described her features, her dress, her manner, and said she had for some time been a member in Zion's Church, naming the class she belonged to. Isabella almost instantly recognized her as a sister in the church, with whom she had knelt at the altar, and with whom she had exchanged the speaking pressure of the hand, in recognition of their spiritual sisterhood; little thinking, at the time, that they were also children of the same earthly parents--even Bomefree and Mau-mau Bett. As inquiries and answers rapidly passed, and the conviction deepened that this was their sister, the very sister they had heard so much of, but had never seen, (for she was the self-same sister that had been locked in the great old fashioned sleigh-box, when she was taken away, never to behold her mother's face again this side the spirit-land, and Michael, the narrator, was the brother who had shared her fate,) Isabella thought, 'D--h! here she was; we met; and was I not, at the time, struck with the peculiar feeling of her hand--the bony hardness so just like mine? and yet I could not know she was my sister; and now I see she looked so like my mother' And Isabella wept, and not alone; Sophia wept, and the strong man, Michael, mingled his tears with theirs. 'Oh Lord,' inquired Isabella, 'what is this slavery, that it can do such dreadful things? what evil can it not do?' Well may she ask; for surely the evils it can and does do, daily and hourly, can never be summed up, till we can see them as they are recorded by him who writes no errors, and reckons without mistake. This account, which now varies so widely in the estimate of different minds, will be viewed alike by all.

Think you, dear reader, when that day comes, the most 'rabid abolitionist' will say--'Behold, I saw all this while on the earth?' Will he not rather say, 'Oh, who has conceived the breadth and depth of this moral malaria, this putrescent plague-spot?' Perhaps the pioneers in the slave's cause will be as much surprised as any to find that with all their looking, there remained so much unseen.

GLEANINGS.

There are some hard things that crossed Isabella's life while in slavery, that she has no desire to publish, for various reasons. First, because the parties from whose hands she suffered them have rendered up their account to a higher tribunal, and their innocent friends alone are living, to have their feelings injured by the recital; secondly, because they are not all for the public ear, from their very nature; thirdly, and not least, because, she says, were she to tell all that happened to her as a slave--all that she knows is 'God's truth'--it would seem to others, especially the uninitiated, so unaccountable, so unreasonable, and what is usually called so unnatural, (though it may be questioned whether people do not always act naturally,) they would not easily believe it. 'Why, no!' she says, 'they'd call me a liar! they would, indeed! and I do not wish to say anything to destroy my own character for veracity, though what I say is strictly true.' Some things have been omitted through forgetfulness, which not having been mentioned in their places, can only be briefly spoken of here;--such as, that her father Bomefree had had two wives before he took Mau mau Bett; one of whom, if not both, were torn from him by the iron hand of the ruthless trafficker in human flesh;--that her husband, Thomas, after one of his wives had been sold away from him, ran away to New York City, where he remained a year or two, before he was discovered and taken back to the prison-house of slavery;--that her master Dumont, when he promised Isabella one year of her time, before the

State should make her free, made the same promise to her husband, and in addition to freedom, they were promised a log cabin for a home of their own; all of which, with the one-thousand-and-one day-dreams resulting therefrom, went into the repository of unfulfilled promises and unrealized hopes;--that she had often heard her father repeat a thrilling story of a little slave-child, which, because it annoyed the family with its cries, was caught up by a white man, who dashed its brains out against the wall. An Indian (for Indians were plenty in that region then) passed along as the bereaved mother washed the bloody corpse of her murdered child, and learning the cause of its death, said, with characteristic vehemence, 'If I had been here, I would have put my tomahawk in his head!' meaning the murderer's.

Of the cruelty of one Hasbrouck.--He had a sick slave-woman, who was lingering with a slow consumption, whom he made to spin, regardless of her weakness and suffering; and this woman had a child, that was unable to walk or talk, at the age of five years, neither could it cry like other children, but made a constant, piteous, moaning sound. This exhibition of helplessness and imbecility, instead of exciting the master's pity, stung his cupidity, and so enraged him, that he would kick the poor thing about like a foot-ball.

Isabella's informant had seen this brute of a man, when the child was curled up under a chair, innocently amusing itself with a few sticks, drag it thence, that he might have the pleasure of tormenting it. She had seen him, with one blow of his foot, send it rolling quite across the room, and down the steps at the door. Oh, how she wished it might instantly die! 'But,' she said, 'it seemed as tough as a moccasin.' Though it did die at last, and made glad the heart of its friends; and its persecutor, no doubt, rejoiced with them, but from very different motives. But the day of his retribution was not far off-- for he sickened, and his reason fled. It was fearful to hear his old slave soon tell how, in the day of his calamity, she treated him.

She was very strong, and was therefore selected to support her master, as he sat up in bed, by putting her arms around, while she stood behind him. It was then that she did her best to wreak her vengeance on him. She would clutch his feeble frame in her iron grasp, as in a vice; and, when her mistress did not see, would give him a squeeze, a shake, and lifting him up, set him down again, as hard as possible. If his breathing betrayed too tight a grasp, and her mistress said, 'Be careful, don't hurt him, Soan!' her ever-ready answer was, 'Oh no, Missus, no,' in her most pleasant tone--and then, as soon as Missus's eyes and ears were engaged away, another grasp--another shake--another bounce. She was afraid the disease alone would let him recover,--an event she dreaded more than to do wrong herself. Isabella asked her, if she were not afraid his spirit would haunt her. 'Oh, no,' says Soan; 'he was so wicked, the devil will never let him out of hell long enough for that.'

Many slaveholders boast of the love of their slaves. How would it freeze the blood of some of them to know what kind of love rankles in the bosoms of slaves for them! Witness the attempt to poison Mrs. Calhoun, and hundreds of similar cases. Most 'surprising' to every body, because committed by slaves supposed to be so grateful for their chains.

These reflections bring to mind a discussion on this point, between the writer and a slaveholding friend in Kentucky, on Christmas morning, 1846. We had asserted, that until mankind were far in advance of what they now are, irresponsible power over our fellow-beings would be, as it is, abused. Our friend declared it his conviction, that the cruelties of slavery existed chiefly in imagination, and that no person in D--County, where we then were, but would be above ill-treating a helpless slave. We answered, that if his belief was well-founded, the people in Kentucky were greatly in advance of the people of New England--for we would not dare say as much as that of any school-district there, letting alone counties. No, we would not answer for our own conduct even on so delicate a point.

The next evening, he very magnanimously overthrew his own position and established ours, by informing us that, on the morning previous, and as near as we could learn, at the very hour in which we were earnestly discussing the probabilities of the case, a young woman of fine appearance, and high standing in society, the pride of her husband, and the mother of an infant daughter, only a few miles from us, ay, in D-- County, too, was actually beating in the skull of a slave-woman called Tabby; and not content with that, had her tied up and whipped, after her skull was broken, and she died hanging to the bedstead, to which she had been fastened. When informed that Tabby was dead, she answered, 'I am glad of it, for she has worried my life out of me.' But Tabby's highest good was probably not the end proposed by Mrs. M--, for no one supposed she meant to kill her. Tabby was considered quite lacking in good sense, and no doubt belonged to that class at the South, that are silly enough to 'die of moderate correction.'

A mob collected around the house for an hour or two, in that manner expressing a momentary indignation. But was she treated as a murderess? Not at all! She was allowed to take boat (for her residence was near the beautiful Ohio) that evening, to spend a few months with her absent friends, after which she returned and remained with her husband, no one to 'molest or make her afraid.'

Had she been left to the punishment of an outraged conscience from right motives, I would have 'rejoiced with exceeding joy.' But to see the life of one woman, and she a murderess, put in the balance against the lives of three millions of innocent slaves, and to contrast her punishment with what I felt would be the punishment of one who was merely suspected of being an equal friend of all mankind, regardless of color or condition, caused my blood to stir within me, and my heart to sicken at the thought. The husband of Mrs. M--was absent from home, at the time alluded to; and when he arrived, some weeks afterwards, bringing beautiful presents to his cherished companion, he beheld his once happy home deserted, Tabby murdered and buried in the garden, and the wife of his bosom, and the mother of his child, the doer of the dreadful deed, a murderess!

When Isabella went to New York city, she went in company with a Miss Grear, who introduced her to the family of Mr. James Latourette, a wealthy merchant, and a Methodist in religion; but who, the latter part of his life, felt that he had outgrown ordinances, and advocated free meetings, holding them at his own dwelling-house for several years previous to his death. She worked for them, and they generously gave her a home while she labored for others, and in their kindness made her as one of their own.

At that time, the 'moral reform' movement was awakening the attention of the benevolent in that city. Many women, among whom were Mrs. Latourette and Miss Grear, became deeply interested in making an attempt to reform their fallen sisters, even the most degraded of them; and in this enterprise of labor and danger, they enlisted Isabella and others, who for a time put forth their most zealous efforts, and performed the work of missionaries with much apparent success. Isabella accompanied those ladies to the most wretched abodes of vice and misery, and sometimes she went where they dared not follow. They even succeeded in eatablishing prayer-meetings in several places, where such a thing might least have been expected.

But these meetings soon became the most noisy, shouting, ranting, and boisterous of gatherings; where they became delirious with excitement, and then exhausted from over-action. Such meetings Isabel had not much sympathy with, at best. But one evening she attended one of them, where the members of it, in a fit of ecstasy, jumped upon her cloak in such a manner as to drag her to the floor--and then, thinking she had fallen in a spiritual trance, they increased their glorifications on her account,--jumping, shouting, stamping, and clapping of hands; rejoicing so much over her spirit, and so entirely overlooking her body, that she suffered much, both from fear and bruises; and ever after refused to attend any more such meetings, doubting much whether God had anything to do with such worship.

THE MATTHIAS DELUSION.

We now come to an eventful period in the life of Isabella, as identified with one of the most extraordinary religious delusions of modern times; but the limits prescribed for the present work forbid a minute narration of all the occurrences that transpired in relation to it.

After she had joined the African Church in Church street, and during her membership there, she frequently attended Mr. Latourette's meetings, at one of which, Mr. Smith invited her to go to a prayer-meeting, or to instruct the girls at the Magdalene Asylum, Bowery Hill, then under the protection of Mr. Pierson, and some other persons, chiefly respectable females. To reach the Asylum, Isabella called on Katy, Mr. Pierson's colored servant, of whom she had some knowledge. Mr. Pierson saw her there, conversed with her, asked her if she had been baptized, and was answered, characteristically, 'by the Holy Ghost.' After this, Isabella saw Katy several times, and occasionally Mr. Pierson, who engaged her to keep his house while Katy went to Virginia to see her children. This engagement was considered an answer to prayer by Mr. Pierson, who had both fasted and prayed on the subject, while Katy and Isabella appeared to see in it the hand of God.

Mr. Pierson was characterized by a strong devotional spirit, which finally became highly fanatical. He assumed the title of Prophet, asserting that God had called him in an omnibus, in these words:--'Thou art

Elijah, the Tishbite. Gather unto me all the members of Israel at the foot of Mount Carmel'; which he understood as meaning the gathering of his friends at Bowery Hill. Not long afterward, he became acquainted with the notorious Matthias, whose career was as extraordinary as it was brief. Robert Matthews, or Matthias, (as he was usually called,) was of Scotch extraction, but a native of Washington county, New York, and at that time about forty-seven year of age. He was religiously brought up, among the Anti-Burghers, a sect of Presbyterians; the clergyman, the Rev. Mr. Bevridge, visiting the family after the manner of the church, and being pleased with Robert, put his hand on his head, when a boy, and pronounced a blessing, and this blessing, with his natural qualities, determined his character; for he ever after thought he should be a distinguished man. Matthias was brought up a farmer till nearly eighteen years of age, but acquired indirectly the art of a carpenter,

without any regular apprenticeship, and showed considerable mechanical skill. He obtained property from his uncle, Robert Thompson, and then he went into business as a store-keeper, was considered respectable, and became a member of the Scotch Presbyterian Church. He married in 1813, and continued in business in Cambridge. In 1816, he ruined himself by a building speculation, and the derangement of the currency which denied bank facilities, and soon after he came to New York with his family, and worked at his trade. He afterwards removed to Albany, and became a hearer at the Dutch Reformed Church, then under Dr. Ludlow's charge. He was frequently much excited on religious subjects.

In 1829, he was well known, if not for street preaching, for loud discussions and pavement exhortations, but he did not make set sermons. In the beginning of 1830, he was only considered zealous; but in the same year he prophesied the destruction of the Albanians and their capital, and while preparing to shave, with the Bible before him, he suddenly put down the soap and exclaimed, 'I have found it! I have found a text which proves that no man who shaves his beard can be a true Christian;' and shortly afterwards, without shaving, he went to the Mission House to deliver an address which he had promised, and in this address he proclaimed his new character, pronounced vengeance on the land, and that the law of God was the only rule of government, and that he was commanded to take possession of the world in the name of the King of kings. His harangue was cut short by the trustees putting out the lights. About this time, Matthias laid by his implements of industry, and in June, he advised his wife to fly with him from the destruction which awaited them in the city; and on her refusal, partly on account of Matthias calling himself a Jew, whom she was unwilling to retain as a husband, he left her, taking some of the children to his sister in Argyle, forty miles from Albany. At Argyle he entered the church and interrupted the minister, declaring the congregation in darkness, and warning them to repentance. He was, of course, taken out of the church, and as he was advertised in the Albany papers, he was sent back to his family. His beard had now obtained a respectable length, and thus he attracted attention, and easily obtained an audience in the streets. For this he was sometimes arrested, once by mistake for Adam Paine, who collected the crowd, and then left Matthias with it on the approach of the officers. He repeatedly urged his wife to accompany him on a mission to convert the world, declaring that food could be obtained from the roots of the forest, if not administered otherwise. At this time he assumed the name of Matthias, called himself a Jew, and set out on a mission, taking a western course, and visiting a brother at Rochester, a skilful mechanic, since dead. Leaving his brother, he proceeded on his mission over the Northern States, occasionally returning to Albany.

After visiting Washington, and passing through Pennsylvania, he came to New York. His appearance at that time was mean, but grotesque, and his sentiments were but little known.

On May the 5th, 1832, he first called on Mr. Pierson, in Fourth street, in his absence. Isabella was alone in the house, in which she had lived since the previous autumn. On opening the door, she, for the first time, beheld Matthias, and her early impression of seeing Jesus in the flesh rushed into her mind. She heard his inquiry, and invited him into the parlor; and being naturally curious, and much excited, and possessing a good deal of tact, she drew him into conversation, stated her own opinions, and heard his replies and explanations. Her faith was at first staggered by his declaring himself a Jew; but on this point she was relieved by his saying, 'Do you not remember how Jesus prayed?' and repeated part of the Lord's prayer, in proof that the Father's kingdom was to come, and not the Son's. She then understood him to be a converted Jew, and in the conclusion she says she 'felt as if God had sent him to set up the kingdom.' Thus Matthias at once secured the good will of Isabella, and we may suppose obtained from her some information in relation to Mr. Pierson, especially that Mrs. Pierson declared there was no true church, and approved of Mr. Pierson's preaching. Matthias left the house, promising to return on Saturday evening. Mr. P. at this time had not seen Matthias.

Isabella, desirous of hearing the expected conversation between Matthias and Mr. Pierson on Saturday, hurried her work, got it finished, and was permitted to be present. Indeed, the sameness of belief made her familiar with her employer, while her attention to her work, and characteristic faithfulness, increased his confidence. This intimacy, the result of holding the same faith, and the principle afterwards adopted of having but one table, and all things in common, made her at once the domestic and the equal, and the depositary of very curious, if not valuable information. To this object, even her color assisted. Persons who have travelled in the South know the manner in which the colored people, and especially slaves, are treated; they are scarcely regarded as being present. This trait in our American character has been frequently noticed by foreign travellers. One English lady remarks

that she discovered, in course of conversation with a Southern married gentleman, that a colored girl slept in his bedroom, in which also was his wife; and when he saw that it occasioned some surprise, he remarked, 'What would he do if he wanted a glass of water in the night?' Other travellers have remarked that the presence of colored people never seemed to interrupt conversation of any kind for one moment. Isabella, then, was present at the first interview between Matthias and Pierson. At this interview, Mr. Pierson asked Matthias if he had a family, to which he replied in the affirmative; he asked him about his beard, and he gave a scriptural reason, asserting also that the Jews did not shave, and that Adam had a beard. Mr. Pierson detailed to Matthias his experience, and Matthias gave his, and they mutually discovered that they held the same sentiments, both admitting the direct influence of the Spirit, and the transmission of spirits from one body to another. Matthias admitted the call of Mr. Pierson, in the omnibus in Wall street, which, on this occasion, he gave in these words:--'Thou art Elijah the Tishbite, and thou shalt go before me in the spirit and power of Elias, to prepare my way before me.' And Mr. Pierson admitted Matthias' call, who completed his declaration on the 20th of June, in Argyle, which, by a curious coincidence, was the very day on which Pierson had received his call in the omnibus. Such singular coincidences have a powerful effect on excited minds. From that discovery,

Pierson and Matthias rejoiced in each other, and became kindred spirits--Matthias, however, claiming to be the Father, or to possess the spirit of the Father--he was God upon earth, because the spirit of God dwelt in him; while Pierson then understood that his mission was like that of John the Baptist, which the name Elias meant. This conference ended with an invitation to supper, and Matthias and Pierson washing each other's feet. Mr. Pierson preached on the following Sunday, but after which, he declined in favor of Matthias, and some of the party believed that the 'kingdom had then come.'

As a specimen of Matthias' preaching and sentiments, the following is said to be reliable:

'The spirit that built the Tower of Babel is now in the world--it is the spirit of the devil. The spirit of man never goes upon the clouds; all who think so are Babylonians. The only heaven is on the earth. All who are ignorant of truth are Ninevites. The Jews did not crucify Christ--it was the Gentiles. Every Jew has his guardian angel attending him in this world. God don't speak through preachers; he speaks through me, his prophet.

'"John the Baptist," (addressing Mr. Pierson,) "read the tenth chapter of Revelations." After the reading of the chapter, the prophet resumed speaking, as follows:--

'Ours is the mustard-seed kingdom which is to spread all over the earth. Our creed is truth, and no man can find truth unless he obeys John the Baptist, and comes clean into the church.

'All real men will be saved; all mock men will be damned. When a person has the Holy Ghost, then he is a man, and not till then. They who teach women are of the wicked. The communion is all nonsense; so is prayer. Eating a nip of bread and drinking a little wine won't do any good. All who admit members into their church, and suffer them to hold their lands and houses, their sentence is, "Depart, ye wicked, I know you not." All females who lecture their husbands, their sentence is the same. The sons of truth are to enjoy all the good things of this world, and must use their means to bring it about. Every thing that has the smell of woman will be destroyed. Woman is the capsheaf of the abomination of desolation--full of all deviltry. In a short time, the world will take fire and dissolve; it is combustible already. All women, not obedient, had better become so as soon as possible, and let the wicked spirit depart, and become temples of truth. Praying is all mocking. When you see any one wring the neck of a fowl, instead of cutting off its head, he has not got the Holy Ghost. (Cutting gives the least pain.)

'All who eat swine's flesh are of the devil; and just as certain as he eats it, he will tell a lie in less than half an hour. If you eat a piece of pork, it will go crooked through you, and the Holy Ghost will not stay in you, but one or the other must leave the house pretty soon.

The pork will be as crooked in you as rams' horns, and as great a nuisance as the hogs in the street.

'The cholera is not the right word; it is choler, which means God's wrath. Abraham, Isaac, and Jacob are now in this world; they did not go up in the clouds, as some believe--why should they go there? They don't want to go there to box the compass from one place to another. The Christians now-a-days are for setting up the Son's kingdom. It is not his; it is the Father's kingdom. It puts me in mind of the man in the country, who took his son in business, and had his sign made, "Hitchcock & Son;" but the son wanted it "Hitchcock & Father"--and that is the way with your Christians. They talk of the Son's kingdom first, and not the Father's kingdom.'

Matthias and his disciples at this time did not believe in a resurrection of the body, but that the spirits of the former saints would enter the bodies of the present generation, and thus begin heaven upon earth, of which he and Mr. Pierson were the first fruits.

Matthias made the residence of Mr. Pierson his own; but the latter, being apprehensive of popular violence in his house, if Matthias remained there, proposed a monthly allowance to him, and advised him to occupy another dwelling. Matthias accordingly took a house in Clarkson street, and then sent for his family at Albany, but they declined coming to the city. However, his brother George complied with a similar offer, bringing his family with him, where they found very comfortable quarters. Isabella was employed to do the housework. In May, 1833, Matthias left his house, and placed the furniture, part of which was Isabella's, elsewhere, living himself at the hotel corner of Marketfield and West streets. Isabella found employment at Mr. Whiting's, Canal street, and did the washing for Matthias by Mrs. Whiting's permission.

Of the subsequent removal of Matthias to the farm and residence of Mr. B. Folger, at Sing Sing, where he was joined by Mr. Pierson, and others laboring under a similar religious delusion--the sudden, melancholy and somewhat suspicious death of Mr. Pierson, and the arrest of Matthias on the charge of his murder, ending in a verdict of not guilty--the criminal connection that subsisted between Matthias, Mrs. Folger, and other membes of the 'Kingdom,' as 'match-spirits'--the final dispersion of this deluded company, and the voluntary exilement of Matthias in the far West, after his release--&c. &c., we do not deem it useful or necessary to give any particulars. Those who are curious to know what there transpired are referred to a work published in New York in 1835, entitled 'Fanaticism; its Sources and Influence; illustrated by the simple Narrative of Isabella, in the case of Matthias, Mr. and Mrs. B. Folger, Mr. Pierson, Mr. Mills, Catharine, Isabella, &c. &c. By G. Vale, 84 Roosevelt street.' Suffice it to say, that while Isabella was a member of the household at Sing Sing, doing much laborious service in the spirit of religious disinterestedness, and gradually getting her vision purged and her mind cured of its illusions, she happily escaped the contamination that surrounded her,-- assiduously endeavoring to discharge all her duties in a becoming manner.

FASTING.

When Isabella resided with Mr. Pierson, he was in the habit of fasting every Friday; not eating or drinking anything from Thursday evening to six o'clock on Friday evening.

Then, again, he would fast two nights and three days, neither eating nor drinking; refusing himself even a cup of cold water till the third day at night, when he took supper again, as usual.

Isabella asked him why he fasted. He answered, that fasting gave him great light in the things of God; which answer gave birth to the following train of thought in the mind of his auditor:--'Well, if fasting will give light inwardly and spiritually, I need it as much as any body,--and I'll fast too. If Mr. Pierson needs to fast two nights and three days, then I, who need light more than he does, ought to fast more, and I will fast three nights and three days.'

This resolution she carried out to the letter, putting not so much as a drop of water in her mouth for three whole days and nights. The fourth morning, as she arose to her feet, not having power to stand, she fell to the floor; but recovering herself sufficiently, she made her way to the pantry, and feeling herself quite voracious, and fearing that she might now offend God by her voracity, compelled herself to breakfast on dry bread and water--eating a large six-penny loaf before she felt at all stayed or satisfied. She says she did get light, but it was all in her body and none in her mind--and this lightness of body lasted a long time. Oh! she was so light, and felt so well, she could 'skim around like a gull.'

THE CAUSE OF HER LEAVING THE CITY.

The first years spent by Isabella in the city, she accumulated more than enough to supply all her wants, and she placed all the overplus in the Savings' Bank. Afterwards, while living with Mr. Pierson, he prevailed on her to take it thence, and invest it in a common fund which he was about establishing, as a fund to be drawn from by all the faithful; the faithful, of course, were the handful that should subscribe to his peculiar creed. This fund, commenced by Mr. Pierson, afterwards became part and parcel of the kingdom of which Matthias assumed to be head; and at the breaking up of the kingdom, her little property was merged in the general ruin--or went to enrich those who profited by the loss of others, if any such there were. Mr. Pierson and others had so assured her, that the fund would supply all her wants, at all times, and in all emergencies, and to the end of life, that she became perfectly careless on the subject--asking for no interest when she drew her money from the bank, and taking no account of the sum she placed in the fund. She recovered a few articles of furniture from the wreck of the kingdom, and received a small sum of money from Mr. B. Folger, as the price of Mrs. Folger's attempt to convict her of murder. With this to start upon, she commenced anew her labors, in the hope of yet being able to accumulate a sufficiency to make a little home for herself, in her advancing age. With this stimulus before her, she toiled hard, working early and late, doing a great deal for a little money, and turning her hand to almost any thing that promised good pay. Still, she did not prosper; and somehow, could not contrive to lay by a single dollar for a 'rainy day.'

When this had been the state of her affairs some time, she suddenly paused, and taking a retrospective view of what had passed, inquired within herself, why it was that, for all her unwearied labors, she had nothing to show; why it was that others, with much less care and labor, could hoard up treasures for themselves and children? She became more and more convinced, as she reasoned, that everything she had undertaken in the city of New York had finally proved a failure; and where her hopes had been raised the highest, there she felt the failure had been the greatest, and the disappointment most severe.

After turning it in her mind for some time, she came to the conclusion, that she had been taking part in a great drama, which was, in itself, but one great system of robbery and wrong. 'Yes,' she said, 'the rich rob the poor, and the poor rob one another.' True, she had not received labor from others, and stinted their pay, as she felt had been practised against her; but she had taken their work from them, which was their only means to get money, and was the same to them in the end. For instance--a gentleman where she lived would give her a half dollar to hire a poor man to clear the new-fallen snow from the steps and side-walks. She would arise early, and perform the labor herself, putting the money into her own pocket. A poor man would come along, saying she ought to have let him have the job; he was poor, and needed the pay for his family. She would harden her heart against him, and answer--'I am poor too, and I need it for mine.' But, in her retrospection, she thought of all the misery she might have been adding to, in her selfish grasping, and it troubled her conscience sorely; and this insensibility to the claims of human brotherhood, and the wants of the destitute and wretched poor, she now saw, as she never had done before, to be unfeeling, selfish and wicked. These reflections and convictions gave rise to a sudden revulsion of feeling in the heart of Isabella, and she began to look upon money and property with great indifference, if not contempt--being at that time unable, probably, to discern any difference between a miserly grasping at and hoarding of money and means, and a true use of the good things of this life for one's own comfort, and the relief of such as she might be enabled to befriend and assist. One thing she was sure of--that the precepts, 'Do unto others as ye would that others should do unto you,' 'Love your neighbor as yourself,' and so forth, were maxims that had been but little thought of by herself, or practised by those about her.

Her next decision was, that she must leave the city; it was no place for her; yea, she felt called in spirit to leave it, and to travel east and lecture. She had never been further east than the city, neither had she any friends there of whom she had particular reason to expect anything; yet to her it was plain that her mission lay in the east, and that she would find friends there. She determined on leaving; but these determinations and convictions she kept close locked in her own breast, knowing that if her children and friends were aware of it, they would make such an ado about it as would render it very unpleasant, if not distressing to all parties. Having made what preparations for leaving she deemed necessary,--which was, to put up a few articles of clothing in a pillow-case, all else being deemed an unnecessary encumbrance,--about an hour before she left, she informed Mrs. Whiting, the woman of the house where she was stopping, that her name was no longer Isabella, but SOJOURNER; and that she was going east. And to her inquiry, 'What are you going east for?' her answer was, 'The Spirit calls me there, and I must go.'

She left the city on the morning of the 1st of June, 1843, crossing over to Brooklyn, L. I.; and taking the rising sun for her only compass and guide, she 'remembered Lot's wife,' and hoping to avoid her fate, she resolved not to look back till she felt sure the wicked city from which she was fleeing was left too far behind to be visible in the distance; and when she first ventured to look back, she could just discern the blue cloud of smoke that hung over it, and she thanked the Lord that she was thus far removed from what seemed to her a second Sodom.

She was now fairly started on her pilgrimage; her bundle in one hand, and a little basket of provisions in the other, and two York shillings in her purse--her heart strong in the faith that her true work lay before her, and that the Lord was her director; and she doubted not he would provide for and protect her, and that it would be very censurable in her to burden herself with anything more than a moderate supply for her then present needs. Her mission was not merely to travel east, but to 'lecture,' as she designated it; 'testifying of the hope that was in her'--exhorting the people to embrace Jesus, and refrain from sin, the nature and origin of which she explained to them in accordance with her own most curious and original views. Through her life, and all its chequered changes, she has ever clung fast to her first permanent impressions on religious subjects.

Wherever night overtook her, there she sought for lodgings--free, if she might--if not, she paid; at a tavern, if she chanced to be at one--if not, at a private dwelling; with the rich, if they would receive her--if not, with the poor.

But she soon discovered that the largest houses were nearly always full; if not quite full, company was soon expected; and that it was much easier to find an unoccupied corner in a small house than in a large one; and if a person possessed but a miserable roof over his head, you might be sure of a welcome to part of it.

But this, she had penetration enough to see, was quite as much the effect of a want of sympathy as of benevolence; and this was also very apparent in her religious conversations with people who were strangers to her. She said, 'she never could find out that the rich had any religion. If I had been rich and accomplished, I could; for the rich could always find religion in the rich, and I could find it among the poor.'

At first, she attended such meetings as she heard of, in the vicinity of her travels, and spoke to the people as she found them assembled. Afterwards, she advertised meetings of her own, and held forth to large audiences, having, as she said, 'a good time.'

When she became weary of travelling, and wished a place to stop a while and rest herself, she said some opening for her was always near at hand; and the first time she needed rest, a man accosted her as she was walking, inquiring if she was looking for work. She told him that was not the object of her travels, but that she would willingly work a few days, if any one wanted. He requested her to go to his family, who were sadly in want of assistance, which he had been thus far unable to supply. She went to the house where she was directed, and was received by his family, one of whom was ill, as a 'God-send;' and when she felt constrained to resume her journey, they were very sorry, and would fain have detained her longer; but as she urged the necessity of leaving, they offered her what seemed in her eyes a great deal of money as a remuneration for her labor, and an expression of their gratitude for her opportune assistance; but she would only receive a very little of it; enough, as she says, to enable her to pay tribute to Cæsar, if it was demanded of her; and two or three York shillings at a time were all she allowed herself to take;

and then, with purse replenished, and strength renewed, she would once more set out to perform her mission.

THE CONSEQUENCES OF REFUSING A TRAVELLER A NIGHT'S LODGING.

As she drew near the centre of the Island, she commenced, one evening at nightfall, to solicit the favor of a night's lodging. She had repeated her request a great many, it seemed to her some twenty times, and as many times she received a negative answer. She walked on, the stars and the tiny horns of the new moon shed but a dim light on her lonely way, when she was familiarly accosted by two Indians, who took her for an acquaintance. She told them they were mistaken in the person; she was a stranger there, and asked them the direction to a tavern. They informed her it was yet a long way--some two miles or so; and inquired if she were alone. Not wishing for their protection, or knowing what might be the character of their kindness, she answered, 'No, not exactly,' and passed on. At the end of a weary way, she came to the tavern,--or, rather, to a large building, which was occupied as court-house, tavern, and jail,--and on asking for a night's lodging, was informed she could stay, if she would consent to be locked in. This to her mind was an insuperable objection. To have a key turned on her was a thing not to be thought of, at least not to be endured, and she again took up her line of march, preferring to walk beneath the open sky, to being locked up by a stranger in such a place. She had not walked far, before she heard the voice of a woman under an open shed; she ventured to accost her, and inquired if she knew where she could get in for the night. The woman answered, that she did not, unless she went home with them; and turning to her 'good man,' asked him if the stranger could not share their home for the night, to which he cheerfully assented. Sojourner thought it evident he had been taking a drop too much, but as he was civil and good-natured, and she did not feel inclined to spend the night alone in the open air, she felt driven to the necessity of accepting their hospitality, whatever it might prove to be. The woman soon informed her that there was a hall in the place, at which they would like to drop in a while, before they went to their home.

Balls being no part of Sojourner's mission, she was not desirous of attending; but her hostess could be satisfied with nothing short of a taste of it, and she was forced to go with her, or relinquish their company at once, in which move there might be more exposure than in accompanying her. She went, and soon found herself surrounded by an assemblage of people, collected from the very dregs of society, too ignorant and degraded to understand, much less entertain, a high or bright idea,-- in a dirty hovel, destitute of every comfort, and where the fumes of whisky were abundant and powerful.

Sojourner's guide there was too much charmed with the combined entertainments of the place to be able to tear herself away, till she found her faculties for enjoyment failing her, from a too free use of liquor; and she betook herself to bed till she could recover them. Sojourner, seated in a corner, had time for many reflections, and refrained from lecturing them in obedience to the recommendation, 'Cast not your pearls,' &c. When the night was far spent, the husband of the sleeping woman aroused the sleeper, and reminded her that she was not very polite to the woman she had invited to sleep at her house, and of the propriety of returning home. They once more emerged into the pure air, which to our friend Sojourner, after so long breathing the noisome air of the ball-room, was most refreshing and grateful. Just as day dawned, they reached the place they called their home. Sojourner now saw that she had lost nothing in the shape of rest by remaining so long at the ball, as their miserable cabin afforded but one bunk or pallet for sleeping; and had there been many such, she would have preferred sitting up all night to occupying one like it. They very politely offered her the bed, if she would use it; but civilly declining, she waited for morning with an eagerness of desire she never felt before on the subject, and was never more happy than when the eye of day shed its golden light once more over the earth. She was once more free, and while day-light should last, independent, and needed no invitation to pursue her journey. Let these facts teach us, that every pedestrian in the world is not a vagabond, and that it is a dangerous thing to compel any one to receive that hospitality from the vicious and abandoned which they should have received from us,--as thousands can testify, who have thus been caught in the snares of the wicked.

The fourth of July, Isabella arrived at Huntingdon; from thence she went to Cold Springs, where she found the people making preparations for a mass temperance-meeting. With her usual alacrity, she entered into their labors, getting up dishes a la New York, greatly to the satisfaction of those she assisted. After remaining at Cold Springs some three weeks, she returned to Huntingdon, where she took boat for Connecticut. Landing at Bridgeport, she again resumed her travels towards the north-east, lecturing some, and working some, to get wherewith to pay tribute to Cæsar, as she called it; and in this manner she presently came to the city of New Haven, where she found many meetings, which she attended--at some of which, she was allowed to express her views freely, and without reservation. She also called meetings expressly to give herself an opportunity to be heard; and found in the city many true friends of Jesus, as she judged, with whom she held communion of spirit, having no preference for one sect more than another, but being well satisfied with all who gave her evidence of having known or loved the Saviour.

After thus delivering her testimony in this pleasant city, feeling she had not as yet found an abiding place, she went from thence to Bristol, at the request of a zealous sister, who desired her to go to the latter place, and hold a religious conversation with some friends of hers there. She went as requested, found the people kindly and religiously disposed, and through them she became acquainted with several very interesting persons.

A spiritually-minded brother in Bristol, becoming interested in her new views and original opinions, requested as a favor that she would go to Hartford, to see and converse with friends of his there. Standing ready to perform any service in the Lord, she went to Hartford as desired, bearing in her hand the following note from this brother:--

'SISTER,--I send you this living messenger, as I believe her to be one that God loves. Ethiopia is stretching forth her hands unto God. You can see by this sister, that God does by his Spirit alone teach his own children things to come. Please receive her, and she will tell you some new things. Let her tell her story without interrupting her, and give close attention, and you will see she has got the lever of truth, that God helps her to pry where but few can. She cannot read or write, but the law is in her heart.

'Send her to brother--, brother--, and where she can do the most good.

'From your brother,

H. L. B.'

SOME OF HER VIEWS AND REASONINGS.

As soon as Isabella saw God as an all-powerful, all-pervading spirit, she became desirous of hearing all that had been written of him, and listened to the account of the creation of the world and its first inhabitants, as contained in the first chapters of Genesis, with peculiar interest. For some time she received it all literally, though it appeared strange to her that 'God worked by the day, got tired, and stopped to rest,' &c. But after a little time, she began to reason upon it, thus--'Why, if God works by the day, and one day's work tires him, and he is obliged to rest, either from weariness or on account of darkness, or if he waited for the "cool of the day to walk in the garden," because he was inconvenienced by the heat of the sun, why then it seems that God cannot do as much as I can; for I can bear the sun at noon, and work several days and nights in succession without being much tired. Or, if he rested nights because of the darkness, it is very queer that he should make the night so dark that he could not see himself. If I had been God, I would have made the night light enough for my own convenience, surely.' But the moment she placed this idea of God by the side of the impression she had once so suddenly received of his inconceivable greatness and entire spirituality, that moment she exclaimed mentally, 'No, God does not stop to rest, for he is a spirit, and cannot tire; he cannot want for light, for he hath all light in himself. And if "God is all in all," and "worketh all in all," as I have heard them read, then it is impossible he should rest at all; for if he did, every other thing would stop and rest too; the waters would not flow, and the fishes could not swim; and all motion must cease. God could have no pauses in his work, and he needed no Sabbaths of rest. Man might need them, and he should take them when he needed them, whenever he required rest. As it regarded the worship of God, he was to be worshipped at all times and in all places; and one portion of time never seemed to her more holy than another.'

These views, which were the result of the workings of her own mind, assisted solely by the light of her own experience and very limited knowledge, were, for a long time after their adoption, closely locked in her own breast, fearing lest their avowal might bring upon her the imputation of 'infidelity,'--the usual charge preferred by all religionists, against those who entertain religious views and feelings differing materially from their own. If, from their own sad experience, they are withheld from shouting the cry of 'infidel,' they fail not to see and to feel, ay, and to say, that the dissenters are not of the right spirit, and that their spiritual eyes have never been unsealed.

While travelling in Connecticut, she met a minister, with whom she held a long discussion on these points, as well as on various other topics, such as the origin of all things, especially the origin of evil, at the same time bearing her testimony strongly against a paid ministry. He belonged to that class, and, as a matter of course, as strongly advocated his own side of the question.

I had forgotten to mention, in its proper place, a very important fact, that when she was examining the Scriptures, she wished to hear them without comment; but if she employed adult persons to read them to her, and she asked them to read a passage over again, they invariably commenced to explain, by giving her their version of it; and in this way, they tried her feelings exceedingly. In consequence of this, she ceased to ask adult persons to read the Bible to her, and substituted children in their stead. Children, as soon as they could read distinctly, would re-read the same sentence to her, as often as she wished, and without comment; and in that way she was enabled to see what her own mind could make out of the record, and that, she said, was what she wanted, and not what others thought it to mean. She wished to compare the teachings of the Bible with the witness within her; and she came to the conclusion, that the spirit of truth spoke in those records, but that the recorders of those truths had intermingled with them ideas and suppositions of their own. This is one among the many proofs of her energy and independence of character.

When it became known to her children, that Sojourner had left New York, they were filled with wonder and alarm. Where could she have gone, and why had she left? were questions no one could answer satisfactorily. Now, their imaginations painted her as a wandering maniac--and again they feared she had been left to commit suicide; and many were the tears they shed at the loss of her.

But when she reached Berlin, Conn., she wrote to them by amanuensis, informing them of her whereabouts, and waiting an answer to her letter; thus quieting their fears, and gladdening their hearts once more with assurances of her continued life and her love.

THE SECOND ADVENT DOCTRINES.

In Hartford and vicinity, she met with several persons who believed in the 'Second Advent' doctrines; or, the immediate personal appearance of Jesus Christ. At first she thought she had never heard of 'Second Advent.' But when it was explained to her, she recollected having once attended Mr. Miller's meeting in New York, where she saw a great many enigmatical pictures hanging on the wall, which she could not understand, and which, being out of the reach of her understanding, failed to interest her. In this section of country, she attended two camp meetings of the believers in these doctrines--the 'second advent' excitement being then at its greatest height. The last meeting was at Windsor Lock. The people, as a matter of course, eagerly inquired of her concerning her belief, as it regarded their most important tenet. She told them it had not been revealed to her; perhaps, if she could read, she might see it differently. Sometimes, to their eager inquiry, 'Oh, don't you believe the Lord is coming?' she answered, 'I believe the Lord is as near as he can be, and not be it.' With these evasive and non-exciting answers, she kept their minds calm as it respected her unbelief, till she could have an opportunity to hear their views fairly stated, in order to judge more understandingly of this matter, and see if, in her estimation, there was any good ground for expecting an event which was, in the minds of so many, as it were, shaking the very foundations of the universe. She was invited to join them in their religious exercises, and accepted the invitation--praying, and talking in her own peculiar style, and attracting many about her by her singing.

When she had convinced the people that she was a lover of God and his cause, and had gained a good standing with them, so that she could get a hearing among them, she had become quite sure in her own mind that they were laboring under a delusion, and she commenced to use her influence to calm the fears of the people, and pour oil upon the troubled waters. In one part of the grounds, she found a knot of people greatly excited: she mounted a stump and called out, 'Hear! hear!' When the people had gathered around her, as they were in a state to listen to anything new, she addressed them as 'children,' and asked them why they made such a 'To-do;--are you not commanded to "watch and pray?" You are neither watching nor praying.' And she bade them, with the tones of a kind mother, retire to their tents, and there watch and pray, without noise or tumult, for the Lord would not come to such a scene of confusion; 'the Lord came still and quiet.' She assured them, 'the Lord might come, move all through the camp, and go away again, and they never know it,' in the state they then were.

They seemed glad to seize upon any reason for being less agitated and distressed, and many of them suppressed their noisy terror, and retired to their tents to 'watch and pray;' begging others to do the same, and listen to the advice of the good sister. She felt she had done some good, and then went to listen further to the preachers. They appeared to her to be doing their utmost to agitate and excite the people, who were already too much excited; and when she had listened till her feelings would let her listen silently no longer, she arose and addressed the preachers. The following are specimens of her speech:--

'Here you are talking about being "changed in the twinkling of an eye." If the Lord should come, he'd change you to nothing! for there is nothing to you.

'You seem to be expecting to go to some parlor away up somewhere, and when the wicked have been burnt, you are coming back to walk in triumph over their ashes--this is to be your New Jerusalem!! Now I can't see anything so very nice in that, coming back to such a muss as that will be, a world covered with the ashes of the wicked! Besides, if the Lord comes and burns--as you say he will--I am not going away; I am going to stay here and stand the fire, like Shadrach, Meshach, and Abednego! And Jesus will walk with me through the fire, and keep me from harm. Nothing belonging to God can burn, any more than God himself; such shall have no need to go away to escape the fire! No, I shall remain. Do you tell me that God's children can't stand fire?' And her manner and tone spoke louder than words, saying, 'It is absurd to think so!'

The ministers were taken quite aback at so unexpected an opposer, and one of them, in the kindest possible manner, commenced a discussion with her, by asking her questions, and quoting scripture to her; concluding finally, that although she had learned nothing of the great doctrine which was so exclusively occupying their minds at the time, she had learned much that man had never taught her.

At this meeting, she received the address of different persons, residing in various places, with an invitation to visit them. She promised to go soon to Cabotville, and started, shaping her course for that place. She arrived at Springfield one evening at six o'clock, and immediately began to search for a lodging for the night. She walked from six till past nine, and was then on the road from Springfield to Cabotville, before she found any one sufficiently hospitable to give her a night's shelter under their roof. Then a man gave her twenty-five cents, and bade her go to a tavern and stay all night. She did so, returning in the morning to thank him, assuring him she had put his money to its legitimate use. She found a number of the friends she had seen at Windsor when she reached the manufacturing town of Cabotville, (which has lately taken the name of Chicopee,) and with them she spent a pleasant week or more; after which, she left them to visit the Shaker village in Enfield. She LOW began to think of finding a resting place, at least, for a season; for she had performed quite a long journey, considering she had walked most of the way; and she had a mind to look in upon the Shakers, and see how things were there, and whether there was any opening there for her. But on her way back to Springfield, she called at a house and asked for a piece of bread; her request was granted, and she was kindly invited to tarry all night, as it was getting late, and she would not be able to stay at every house in that vicinity, which invitation she cheerfully accepted. When the man of the house came in, he recollected having seen her at the camp-meeting, and repeated some conversations, by which she recognized him again. He soon proposed having a meeting that evening, went out and notified his friends and neighbors, who came together, and she once more held forth to them in her peculiar style. Through the agency of this meeting, she became acquainted with several people residing in Springfield, to whose houses she was cordially invited, and with whom she spent some pleasant time.

One of these friends, writing of her arrival there, speaks as follows. After saying that she and her people belonged to that class of persons who believed in the second advent doctrines; and that this class, believing also in freedom of speech and action, often found at their meetings many singular people, who did not agree with them in their principal doctrine; and that, being thus prepared to hear new and strange things, 'They listened eagerly to Sojourner, and drank in all she said;'--and also, that she 'soon became a favorite among them; that when she arose to speak in their assemblies, her commanding figure and dignified manner hushed every trifler into silence, and her singular and sometimes uncouth modes of expression never provoked a laugh, but often were the whole audience melted into tears by her touching stories.' She also adds, 'Many were the lessons of wisdom and faith I have delighted to learn from her.' . . . . 'She continued a great favorite in our meetings, both on account of her remarkable gift in prayer, and still more remarkable talent for singing, . . . and the aptness and point of her remarks, frequently illustrated by figures the most original and expressive.

'As we were walking the other day, she said she had often thought what a beautiful world this would be, when we should see everything right side up. Now, we see everything topsy-turvy, and all is confusion.' For a person who knows nothing of this fact in the science of optics, this seemed quite a remarkable idea.

'We also loved her for her sincere and ardent piety, her unwavering faith in God, and her contempt of what the world calls fashion, and what we call folly.

'She was in search of a quiet place, where a way-worn traveller might rest. She had heard of Fruitlands, and was inclined to go there; but the friends she found here thought it best for her to visit Northampton. She passed her time, while with us, working wherever her work was needed, and talking where work was not needed.

'She would not receive money for her work, saying she worked for the Lord; and if her wants were supplied, she received it as from the Lord.

'She remained with us till far into winter, when we introduced her at the Northampton Association.' . . . .

'She wrote to me from thence, that she had found the quiet resting place she had so long desired. And she has remained there ever since.'

ANOTHER CAMP-MEETING.

When Sojourner had been at Northampton a few months, she attended another camp-meeting, at which she performed a very important part.

A party of wild young men, with no motive but that of entertaining themselves by annoying and injuring the feelings of others, had assembled at the meeting, hooting and yelling, and in various ways interrupting the services, and causing much disturbance. Those who had the charge of the meeting, having tried their persuasive powers in vain, grew impatient and tried threatening.

The young men, considering themselves insulted, collected their friends, to the number of a hundred or more, dispersed themselves through the grounds, making the most frightful noises, and threatening to fire the tents. It was said the authorities of the meeting sat in grave consultation, decided to have the ringleaders arrested, and sent for the constable, to the great displeasure of some of the company, who were opposed to such an appeal to force and arms. Be that as it may, Sojourner, seeing great consternation depicted in every countenance, caught the contagion, and, ere she was aware, found herself quaking with fear.

Under the impulse of this sudden emotion, she fled to the most retired corner of a tent, and secreted herself behind a trunk, saying to herself, 'I am the only colored person here, and on me, probably, their wicked mischief will fall first, and perhaps fatally.' But feeling how great was her insecurity even there, as the very tent began to shake from its foundations, she began to soliloquize as follows:--

'Shall I run away and hide from the Devil? Me, a servant of the living God? Have I not faith enough to go out and quell that mob, when I know it is written--"One shall chase a thousand, and two put ten thousand to flight"? I know there are not a thousand here; and I know I am a servant of the living God. I'll go to the rescue, and the Lord shall go with and protect me.

'Oh,' said she, 'I felt as if I had three hearts! and that they were so large, my body could hardly hold them!'

She now came forth from her hiding-place, and invited several to go with her and see what they could do to still the raging of the moral elements. They declined, and considered her wild to think of it.

The meeting was in the open fields--the full moon shed its saddened light over all--and the woman who was that evening to address them was trembling on the preachers' stand. The noise and confusion were now terrific. Sojourner left the tent alone and unaided, and walking some thirty rods to the top of a small rise of ground, commenced to sing, in her most fervid manner, with all the strength of her most powerful voice, the hymn on the resurrection of Christ--

It was early in the morning--it was early

in the morning,
Just at the break of day--
When he rose--when he rose--when he rose,
 And went to heaven on a cloud.'

All who have ever heard her sing this hymn will probably remember it as long as they remember her. The hymn, the tune, the style, are each too closely associated with to be easily separated from herself, and when sung in one of her most animated moods, in the open air, with the utmost strength of her most powerful voice, must have been truly thrilling.

As she commenced to sing, the young men made a rush towards her, and she was immediately encircled by a dense body of the rioters, many of them armed with sticks or clubs as their weapons of defence, if not of attack. As the circle narrowed around her, she ceased singing, and after a short pause, inquired, in a gentle but firm tone, 'Why do you come about me with clubs and sticks? I am not doing harm to anyone.' 'We ar'n't a going to hurt you, old woman; we came to hear you sing,' cried many voices, simultaneously. 'Sing to us, old woman,' cries one. 'Talk to us, old woman,' says another. 'Pray, old woman,' says a third. 'Tell us your experience,' says a fourth. 'You stand and smoke so near me, I cannot sing or talk,' she answered.

'Stand back,' said several authoritative voices, with not the most gentle or courteous accompaniments, raising their rude weapons in the air. The crowd suddenly gave back, the circle became larger, as many voices again called for singing, talking, or praying, backed by assurances that no one should be allowed to hurt her--the speakers declaring with an oath, that they would 'knock down' any person who should offer her the least indignity.

She looked about her, and with her usual discrimination, said inwardly--'Here must be many young men in all this assemblage, bearing within them hearts susceptible of good impressions. I will speak to them.' She did speak; they silently heard, and civilly asked her many questions. It seemed to her to be given her at the time to answer them with truth and wisdom beyond herself. Her speech had operated on the roused passions of the mob like oil on agitated waters; they were, as a whole, entirely subdued, and only clamored when she ceased to speak or sing. Those who stood in the background, after the circle was enlarged, cried out, 'Sing aloud, old woman, we can't hear.' Those who held the sceptre of power among them requested that she should make a pulpit of a neighboring wagon. She said, 'If I do, they'll overthrow it.' 'No, they sha'n't--he who dares hurt you, we'll knock him down instantly, d--n him,' cried the chiefs. 'No we won't, no we won't, nobody shall hurt you,' answered the many voices of the mob. They kindly assisted her to mount the wagon, from which she spoke and sung to them about an hour. Of all she said to them on the occasion, she remembers only the following:--

'Well, there are two congregations on this ground. It is written that there shall be a separation, and the sheep shall be separated from the goats. The other preachers have the sheep, I have the goats. And I have a few sheep among my goats, but they are very ragged.' This exordium produced great laughter. When she became wearied with talking, she began to cast about her to contrive some way to induce them to disperse. While she paused, they loudly clamored for 'more,' 'more,'--'sing,' 'sing more.' She motioned them to be quiet, and called out to them: 'Children, I have talked and sung to you, as you asked me; and now I have a request to make of you: will you grant it?' 'Yes, yes, yes,' resounded from every quarter. 'Well, it is this,' she answered: 'if I will sing one more hymn for you, will you then go away, and leave us this night in peace?' 'Yes, yes,' came faintly, feebly from a few. 'I repeat it,' says Sojourner, 'and I want an answer from you all, as of one accord. If I will sing you one more, you will go away, and leave us this night in peace?' 'Yes, yes, yes,' shouted many voices, with hearty emphasis. 'I repeat my request once more,' said she, 'and I want you all to answer.' And she reiterated the words again. This time a long, loud 'Yes--yes--yes,' came up, as from the multitudinous mouth of the entire mob. 'AMEN! it is SEALED, repeated Sojourner, in the deepest and most solemn tones of her powerful and sonorous voice. Its effect ran through the multitude, like an electric shock; and the most of them considered themselves bound by their promise, as they might have failed to do under less imposing circumstances. Some of them began instantly to leave; others said, 'Are we not to have one more hymn?' 'Yes,' answered their entertainer, and she commenced to sing:

> 'I bless the Lord I've got my seal--to-day and to-day--
> To slay Goliath in the field--to-day and to-day;
> The good old way is a righteous way,
> I mean to take the kingdom in the good old way.'

While singing, she heard some enforcing obedience to their promise, while a few seemed refusing to abide by it. But before she had quite concluded, she saw them turn from her, and in the course of a few minutes, they were running as fast as they well could in a solid body; and she says she can compare them to nothing but a swarm of bees, so dense was their phalanx, so straight their course, so hurried their march. As they passed with a rush very near the stand of the other preachers, the hearts of the people were smitten with fear, thinking that their entertainer had failed to enchain them longer with her spell, and that they were coming upon them with redoubled and remorseless fury. But they found they were mistaken, and that their fears were groundless; for, before they could well recover from their surprise, every rioter was gone, and not one was left on the grounds, or seen there again during the meeting. Sojourner was informed that as her audience reached the main road, some distance from the tents, a few of the rebellious spirits refused to go on, and proposed returning; but their leaders said, 'No--we have promised to leave--all promised, and we must go, all go, and you shall none of you return again.'

She did not fall in love at first sight with the Northampton Association, for she arrived there at a time when appearances did not correspond with the ideas of associationists, as they had been spread out in their writings; for their phalanx was a factory, and they were wanting in means to carry out their ideas of beauty and elegance, as they would have done in different circumstances. But she thought she would make an effort to tarry with them one night, though that seemed to her no desirable affair. But as soon as she saw that accomplished, literary and refined persons were living in that plain and simple manner, and submitting to the labors and privations incident to such an infant institution, she said, 'Well, if these can live here, I can.' Afterwards, she gradually became pleased with, and attached to, the place and the people, as well she might; for it must have been no small thing to have found a home in a 'Community composed of some of the choicest spirits of the age,' where all was characterized by an equality of feeling, a liberty of thought and speech, and a largeness of soul, she could not have before met with, to the same extent, in any of her wanderings.

Our first knowledge of her was derived from a friend who had resided for a time in the 'Community,' and who, after describing her, and singing one of her hymns, wished that we might see her. But we little thought, at that time, that we should ever pen these 'simple annals' of this child of nature.

When we first saw her, she was working with a hearty good will; saying she would not be induced to take regular wages, believing, as once before, that now Providence had provided her with a never failing fount, from which her every want might be perpetually supplied through her mortal life. In this, she had calculated too fast. For the Associationists found, that, taking everything into consideration, they would find it most expedient to act individually; and again, the subject of this sketch found her dreams unreal, and herself flung back upon her own resources for the supply of her needs. This she might have found more inconvenient at her time of life--for labor, exposure and hardship had made sad inroads upon her iron constitution, by inducing chronic disease and premature old age--had she not remained under the shadow of one,*

* GEORGE W. BENSON.

who never wearies in doing good, giving to the needy, and supplying the wants of the destitute. She has now set her heart upon having a little home of her own, even at this late hour of life, where she may feel a greater freedom than she can in the house of another, and where she can repose a little, after her day of action has passed by. And for such a 'home' she is now dependent on the charities of the benevolent, and to them we appeal with confidence.

Through all the scenes of her eventful life may be traced the energy of a naturally powerful mind--the fearlessness and child-like simplicity of one untrammelled by education or conventional customs--purity of character--an unflinching adherence to principle--and a native enthusiasm, which, under different circumstances, might easily have produced another Joan of Arc.

With all her fervor, and enthusiasm, and speculation, her religion is not tinctured in the least with gloom. No doubt, no hesitation, no despondency, spreads a cloud over her soul; but all is bright, clear, positive, and at times ecstatic. Her trust is in God, and from him she looks for good, and not evil. She feels that 'perfect love casteth out fear.'

Having more than once found herself awaking from a mortifying delusion,--as in the case of the Sing-Sing kingdom,--and resolving not to be thus deluded again, she has set suspicion to guard the door of her heart, and allows it perhaps to be aroused by too slight causes, on certain subjects--her vivid imagination assisting to magnify the phantoms of her fears into gigantic proportions, much beyond their real size; instead of resolutely adhering to the rule we all like best, when it is to be applied to ourselves--that of placing everything we see to the account of the best possible motive, until time and circumstance prove that we were wrong. Where no good motive can be assigned, it may become our duty to suspend our judgment till evidence can be had.

In the application of this rule, it is an undoubted duty to exercise a commendable prudence, by refusing to repose any important trust to the keeping of persons who may be strangers to us, and whose trustworthiness we have never seen tried. But no possible good, but incalculable evil may and does arise from the too common practice of placing all conduct, the source of which we do not fully understand, to the worst of intentions. How often is the gentle, timid soul discouraged, and driven perhaps to despondency, by finding its 'good evil spoken of;' and a well-meant but mistaken action loaded with an evil design!

If the world would but sedulously set about reforming itself on this one point, who can calculate the change it would produce--the evil it would annihilate, and the happiness it would confer! None but an all-seeing eye could at once embrace so vast a result. A result, how desirable! and one that can be brought about only by the most simple process--that of every individual seeing to it that he commit not this sin himself. For why should we all low in ourselves, the very fault we most dislike, when committed against us? Shall we not at least aim at consistency?

Had she possessed less generous self-sacrifice, more knowledge of the world and of business matters in general, and had she failed to take it for granted that others were like herself, and would, when her turn came to need, do as she had done, and find it 'more blessed to give than to receive,' she might have laid by something for the future. For few, perhaps, have ever possessed the power and inclination, in the same degree, at one and the same time, to labor as she has done, both day and night, for so long a period of time. And had these energies been well directed, and the proceeds well husbanded, since she has been her own mistress, they would have given her an independence during her natural life. But her constitutional biases, and her early training, or rather want of training, prevented this result; and it is too late now to remedy the great mistake. Shall she then be left to want? Who will not answer, 'No!'

LAST INTERVIEW WITH HER MASTER.

In the spring of 1849, Sojourner made a visit to her eldest daughter, Diana, who has ever suffered from ill health, and remained with Mr. Dumont, Isabella's humane master. She found him still living, though advanced in age, and reduced in property, (as he had been for a number of years,) but greatly enlightened on the subject of slavery. He said he could then see, that 'slavery was the wickedest thing in the world, the greatest curse the earth had ever felt--that it was then very clear to his mind that it was so, though, while he was a slaveholder himself, he did not see it so, and thought it was as right as holding any other property.' Sojourner remarked to him, that it might be the same with those who are now slaveholders. 'O, no,' replied he, with warmth, 'it cannot be. For, now, the sin of slavery is so clearly written out, and so much talked against,--(why, the whole world cries out against it!)--that if anyone says he don't know, and has not heard, he must, I think, be a liar. In my slaveholding days, there were few that spoke against it, and these few made little impression on any one. Had it been as it is now, think you I could have held slaves? No! I should not have dared to do it, but should have emancipated every one of them. Now, it is very different; all may hear if they will.'

Yes, reader, if any one feels that the tocsin of alarm, or the anti-slavery trump, must sound a louder note before they can hear it, one would think they must be very hard of hearing--yea, that they belong to that class, of whom it may be truly said, 'they have stopped their ears that they may not hear.'

She received a letter from her daughter Diana, dated Hyde Park, December 19, 1849, which informed her that Mr. Dumont had 'gone West' with some of his sons--that he had taken along with him, probably through mistake, the few articles of furniture she had left with him. 'Never mind,' says Sojourner, 'what we give to the poor, we lend to the Lord.' She thanked the Lord with fervor, that she had lived to hear her master say such blessed things! She recalled the lectures he used to give his slaves, on speaking the truth and being honest, and laughing, she says he taught us not to lie and steal, when he was stealing all the time himself and did not know it! Oh! how sweet to my mind was this confession! And what a confession for a master to make to a slave! A slaveholding master turned to a brother! Poor old man, may the Lord bless him, and all slaveholders partake of his spirit!

SUPERWOMEN

Narrative of Sojourner Truth

PART SECOND.
"BOOK OF LIFE."

PART SECOND.
"BOOK OF LIFE."

THE preceding narrative has given us a partial history of Sojourner Truth. This biography was published not many years after her freedom had been secured to her. Having but recently emerged from the gloomy night of slavery, ignorant and untaught in all that gives value to human existence, she was still suffering from the burden of acquired and transmitted habits incidental to her past condition of servitude. Yet she was one whose life forces and moral perceptions were so powerful and clear-cut that she not only came out from this moral gutter herself, but largely assisted in clevating others of her race from a similar state of degradation. It was the "oil of divine origin" which quickened her soul and fed the vital spark that her own indomitable courage fanned to an undying flame. She was one of the first to enlist in the war against slavery, and fought the battles for freedom by the side of its noble leaders.

A true sentinel, she slumbered not at her post. To hasten the enfranchisement of her own people was the great work to which she consecrated her life; yet, ever responsive to the calls of humanity, she cheerfully lent her aid to the advancement of other reforms, especially woman's rights and temperance.

During the last twenty-five years, she has traveled thousands of miles, lectured in many States of the

Union, spoken in Congress, and has received tokens of friendship such as few can produce. The following article was published in a Washington Sunday paper during the administration of President Lincoln:--

"It was our good fortune to be in the marble room of the senate chamber, a few days ago, when that old land-mark of the past--the representative of the forever-gone age--Sojourner Truth, made her appearance. It was an hour not soon to be forgotten; for it is not often, even in this magnanimous age of progress, that we see reverend senators--even him that holds the second chair in the gift of the Republic--vacate their seats in the hall of State, to extend the hand of welcome, the meed of praise, and substantial blessings, to a poor negro woman, whose poor old form, bending under the burden of nearly four-score and ten years, tells but too plainly that her marvelously strange life is drawing to a close. But it was as refreshing as it was strange to see her who had served in the shackles of slavery in the great State of New York for nearly a quarter of a century before a majority of these senators were born now holding a levee with them in the marble room, where less than a decade ago she would have been spurned from its outer corridor by the lowest menial, much less could she have taken the hand of a senator. Truly, the spirit of progress is abroad in the land, and the leaven of love is working in the hearts of the people, pointing with unerring certainty to the not far distant future, when the ties of affection shall cement all nations, kindred's and tongues into one common brotherhood."

She carries with her a book that she calls the Book of Life, which contains the autographs of many distinguished personages--the good and great of the land. No better idea can be given of the estimation in which she is held than by transcribing these testimonials and giving them to the public. It will be difficult to arrange these accounts in the chronological order of events, but no effort has been spared to furnish correct dates.

In the year 1851, she left her home in Northampton, Mass., for a lecturing tour in Western New York, accompanied by the Hon. George Thompson of England, and other distinguished abolitionists. To advocate the cause of the enslaved at this period was both unpopular and unsafe. Their meetings were frequently disturbed or broken up by the pro-slavery mob, and their lives imperiled. At such times, Sojourner fearlessly maintained her ground, and by her dignified manner and opportune remarks would disperse the rabble and restore order.

She spent several months in Western New York, making Rochester her headquarters. Leaving this State, she traveled westward, and the next glimpse we get of her is in a Woman's Rights Convention at Akron, Ohio. Mrs. Frances D. Gage, who presided at that meeting, relates the following:--

"The cause was unpopular then. The leaders of the movement trembled on seeing a tall, gaunt black woman, in a gray dress and white turban, surmounted by an uncouth sun-bonnet, march deliberately into the church, walk with the air of a queen up the aisle, and take her seat upon the pulpit steps. A buzz of disapprobation was heard all over the house, and such words as these fell upon listening ears:--

"'An abolition affair!' 'Woman's rights and niggers!' 'We told you so!' 'Go it, old darkey!'

"I chanced upon that occasion to wear my first laurels in public life as president of the meeting. At my request, order was restored and the business of the hour went on. The morning session was held; the evening exercises came and went. Old Sojourner, quiet and reticent as the 'Libyan Statue,' sat crouched against the wall on the corner of the pulpit stairs, her sun-bonnet shading her eyes, her elbows on her knees, and her chin resting upon her broad, hard palm. At intermission, she was busy, selling 'The Life of Sojourner Truth,' a narrative of her own strange and adventurous life. Again and again timorous and trembling ones came to me and said with earnestness, 'Do n't let her speak, Mrs. Gage, it will ruin us. Every newspaper in the land will have our cause mixed with abolition and niggers, and we shall be utterly denounced.' My only answer was, 'We shall see when the time comes.'

"The second day the work waxed warm. Methodist, Baptist, Episcopal, Presbyterian, and Universalist ministers came in to hear and discuss the resolutions presented. One claimed superior rights and privileges for man on the ground of superior intellect; another, because of the manhood of Christ. 'If God had desired the equality of woman, he would have given some token of his will through the birth, life, and death of the Saviour.' Another gave us a theological view of the sin of our first mother. There were few women in those days that dared to 'speak in meeting,' and the august teachers of the people were seeming to get the better of us, while the boys in the galleries and the sneerers among the pews were hugely enjoying the discomfiture, as they supposed, of the 'strong minded.' Some of the tender-skinned friends were on the point of losing dignity, and the atmosphere of the convention betokened a storm.

"Slowly from her seat in the corner rose Sojourner Truth, who, till now, had scarcely lifted her head. 'Do n't let her speak!' gasped half a dozen in my ear. She moved slowly and solemnly to the front, laid her old bonnet at her feet, and turned her great, speaking eyes to me. There was a hissing sound of disapprobation above and below. I rose and announced 'Sojourner Truth,' and begged the audience to keep silence for a few moments. The tumult subsided at once, and every eye was fixed on this almost Amazon form, which stood nearly six feet high, head erect, and eye piercing the upper air, like one in a dream. At her first word, there was a profound hush. She spoke in deep tones, which, though not loud, reached every ear in the house, and away through the throng at the doors and windows:--

"'Well, chilern, whar dar is so much racket dar must be something out o' kilter. I tink dat 'twixt de niggers of de Souf and de women at de Norf all a talkin' 'bout rights, de white men will be in a fix pretty soon. But what's all dis here talkin' 'bout? Dat man ober dar say dat women needs to be helped into carriages, and lifted ober ditches, and to have de best place every whar. Nobody eber help me into carriages, or ober mud puddles, or gives me any best place [and raising herself to her full hight and her voice to a pitch like rolling thunder, she asked], and ar'n't I a woman? Look at me! Look at my arm! [And she bared her right arm to the shoulder, showing her tremendous muscular power.] I have plowed, and planted, and gathered into barns, and no man could head me--and ar'n't I a woman? I could work as much and eat as much as a man (when I could get it), and bear de lash as well--and ar'n't I a woman? I have borne thirteen chilern and seen 'em mos' all sold off into slavery, and when I cried out with a mother's grief, none but Jesus heard--and ar'n't I a woman? Den dey talks 'bout dis ting in de head--what dis dey call it?' 'Intellect,' whispered some one near. 'Dat's it honey. What's dat got to do with women's rights or niggers' rights? If my cup won't hold but a pint and yourn holds a quart, would n't ye be mean not to let me have my little half-measure full?' And she pointed her significant finger and sent a keen glance at the minister who had made the argument. The cheering was long and loud.

"'Den dat little man in black dar, he say women can't have as much rights as man, cause Christ want a woman. Whar did your Christ come from?' Rolling thunder could not have stilled that crowd as did those deep, wonderful tones, as she stood there with outstretched arms and eye of fire. Raising her voice still louder, she repeated, 'Whar did your Christ come from? From God and a woman. Man had nothing to do with him.' Oh! what a rebuke she gave the little man.

"'Turning again to another objector, she took up the defense of mother Eve. I cannot follow her through it all. It was pointed, and witty, and solemn, eliciting at almost every sentence deafening applause; and she ended by asserting that 'if de fust woman God ever made was strong enough to turn the world upside down, all 'lone, dese togedder [and she glanced her eye over us], ought to be able to turn it back and get it right side up again, and now dey is asking to do it, de men better let em.' Long-continued cheering. 'Bleeged to ye for hearin' on me, and now ole Sojourner ha'n't got nothing more to say.'

"Amid roars of applause, she turned to her corner, leaving more than one of us with streaming eyes and hearts beating with gratitude. She had taken us up in her strong arms and carried us safely over the slough of difficulty, turning the whole tide in our favor. I have never in my life seen anything like the magical influence that subdued the mobbish spirit of the day and turned the jibes and sneers of an excited crowd into notes of respect and admiration. Hundreds rushed up to shake hands, and congratulate the glorious old mother and bid her God speed on her mission of 'testifying again concerning the wickedness of this 'ere people.'"

Mrs. Gage also in the same article relates the folowing:--

"Once upon a Sabbath in Michigan an abolition meeting was held. Parker Pillsbury was speaker, and criticized freely the conduct of the churches regarding slavery. While he was speaking there came up a fearful thunder storm. A young Methodist arose, and interrupting the speaker, said he felt alarmed; he felt as if God's judgment was about to fall on him for daring to sit and hear such blasphemy; that it made his hair almost rise with terror. Here a voice, sounding above the rain that beat upon the roof, the sweeping surge of the winds, the crashing of the limbs of trees, the swaying of branches, and the rolling of thunder, spoke out: 'Chile, do n't be skeered; you are not going to be harmed. I do n't speck God's ever hearn tell on ye.' It was all she said, but it was enough."

She remained two years in the State of Ohio, going from town to town, attending conventions, and holding meetings of her own. Marius Robinson, of Salem, Ohio, editor of the Anti-Slavery Bugle, whose clarion notes never faltered in freedom's cause, was her friend and co-laborer. She toiled on in this field perseveringly, sowing the seeds of truth in the hearts of the people, and patiently awaiting the time when she should help gather in the sheaves of a ripened harvest. At this time she attracted but little attention outside a charmed circle of reformers whose mighty moral power was the lever which eventually overthrew the institution of American slavery.

About the year 1856, she came to Battle Creek and bought a house and lot, since which time her home has been in Michigan. She still continued her itinerant life, spending much of her time in the neighboring States, especially in Indiana, which she felt needed her missionary efforts. An account of one of her meetings held in the northern part of that State has been kindly furnished us by her friend, Parker Pillsbury, accompanied by a note from himself.

"I inclose a communication from the Boston Liberator, of Oct. 5, 1858, relating to Sojourner Truth. The wondrous experiences of that most remarkable woman would make a library, if not indeed a literature, could they all be gathered and spread before the world. I was much in her company for several years in the anti-slavery conflict, and have often seen her engaged in what seemed most unequal combat with the defenders of slavery and foes of freedom; but I never saw her when she did not, as in the instance given below, scatter her enemies with dismay and confusion, winning more than victory in every battle.

P. P."

"PRO-SLAVERY IN INDIANA.

"SILVER LAKE, Kosciusko Co., Ind.,
"October 1, 1858.

"FRIEND W. L. GARRISON:--Sojourner Truth, an elderly colored woman, well known throughout the Eastern States, is now holding a series of anti-slavery meetings in Northern Indiana. Sojourner comes well recommended by H. B. Stowe, yourself, and others, and was gladly received and welcomed by the friends of the slave in this locality. Her progress in knowledge, truth, and righteousness is very remarkable, especially when we consider her former low estate as a slave. The border-ruffian Democracy of Indiana, however, appear to be jealous and suspicious of every anti-slavery movement. A rumor was immediately circulated that Sojourner was an impostor; that she was, indeed, a man disguised in women's clothing. It appears, too, from what has since transpired, that they suspected her to be a mercenary hireling of the Republican party.

"At her third appointed meeting in this vicinity, which was held in the meeting-house of the United Brethren, a large number of democrats and other pro-slavery persons were present. At the close of the meeting, Dr. T. W. Strain, the mouthpiece of the slave Democracy, requested the large congregation to 'hold on,' and stated that a doubt existed in the minds of many persons present respecting the sex of the speaker, and that it was his impression that a majority of them believed the speaker to be a man. The doctor also affirmed (which was not believed by the friends of the slave) that it was for the speaker's special benefit that he now demanded that Sojourner submit her breast to the inspection of some of the ladies present, that the doubt might be removed by their testimony. There were a large number of ladies present, who appeared to be ashamed and indignant at such a proposition. Sojourner's friends, some of whom had not heard the rumor, were surprised and indignant at such ruffianly surmises and treatment.

"Confusion and uproar ensued, which was soon suppressed by Sojourner, who, immediately rising, asked them why they suspected her to be a man. The Democracy answered, 'Your voice is not the voice of a woman, it is the voice of a man, and we believe you are a man.' Dr. Strain called for a vote, and a boisterous 'Aye,' was the result. A negative vote was not called for. Sojourner told them that her breasts had suckled many a white babe, to the exclusion of her own offspring; that some of those white babies had grown to man's estate; that, although they had sucked her colored breasts, they were, in her estimation, far more manly than they (her persecutors) appeared to be; and she quietly asked them, as she disrobed her bosom, if they, too, wished to suck! In vindication of her truthfulness, she told them that she would show her breast to the whole congregation; that it was not to her shame that she uncovered her breast before them, but to their shame. Two young men (A. Badgely and J. Horner) stepped forward while Sojourner exposed her naked breast to the audience. I heard a democrat say, as we were returning home from meeting, that Dr. Strain had, previous to the examination, offered to bet forty dollars that Sojourner was a man! So much for the physiological acumen of a western physician.

"As 'agitation of thought is the beginning of wisdom,' we hope that Indiana will yet be redeemed.

"Yours, truly, for the slave,

"WILLIAM HAYWARD."

The late lamented Josephine Griffing, whose loyal services in support of the Union, and untiring labors for the colored race, entitles her to a monument at the nation's cost, was often associated with Sojourner in anti-slavery times, and was invited to hold meetings with her in Angola and vicinity in the autumn of 1862. The slave-holding spirit was now fully aroused in Indiana, and very bitter toward the negro. A law had recently been passed forbidding their entering the State or remaining in it. This law was unconstitutional, nevertheless the democrats had enforced it and endeavored to enforce it in Sojourner's case. A warrant was made out and she was arrested for both offenses. Mrs. Griffing undertook her defense alone, outwitted and beat the enemy. Sojourner, nothing daunted, determined to remain and carry out the programme. For a time her meetings were much disturbed. When she arose to speak, the democrats would cry, "Down with you! We think the niggers have done enough! We will not hear you speak! Stop your mouth! &c., &c." She told them that the Union people would soon make them stop their mouths. The Union home guard took her into custody to protect her from being thrown into jail by the rebels.

A meeting was appointed at the town-house in Angola, but the democrats threatened to burn the building if she attempted to speak in it. To this she made answer, "Then I will speak upon the ashes." Describing this meeting, she says:--

"The ladies thought I should be dressed in uniform as well as the captain of the home guard, whose prisoner I was and who was to go with me to the meeting. So they put upon me a red, white, and blue shawl, a sash and apron to match, a cap on my head with a star in front, and a star on each shoulder. When I was dressed I looked in the glass and was fairly frightened." Said I, "It seems I am going to battle." My friends advised me to take a sword or pistol. I replied, "I carry no weapon; the Lord will reserve [preserve] me without weapons. I feel safe even in the midst of my enemies; for the truth is powerful and will prevail."

"When we were ready to go, they put me into a large, beautiful carriage with the captain and other gentlemen, all of whom were armed. The soldiers walked by our side and a long procession followed. As we neared the courthouse, looking out of the window, I saw that the building was surrounded by a great crowd. I felt as I was going against the Philistines and I prayed the Lord to reliver [deliver] me out of their hands. But when the rebels saw such a mighty army coming, they fled, and by the time we arrived they were scattered over the fields, looking like a flock of frightened crows, and not one was left but a small boy, who sat upon the fence, crying, 'Nigger, nigger!'

"We now marched into the court-house, escorted by double files of soldiers with presented arms. The band struck up the 'Star Spangled Banner,' in which I joined and sang with all my might, while amid flashing bayonets and waving banners our party made its way to the platform upon which I went and advocated free speech with more zeal than ever before, and without interruption. At the close of the meeting, I was conducted to the house of the esquire for safety, as my friends feared the mob might return and make us trouble; but the day passed without farther annoyance.

"I spent some of the time at Pleasant Lake with Mr. Roby's family; but Mr. Roby was arrested for entertaining me, tried and acquitted. Another friend, Mr. Fox, was taken up for encouraging me to remain in the State and summoned to appear at the district court, but was found 'not guilty.'

"One day whilst I was at Mr. Roby's, two ladies drove up in haste and earnestly desired me to leave, saying the rebels were near by--coming to take me--

whereupon I went home with them. But they, becoming more alarmed, advised me to seek safety in some woods not far away, by offering to go with me. This I positively refused to do, and told them I would sooner go to jail. I stood my ground and the rebel constable came with a warrant to take me; but a Union officer, following closely behind him, stepped up and read some papers showing that I was his prisoner. At this turn of affairs the rebel officer looked very much disgusted, and turning to go, said, 'I ain't going to bother my head with niggers, I'll resign my office first.' Then the home guard marched up to our house, playing upon the fife and drum, and gave loud cheers for Sojourner, Free Speech, and the Union.

"The last time I was arrested, the constable asked if I would appear at court, or if he should take me along with him. My friends assured him that they would be responsible for my appearance. When the day for my trial came, a great many went with me, some of the best families in the county, among whom were Dr. Gale, Dr. Moss and family, Thomas Moss and family, Mr. Roby, Mrs. Griffing, and many other noble people whose names I cannot now recall, but the memory of whose friendship will be cherished whilst memory remains.

"My enemies, thinking I would probably run away, had made no preparation for the trial; but when they saw us come, hunted around and procured a shabby room into which I went with a few friends and waited for some one to appear against me. After a while, two half-drunken lawyers, who looked like the scrapings of the

Democratic party, made their appearance, eyed us for a few moments, then left. Presently we saw them enter a tavern across the way, and this ended the trial.

"We now went to the house of a friend and had a grand picnic. I returned home after a month of hard labor in Indiana, which I believe did much for the cause of human freedom."

Mrs. Griffing, writing to the Anti-Slavery Standard, says, "Our meetings are largely attended by persons from every part of the county; especially by the most noble-hearted women, whose presence has produced a marked impression and has done more toward establishing a free government than would the killing of a hundred of Ellsworth's Zouaves. The lines are now being drawn as they never were by political maneuver, and as they cannot be by the cold steel alone, because it is a blow at slavery. 'Cannon balls may aid the truth, but thought's a weapon stronger.'

"Slavery has made a conquest in this county by the suppression of free speech, and freedom must make her conquest by the steadfast support of free speech. There was not manhood enough in the county last fall to protect an anti-slavery meeting at the county-seat; now there are a hundred men who would spill their blood sooner than surrender the right of even Sojourner. At all of our meetings we have been told that armed men were in our midst and had declared they would blow out our brains."

In the winter and spring of 1863, Sojourner was ill for many weeks and her finances becoming exhausted, she prayed the Lord to send an angel to relieve her wants. Soon after, a friend called bringing all needful supplies, to whom she said, "I just asked the Lord to send one of his chosen angels to me," and smiling added, "I knew he would think of you first."

Her case was made known to the public through the columns of the Anti-Slavery Standard and generous donations were forwarded to her. The following articles were published at the time:--

"SOJOURNER TRUTH.

"OLIVER JOHNSON:--

"Dear Friend--Again I would ask permission, through your paper, to return thanks to friends whose hearts have been moved to give aid and comfort to our 'venerable friend and teacher,' Sojourner Truth. She desires me to say that she cannot rest until all know how truly grateful she is for their kind assistance. She says her heart is full of praises and prayer, and sometimes she thinks her cup of happiness is about to run over, and she prays de Lord to pour it on to some of her friends. Would that some people had the power and goodness of heart to extract happiness from material surroundings in proportion to their possessions, as Sojourner has. A much better world would this be.

"When the kind and excellent letter reached her from Samuel May and wife, of Leicester, Mass., accompanied with donations from Ireland, she was greatly surprised, and expressions of deep gratitude came in rapid succession. Finally, she concluded that no on earth was ever so blessed before, and she was quite sure 'de Lord never sent his angels from so great a distance, even in 'Lijah's day.' She wondered who ever heard of Sojourner way in Ireland, and when she thought that they were friends whom she had never seen, she was quite overcome with joy, and thought the goodness of the Lord was greater than she could understand.

'She wishes you to print the name of her grandson, James Caldwell, of the 54th, thinking that some one may go and see him.

'She wishes her friends to know that her health is better than it was some time since. She says she has budded out wid de trees, but may fall wid de autumn leaves.'

"PHEBE H. M. STICKNEY."

"NAMES OF DONORS.

- Mrs. Edmundson, Dublin, Ireland.
- Mrs. Anne Allen, Dublin, Ireland.
- Richard D. Webb, Dublin, Ireland.
- Sarah R. May, Leicester, Mass.
- Samuel May, Jr., Leicester, Mass.
- Mrs. Goss, New York.
- W. H. Burleigh, New York.
- George W. Bungay, New York.
- Oliver Johnson, New York.
- Theodore Tilton, New York.
- 'Freedman's Relief Society,' Worcester, Mass.
- Miss Ladd,
- Mrs. Miller,

- Mr. and Mrs. Twam,
- Dr. Church and wife,
- Mrs. John Hull,
- Mrs. Maria Brown and Stillman,
- Miss Laura Stebbins,
- Mrs. Charles Hastings,
- Mrs. Griffing,
- Mrs. Samson and Mrs. Eliot,
- Mrs. John Hamilton,"

"To the Editor of the *National Anti-Slavery Standard*:

"This extraordinary woman still lives. When the letter of Phebe M. Stickney came to us at our home on the prairies in Iowa, suggesting pecuniary comfort for the blessed old saint in the sunset of her remarkable and useful life, I never remember to have regretted more that I had so little at command to bestow. The Standard, however, reports the names of a number of friends who were ready and willing to minister to her necessities. I hope others will do likewise. Few, if any, in the land are more worthy. Hers has been a life of pre-eminent devotion to the sacred cause or liberty and purity.

"The graphic sketch of her by the author of 'Uncle Tom's Cabin' has doubtless been read with interest by thousands. No pen, however, can give an adequate idea of Sojourner Truth. This unlearned African woman, with her deep religious and trustful nature burning in her soul like fire, has a magnetic power over an audience perfectly astounding. I was once present in a religious meeting where some speaker had alluded to the government of the United States, and had uttered sentiments in favor of its Constitution. Sojourner stood, erect and tall, with her white turban on her head, and in a low and subdued tone of voice began by saying: 'Children, I talks to God and God talks to me.' I goes out and talks to God in de fields and de woods. [The weevil had destroyed thousands of acres of wheat in the West that year.] Dis morning I was walking out, and I got over de fence. I saw de wheat a holding up its head, looking very big. I goes up and takes holt ob it. You b'lieve it, dere was no wheat dare? I says, God [speaking the name in a voice of reverence peculiar to herself], what is de matter wid dis wheat? and he says to me, "Sojourner, dere is a little weasel in it." Now I hears talkin' about de Constitution and de rights of man. I comes up and I takes hold of dis Constitution. It looks mighty big, and I feels for my rights, but der aint any dare. Den I says, God, what ails dis Constitution? He says to me, "Sojourner, dere is a little weasel in it."' The effect upon the multitude was irresistible.

"On a dark, cloudy morning, while she was our guest, she was sitting, as she often was wont to do, with her cheeks upon her palms, her elbows on her knees; she lifted up her head as though she had just wakened from a dream, and said, 'Friend Dugdale, poor old Sojourner can't read a word, will you git me de Bible and read me a little of de Scripter?' Oh, yes, Sojourner, gladly, said I. I opened to Isaiah, the 59th chapter. She listened as though an oracle was speaking. When I came to the words, None calleth for justice, nor any pleadeth for truth; your hands are defiled with blood, and your fingers with iniquity; they conceive mischief, and bring forth iniquity; they hatch cockatrice's eggs, and weave the spider's web; he that eateth of their eggs dieth, and that which is crushed breaketh out into a viper, she could restrain herself no longer, and, bringing her great palms together with an emphasis that I shall never forget, she exclaimed, 'Is dat thare? "It shall break out into a viper." Yes, God told me dat. I never heard it read afore, now I know it double!' Of course her mind was directed to the heinous institution of American slavery, and she regarded these terrible words of the seer as prophetic concerning its fearful consequences.

"On one occasion, in a large reform meeting, where many able and efficient public speakers were present, Sojourner sat in the midst. One man, in defiance of propriety, was wasting the time of the meeting by distasteful and indelicate declamation. Some, in despair of his ending, were leaving the meeting. Others, mortified and distressed, were silently enduring, while the 'flea of the Convention,' continued to bore it, nothing daunted. Just at a point where he was forced to suspend long enough to take in a long breath, Sojourner, who had been sitting in the back part of the house with her head bowed, and groaning in spirit, raised up her tall figure before him, and, putting her eyes upon him, said, 'Child, if de people has no whar to put it, what is de use? Sit down, child, sit down!' The man dropped as if he had been shot, and not another word was heard from him.

"A friend related the following anecdote to me: In that period of the anti-slavery movement when mobocratic violence was often resorted to, one of its most talented and devoted advocates, after an able address, was followed by a lawyer, who appealed to the lowest sentiments--was scurrilous and abusive in the superlative degree. Alluding to the colored race, he compared them to monkeys, baboons, and ourang-outangs. When he was about closing his inflammatory speech, Sojourner quietly drew near to the platform and whispered in the ear of the advocate of her people, 'Do n't dirty your hands wid dat critter; let me 'tend to him!' The speaker knew it was safe to trust her. 'Children,' said she, straightening herself to her full hight, 'I am one of dem monkey tribes. I was born a slave. I had de dirty work to do--de scullion work. Now I am going to 'ply to dis critter'--pointing her long, bony finger with withering scorn at the petty lawyer. 'Now in de course of my time I has done a great deal of dirty scullion work, but of all de dirty work I ever done, dis is de scullionist and de dirtiest.' Peering into the eyes of the auditory with just such a look as she could give, and that no one could imitate, she continued: 'Now, children, do n't you pity me?' She had taken the citadel by storm. The whole audience shouted applause, and the negro-haters as heartily as any.

"I was present at a large religious convention. Love in the family had been portrayed in a manner to touch the better nature of the auditory. Just as the meeting was about to close, Sojourner stood up. Tears were coursing down her furrowed cheeks. She said: 'We has heerd a great deal about love at home in de family. Now, children, I was a slave, and my husband and my children was sold from me.' The pathos with which she uttered these words made a deep impression upon the meeting. Pausing a moment, she added: 'Now, husband and children is all gone, and what has 'come of de affection I had for dem? Dat is de question before de house!' The people smiled amidst a baptism of tears.

"Let food and raiment be given her. There are many in the land who will be made richer by seeing that this noble woman shares their bounty; and then, when her Lord shall come to talk with her, and take her into his presence chamber, and shall say, 'Sojourner, lacked thou anything?' she may answer, 'Nothing, Lord, either for body or soul.'

"J. A. D.

"Near Mt. Pleasant, Iowa, 1863."

In April, 1863, a lengthy account of Sojourner's life was published in the Atlantic Monthly, entitled, "Sojourner Truth, the Libyan Sibyl," written by Mrs. H. B. Stowe. This graphic sketch not only gave Sojourner greater notoriety, but added fresh laurels to Mrs. Stowe's increasing fame as an authoress. The description of her person and the portrayal of her character are so vivid that it finds a fitting place in her Book of Life, and is here fully given.

SOJOURNER TRUTH, THE LIBYAN SIBYL.

Many years ago, the few readers of radical abolitionist papers must often have seen the singular name of Sojourner Truth, announced as a frequent speaker at anti-slavery meetings, and as traveling on a sort of self-appointed agency through the country. I had myself often remarked the name, but never met the individual. On one occasion, when our house was filled with company, several eminent clergymen being our guests, notice was brought up to me that Sojourner Truth was below, and requested an interview. Knowing nothing of her but her singular name, I went down, prepared to make the interview short, as the pressure of many other engagements demanded.

When I went into the room, a tall, spare form arose to meet me. She was evidently a full-blooded African, and though now aged and worn with many hardships, still gave the impression of a physical development, which in early youth must have been as fine a specimen of the torrid zone as Cumberworth's celebrated statuette of the Negro Woman at the Fountain. Indeed, she so strongly reminded me of that figure, that, when I recall the events of her life, as she narrated them to me, I imagine her as a living, breathing impersonation of that work of art.

I do not recollect ever to have been conversant with anyone who had more of that silent and subtle power which we call personal presence than this woman. In the modern spiritualistic phraseology, she would be described as having a strong sphere. Her tall form, as she rose up before me, is still vivid to my mind. She was dressed in some stout, grayish stuff, neat and clean, though dusty from travel. On her head she wore a bright Madras handkerchief, arranged as a turban, after the manner of her race. She seemed perfectly self-possessed and at her ease; in fact, there was almost an unconscious superiority, not unmixed with a solemn twinkle of humor, in the odd, composed manner in which she looked down on me. Her whole air had at times a gloomy sort of drollery which impressed one strangely.

"So this is you," she said.

"Yes," I answered.

"Well, honey, de Lord bless ye! I jes' thought I'd like to come an' have a look at ye. You's heerd o' me, I reckon?" she added.

"Yes, I think I have. You go about lecturing, do you not?'

"Yes, honey, that's what I do. The Lord has made me a sign unto this nation, an' I go round a-testifyin,' an' showin' on em' their sins agin my people."

So saying, she took a seat, and, stooping over and crossing her arms on her knees, she looked down on the floor, and appeared to fall into a sort of reverie. Her great, gloomy eyes and her dark face seemed to work with some undercurrent of feeling; she sighed deeply, and occasionally broke out,

"O Lord! O Lord! Oh, the tears, an' the groans, an' the moans, O Lord!"

I should have said that she was accompanied by a little grandson of ten years--the fattest, jolliest woolly-headed little specimen of Africa that one can imagine. He was grinning and showing his glistening white teeth in a state of perpetual merriment, and at this moment broke out into an audible giggle, which disturbed the reverie into which his relative was falling.

She looked at him with an indulgent sadness, and then at me.

"Laws, ma'am, he don't know nothin' about it, he don't. Why, I've seen them poor critters beat an' 'bused an' hunted, brought in all torn--ears hangin' all in rags, where the dogs been a bitin' of 'em!"

This set off our little African Puck into another giggle, in which he seemed perfectly convulsed. She surveyed him soberly, without the slightest irritation.

"Well, you may bless the Lord, you can laugh; but I tell you, 't wa'n't no laughin' matter.

By this time I thought her manner so original that it might be worth while to call down my friends; and she seemed perfectly well pleased with the idea. An audience was what she wanted--it mattered not whether high or low, learned or ignorant. She had things to say, and was ready to say them at all times, and to any one.

I called down Dr. Beecher, Professor Allen, and two or three other clergymen, who, together with my husband and family, made a roomful. No princess could have received a drawing-room with more composed dignity than Sojourner her audience. She stood among them, calm and erect, as one of her own native palm-trees waving alone in the desert. I presented one after another to her, and at last said--

"Sojourner, this is Dr. Beecher. He is a very celebrated preacher."

"Is he?" she said, offering her hand in a condescending manner, and looking down on his white head. "Ye dear lamb, I'm glad to see ye! De Lord bless ye! I loves preachers. I'm a kind o' preacher myself."

"You are?" said Dr. Beecher. "Do you preach from the Bible?"

"No, honey, can't preach from de Bible--can't read a letter."

"Why, Sojourner, what do you preach from, then?"

Her answer was given with a solemn power of voice, peculiar to herself, that hushed everyone in the room.

"When I preaches, I has jest one text to preach from, an' I always preaches from this one. My text is, 'WHEN I FOUND JESUS!'

"Well, you could n't have a better one," said one of the ministers.

She paid no attention to him, but stood and seemed swelling with her own thoughts, and then began this narration:--

"Well, now, I'll jest have to go back an' tell ye all about it. Ye see we was all brought over from Africa, father, an' mother an' I, an' a lot more of us; an' we was sold up an' down, an' hither an' yon; an' I can 'member, when I was a little thing, not bigger than this 'ere,' pointing to her grandson, 'how my ole mammy would sit out o' doors in the evening,' an' look up at the stars an' groan. She'd groan, an groan, an' says I to her,

"'Mammy, what makes you groan so?'

"An' she'd say,

"'Matter enough, chile! I'm groanin' to think o' my poor children: they don't know where I be, an' I don't know where they be; they looks up at the stars, an' I looks up at the stars, but I can't tell where they be.

"'Now,' she said, 'chile, when you 're grown up, you may be sold away from your mother an' all your old friends, an' have great troubles come on ye; an' when you has these troubles come on ye, ye jes' go to God, an' he'll help ye.'

"An says I to her,

"'Who is God, anyhow, mammy?'

"An' says she,

"'Why, chile, you jes' look up dar. It's him that made all dem?'

"Well, I did n't mind much 'bout God in them days. I grew up pretty lively an' strong, an' could row a boat, or ride a horse, or work round, an' do 'most anything.

"At last I got sold away to a real hard massa an' missis. Oh, I tell you they was hard! 'Peared like I could n't please 'em nohow. An' then I thought o' what my old mammy told me about God; an' I thought I'd got into trouble, sure enough, an' I wanted to find God, an' I heerd someone tell a story about a man that met God on a threshin'-floor, an' I thought, well an' good, I'll have a threshin'-floor, too. So I went down in the lot, and I threshed down a place real hard, an' I used to go down there every day, an' pray an' cry with all my might, a prayin' to the Lord to make my massa an' missis better, but it did n't seem to do no good; and so says I, one day,

"'O God, I been a askin' ye, an' askin' ye, an askin' ye, for all this long time, to make my massa an' missis better, an' you do n't do it, an' what can be the reason?

Why, maybe you can't. Well, I should n't wonder if you could n't. Well, now, I tell you, I 'll make a bargain with you. Ef you 'll help me to git away from my massa an' missis, I 'll agree to be good; but ef you do n't help me, I really do n't think I can be. Now,' says I, 'I want to git away; but the trouble's jest here; ef I try to git away in the night, I can't see; an' ef I try to git away in the daytime, they'll see me an' be after me.'

"Then the Lord said to me, 'Git up two or three hours afore daylight, an' start off.'

"An' says I, 'Thank'ee Lord! that's a good thought.'

"So up I got about three o'clock in the mornin', an' I started an' traveled pretty fast, till, when the sun rose, I was clear away from our place an' our folks, an' out o' sight. An' then I begun to think I did n't know nothin' where to go. So I kneeled down, and says I,

"'Well, Lord, you've started me out, an' now please to show me where to go.'

"Then the Lord made a house appear to me, an' he said to me that I was to walk on till I saw that house, an' then go in an' ask the people to take me. An' I traveled all day, an' did n't come to the house till late at night; but when I saw it, sure enough, I went in, an' I told the folks that the Lord sent me; an' they was Quakers, an' real kind they was to me. They jes' took me in an' did for me as kind as ef I 'd been one of 'em; an' after they 'd giv me supper, they took me into a room where there was a great, tall, white bed; an' they told me to sleep there. Well, honey, I was kind o' skeered when they left me alone with that great white bed; 'cause I never had been in a bed in my life. It never came into my mind they could mean me to sleep in it. An' so I jes' camped down under it, on the floor, an' then I slep' pretty well. In the mornin', when they came in, they asked me ef I had n't been asleep; an' I said, 'Yes, I never slep' better.' An' they said, 'Why, you hav n't been in the bed!' An' says I, 'Laws, you did n't think o' sech a thing as my sleepin' in dat 'ar' bed, did you? I never heered o' sech a thing in my life.'

"Well, ye see, honey, I stayed an' lived with 'em. An' now jes' look here: instead o' keepin' my promise an' bein' good, as I told the Lord I would, jest as soon as everything got a goin' easy, I forgot all about God.

"Pretty well do n't need no help; an' I gin up prayin.' I lived there two or three years, an' then the slaves in New York were all set free, 'an ole massa came to our house to make a visit, an' he asked me ef I did n't want to go back an' see the folks on the ole place. An' I told him I did. So he said, ef I 'd jes' git into the wagon with him, he 'd carry me over. Well, jest as I was goin' out to get into the wagon, I met God! an' says I, 'O God, I did n't know as you was so great!' An' I turned right round an' come into the house, an' set down in my room; for 't was God all around me. I could feel it burnin', burnin', burnin' all around me, an' goin' through me; an' I saw I was so wicked, it seemed as ef it would burn me up. An'

I said, 'O somebody, somebody, stand between God an' me! for it burns me!' Then, honey, when I said so, I felt as it were something' like an amberill [umbrella] that came between me an' the light, an' I felt it was somebody--somebody that stood between me an' God; an' it felt cool, like a shade; an' says I, 'Who's this that stands between me an' God? Is it old Cato?' He was a pious old preacher; but then I seemed to see Cato in the light, an' he was all polluted an' vile, like me; an' I said, 'Is it old Sally?' an' then I saw her, an' she seemed jes' so. An' then says I, 'Who is this?' An' then, honey, for a while, it was like the sun shinin' in a pail o' water, when it moves up and down; for I begun to feel t'was somebody that loved me; an' I tried to know him. An' I said, 'I know you! I know you! I know you!' An' then I said, 'I don't know you! I don't know you! I don't know you!' An' when I said, 'I know you, I know you' the light came; an' when I said, 'I do n't know you, I do n't know you,' it went jes' like the sun in a pail o' water. An' finally, somethin' spoke out in me an' said, 'This is Jesus!' An' I spoke out with all my might, an' says I, 'This is Jesus! Glory be to God!' An' then the whole world grew bright, an' the trees they waved an' waved in glory, an' every little bit o' stone on the ground shone like glass; and I shouted an' said, 'Praise, praise, praise to the Lord!' An' I begun to feel sech a love in my soul as I never felt before--love to all creatures. An' then, all of a sudden, it stopped, an' I said, 'Dar's de white folks that have abused you, an' beat you, an' abused your people--think o' them!' But then there came another rush of love through my soul, an' I cried out loud--'Lord, Lord, I can love even de white folks!'

"Honey, I jes' walked round an' round in a dream. Jesus loved me! I knowed it--I felt it. Jesus was my Jesus. Jesus would love me always. I did n't dare tell nobody; 't was a great secret. Everything had been got away from me that I ever had; an' I thought that ef I let white folks know about this, maybe they 'd get Him away--so I said, 'I'll keep this close. I wont let anyone know.'"

"But, Sojourner, had you never been told about Jesus Christ?"

"No, honey. I had n't heerd no preachin'--been to no meetin.' Nobody had n't told me. I'd kind o' heerd of Jesus, but thought he was like Gineral Lafayette, or some o' them. But one night there was a Methodist meetin' somewhere in our parts, an' I went; an' they got up an' begun for to tell der 'speriences: an' de fust one begun to speak. I started, 'cause he told about Jesus. 'Why,' says I to myself, 'dat man 's found him, too!' An' another got up an' spoke, an' I said, 'He's found him, too!' An' finally I said, 'Why, they all know him!' I was so happy! An' then they sung this hymn" (Here Sojourner sang, in a strange, cracked voice, but evidently with all her soul and might, mispronouncing the English, but seeming to derive as much elevation and comfort from bad English as from good):--

"There is a holy city,
A world of light above,
Above the stairs and regions,—

* Starry regions.

Built by the God of love.

"An everlasting temple,
And saints arrayed in white,
There serve their great Redeemer
And dwell with him in light.

"The meanest child of glory
Outshines the radiant sun;
But who can speak the splendor
Of Jesus on his throne?

"Is this the Man of Sorrows
Who stood at Pilate's bar,
Condemned by haughty Herod
And by his men of war?

"He seems a mighty conqueror,
Who spoiled the powers below,
And ransomed many captives
From everlasting woe.

"The hosts of saints around him
Proclaim his work of grace,
The patriarchs and prophets,
And all the godly race,

"Who speak of fiery trials
And tortures on their way;
They came from tribulation
To everlasting day.

"And what shall be my journey,
How long I 'll stay below,

Or what shall be my trials,
Are not for me to know.

"In every day of trouble
I 'll raise my thoughts on high,
I 'll think of that bright temple
And crowns above the sky."

    I put in this whole hymn, because Sojourner, carried away with her own feeling, sang it from beginning to end with a triumphant energy that held the whole circle around her intently listening. She sang with the strong barbaric accent of the native African, and with those indescribable upward turns and those deep gutturals which give such a wild, peculiar power to the negro singing--but above all, with such an overwhelming energy of personal appropriation that the hymn seemed to be fused in the furnace of her feelings and come out recrystallized as a production of her own.

It is said that Rachel was wont to chant the "Marseillaise" in a manner that made her seem, for the time, the very spirit and impersonation of the gaunt, wild, hungry, avenging mob which rose against aristocratic oppression; and in like manner, Sojourner, singing this hymn, seemed to impersonate the fervor of Ethiopia, wild, savage, hunted of all nations, but burning after God in her tropic heart, and stretching her scarred hands toward the glory to be revealed.

"Well, den ye see, after a while I thought I'd go back an' see de folks on de ole place. Well, you know de law had passed dat de culled folks was all free; an' my old missis, she had a daughter married about dis time who went to live in Alabama--an' what did she do but give her my son, a boy about de age of dis yer, for her to take down to Alabama? When I got back to de ole place, they told me about it, an' I went right up to see ole missis, an' says I,

"'Missis, have you been an' sent my son away down to Alabama?'

"'Yes, I have,' says she; 'he's gone to live with your young missis.'

"'Oh, Missis,' says I, 'how could you do it?'

"'Poh!' says she, 'what a fuss you make about a little nigger! Got more of 'em now than you know what to do with.'

"I tell you, I stretched up. I felt as tall as the world!

"'Missis,' says I, 'I'll have my son back agin!'

"She laughed.

"'You will, you nigger? How you goin' to do it? You ha'n't got no money.'

"'No, Missis--but God has--an' you'll see he'll help me!--an' I turned round an' went out.

"Oh, but I was angry to have her speak to me so haughty an' so scornful, as ef my chile was n't worth anything. I said to God, 'O Lord, render unto her double!' It was a dreadful prayer, an' I did n't know how true it would come.

"Well, I did n't rightly know which way to turn; but I went to the Lord, an' I said to him, 'O Lord, ef I was as rich as you be, an' you was as poor as I be, I'd help you--you know I would; and, oh, do help me!' An' I felt sure then that he would.

"Well, I talked with people, an' they said I must git the case before a grand jury. So I went into the town when they was holdin' a court, to see ef I could find any grand jury. An' I stood round the court-house, an' when they was a-comin' out, I walked right up to the grandest lookin' one I could see, an' says I to him:--

"'Sir, be you a grand jury?'

"An' then he wanted to know why I asked, an' I told him all about it; an' he asked me all sorts of questions, an' finally he says to me:--

"'I think, ef you pay me ten dollars, that I'd agree to git your son for you.' An' says he, pointin' to a house over the way, 'You go 'long an' tell your story to the folks in that house, an' I guess they'll give you the money.'

"Well, I went, an' I told them, an' they gave me twenty dollars; an' then I thought to myself, 'Ef ten dollars will git him, twenty dollars will git him sartin.' So I carried it to the man all out, an' said,

"'Take it all--only be sure an' git him.'

"Well, finally they got the boy brought back; an' then they tried to frighten him, an' to make him say that I was n't his mammy, an' that he did n't know me; but they could n't make it out. They gave him to me, an' I took him and carried him home; an' when I came to take off his clothes, there was his poor little back all covered with scars an' hard lumps, where they'd flogged him.

"Well, you see, honey, I told you how I prayed the Lord to render unto her double. Well, it came true; for I was up at ole missis' house not long after, an' I heerd 'em readin' a letter to her how her daughter's husband had murdered her--how he'd thrown her down an' stamped the life out of her, when he was in liquor; an' my ole missis, she give a screech, an fell flat on the floor. Then says I, 'O Lord, I did n't mean all that! You took me up too quick.'

"Well, I went in an' tended that poor critter all night. She was out of her mind--a cryin', an' callin' for her daughter; an' I held her poor ole head on my arm, an' watched for her as ef she'd been my babby. An' I watched by her, an' took care on her all through her sickness after that, an' she died in my arms, poor thing!"

"Well, Sojourner, did you always go by this name?"

"No, 'deed! My name was Isabella; but when I left the house of bondage, I left everything behind. I wa'n't goin' to keep nothin' of Egypt on me, an' so I went to the Lord an' asked him to give me a new name. And the Lord gave me Sojourner, because I was to travel up an' down the land, showin' the people their sins, an' bein' a sign unto them. Afterward I told the Lord I wanted another name, 'cause everybody else had two names; and the Lord gave me Truth, because I was to declare the truth to the people.

"Ye see some ladies have given me a white satin banner," she said, pulling out of her pocket and unfolding a white banner, printed with many texts, such as, "Proclaim liberty throughout all the land unto all the inhabitants thereof," and others of like nature. "Well," she said, "I journeys round to camp-meetin's, an' wherever folks is, an' I sets up my banner, an' then I sings, an' then folks always comes up round me, an' then I preaches to 'em. I tells 'em about Jesus, an' I tells 'em about the sins of this people. A great many always comes to hear me; an' they're right good to me, too, an' say they want to hear me agin."

We all thought it likely; and as the company left her, they shook hands with her, and thanked her for her very original sermon; and one of the ministers was overheard to say to another, "There's more of the gospel in that story than in most sermons."

Sojourner staid several days with us, a welcome guest. Her conversation was so strong, simple, shrewd, and with such a droll flavoring of humor, that the Professor was wont to say of an evening, "Come, I am dull, can't you get Sojourner up here to talk a little?" She would come up into the parlor, and sit among pictures and ornaments, in her simple stuff gown, with her heavy traveling shoes, the central object of attention both to parents and children, always ready to talk or to sing, and putting into the common flow of conversation the keen edge of some shrewd remark.

"Sojourner, what do you think of women's Rights?"

"Well, honey, I 's ben to der meetins, an' harked a good deal. Dey wanted me fur to speak. So I got up. Says I, 'Sisters, I a'n't clear what you'd be after. Ef women want any rights more'n dey's got, why don't dey jes' take 'em, an' not be talkin' about it?' Some on 'em came round me, an' asked why I did n't wear bloomers. An' I told 'em I had bloomers enough when I was in bondage. You see," she said, "dey used to weave what dey called nigger-cloth, an' each one of us got jes' sech a strip, an' had to wear it width-wise. Them that was short got along pretty well, but as for me"--She gave an indescribably droll glance at her long limbs and then at us, and added, "Tell you, I had enough of bloomers in them days."

Sojourner then proceeded to give her views of the relative capacity of the sexes, in her own way.

"S'pose a man's mind holds a quart, an a woman's do n't hold but a pint; ef her pint is full, it's as good as his quart."

Sojourner was fond of singing an extraordinary lyric, commencing,

> "I'm on my way to Canada,
> That cold, but happy, land;
> The dire effects of slavery
> I can no longer stand.

> O righteous Father,
> Do look down on me,
> And help me on to Canada,
> Where colored folks are free!"

The lyric ran on to state that, when the fugitive crosses the Canada line,

> "The queen comes down unto the shore,
> With arms extended wide,
> To welcome the poor fugitive
> Safe onto freedom's side."

In the truth thus set forth she seemed to have the most simple faith.

But her chief delight was to talk of "glory," and to sing hymns whose burden was, and when left to herself, she would often hum these with great delight, nodding her head.

> "O glory, glory, glory,
> Won't you come along with me?"

On one occasion, I remember her sitting at a window singing and fervently keeping time with her head, the little black Puck of a grandson meanwhile amusing himself with ornamenting her red-and-yellow turban with green dandelion curls, which shook and trembled with her emotions, causing him perfect convulsions of delight.

"Sojourner," said the Professor to her, one day, when he heard her singing, "you seem to be very sure about Heaven."

"Well, I be," she answered, triumphantly.

"What makes you so sure there is any Heaven?"

"Well, 'cause I got such a hankerin' arter it in here," she said--giving a thump on her breast with her usual energy.

There was at the time an invalid in the house, and Sojourner, on learning it, felt a mission to go and comfort her. It was curious to see the tall, gaunt, dusky figure stalk up to the bed with such an air of conscious authority, and take on herself the office of consoler with such a mixture of authority and tenderness. She talked as from above--and at the same time, if a pillow needed changing or any office to be rendered, she did it with a strength and handiness that inspired trust. One felt as if the dark, strange woman were quite able to take up the invalid in her bosom, and bear her as a lamb, both physically and spiritually. There was both power and sweetness in that great warm soul and that vigorous frame.

At length, Sojourner, true to her name, departed. She had her mission elsewhere. Where now she is I know not; but she left deep memories behind her.

To these recollections of my own I will add one more anecdote, related by Wendell Phillips.

Speaking of the power of Rachel to move and bear down a whole audience by a few simple words, he said he never knew but one other human being that had that power, and that other was Sojourner Truth.

He related a scene of which he was witness. It was at a crowded public meeting in Faneuil Hall, where Frederick Douglas was one of the chief speakers. Douglas had been describing the wrongs of the black race, and as he proceeded, he grew more and more excited, and finally ended by saying that they had no hope of justice from the whites, no possible hope except in their own right arms. It must come to blood; they must fight for themselves and redeem themselves, or it would never be done.

Sojourner was sitting, tall and dark, on the very front seat, facing the platform; and in the hush of deep feeling, after Douglas sat down, she spoke out in her deep, peculiar voice, heard all over the house,

"Frederick, is God dead?"

The effect was perfectly electrical, and thrilled through the whole house, changing as by a flash the whole feeling of the audience. Not another word she said or needed to say; it was enough.

It is with a sad feeling that one contemplates noble minds and bodies, nobly and grandly formed human beings, that have come to us cramped, scarred, maimed, out of the prison-house of bondage. One longs to know what such beings might have become, if suffered to unfold and expand under the kindly developing influences of education.

It is the theory of some writers that to the African is reserved, in the later and palmier days of the earth, the full and harmonious development of the religious element in man. The African seems to seize on the tropical fervor and luxuriance of Scripture imagery as something native; he appears to feel himself to be of the same blood with those old burning, simple souls, the patriarchs, prophets, and seers, whose impassioned words seem only grafted as foreign plants on the cooler stock of the occidental mind.

I cannot but think that Sojourner with the same culture might have spoken words as eloquent and undying as those of the African Saint Augustine or Tertullian. How grand and queenly a woman she might have been, with her wonderful physical vigor, her great heaving sea of emotion, her power of spiritual conception, her quick penetration, and her boundless energy! We might conceive an African type of woman so largely made and moulded, so much fuller in all the elements of life, physical and spiritual, that the dark hue of the skin should seem only to add an appropriate charm--as Milton says of his Penseroso, whom he imagines

> "Black, but such as in esteem
> Prince Memnon's sister might beseem,
> Or that starred Ethiop queen that strove
> To set her beauty's praise above
> The sea-nymph's."

But though Sojourner Truth has passed away from among us as a wave of the sea, her memory still lives in one of the loftiest and most original works of modern art, the Libyan Sibyl, by Mr. Story, which attracted so much attention in the late World's Exhibition. Some years ago, when visiting Rome, I related Sojourner's history to Mr. Story at a breakfast at his house. Already had his mind begun to turn to Egypt in search of a type of art which should represent a larger and more vigorous development of nature than the cold elegance of Greek lines. His glorious Cleopatra was then in process of evolution, and his mind was working out the problem of her broadly developed nature, of all that slumbering weight and fullness of passion with which this statue seems charged, as a heavy thunder-cloud is charged with electricity.

The history of Sojourner Truth worked in his mind and led him into the deeper recesses of the African nature--those unexplored depths of being and feeling, mighty and dark as the gigantic depths of tropical forests, mysterious as the hidden rivers and mines of that burning continent whose life-history is yet to be. A few days after, he told me that he had conceived the idea of a statue which he should call the Libyan Sibyl. Two years subsequently, I revisited Rome, and found the gorgeous Cleopatra finished, a thing to marvel at, as the creation of a new style of beauty, a new manner of art. Mr. Story requested me to come and repeat to him the history of Sojourner Truth, saying that the conception had never left him. I did so; and a day or two after, he showed me the clay model of the Libyan Sibyl. I have never seen the marble statue; but am told by those who have, that it was by far the most impressive work of art at the Exhibition.

A notice of the two statues from the London Athenæum must supply a description, which I cannot give.

"The Cleopatra and the Sibyl are seated, partly draped, with the characteristic Egyptian gown, that gathers about the torso and falls freely around the limbs; the first is covered to the bosom, the second bare to the hips. Queenly Cleopatra rests back against her chair in meditative ease, leaning her cheek against one hand, whose elbow the rail of the seat sustains; the other is outstretched upon her knee, nipping its forefinger upon the thumb thoughtfully, as though some firm, willful purpose filled her brain, as it seems to set those luxurious features to a smile as if the whole woman 'would.' Upon her head is the coif, bearing in front the mystic uræus, or twining basilisk of sovereignty, while from its sides depend the wide Egyptian lappels, or wings, that fall upon her shoulders. The Sibilla Libica has crossed her knees--an action universally held amongst the ancients as indicative of reticence or secrecy, and of power to bind. A secret-keeping looking dame she is, in the full-bloom proportions of ripe womanhood, wherein choosing to place his figure the sculptor has deftly gone between the disputed point whether these women were blooming and wise in youth, or deeply furrowed with age and burdened with the knowledge of centuries, as Virgil, Livy, and Gellius say. Good artistic example might be quoted on both sides. Her forward elbow is propped upon one knee; and to keep her secrets closer, for this Libyan woman is the closest of all the sibyls, she rests her shut mouth upon one closed palm, as if holding the African mystery deep in the brooding brain that looks out through mournful, warning eyes, seen under the wide shade of the strange horned (Ammonite) crest, that bears the mystery of the Tetragrammaton upon its upturned front. Over her full bosom, mother of myriads as she was, hangs the same symbol. Her face has a Nubian cast, her hair wavy and plaited, as is meet."

We hope to see the day when copies both of the Cleopatra and the Libyan Sibyl shall adorn the Capitol at Washington.

Near the close of the article Mrs. Stowe said, "Sojourner has passed away from among us as a wave of the sea." But as the wave describes larger circles in its outward-bound course, so has her life become more significant as she has been borne forth into the ocean of life. Her work was then but just begun, and her record since that time shows a faith in the power of truth, a devotion in the cause of humanity, and a perseverance in the accomplishment of her purposes which command attention and respect. She had been around "a testifying," but now other duties were superadded. To the great work being done for the soldiers, she lent a helping hand, seeking every opportunity to aid them. The first colored troops that enlisted from Battle Creek encamped in Detroit. As the thanksgiving season approached, Sojourner proposed that the citizens of that city should send the "boys" a dinner, to which they cordially responded. In her soliciting rounds, she met a gentleman whom she invited to donate for the entertainment. He refused to do so, and made some severe remarks about the war, the nigger, &c. Much surprised, she asked him who he was. He replied, "I am the only son of my mother." "I am glad there are no more," said she, and passed on. Several large boxes, containing the luxuries of the season, not forgetting the fattened turkey, were dispatched by the generous people of the town with Sojourner as distributor. Detroit papers spoke of her efforts commendingly.

"GALA DAY AT CAMP WARD.

"ADDRESS BY SOJOURNER TRUTH.--The colored soldiers at Camp Ward had a regular jubilee last Friday. About eleven o'clock a carriage drove up before Col. Bennett's quarters laden with boxes and packages containing all manner of delicacies for 'the boys', sent from Battle Creek. Sojourner Truth, who carries not only a tongue of fire, but a heart of love, was the bearer of these offerings. The Colonel ordered the regiment into line 'in their best' for the presentation, which was made by Sojourner, accompanied by a speech glowing with patriotism, exhortation, and good wishes, which was responded to by rounds of enthusiastic cheers. At the close of the ceremony, Sojourner spent an hour or two among the soldiers in motherly conversation, and assisting in opening the boxes and distributing their contents, which the recipients disposed of with hearty good-will.

"Sunday afternoon, according to appointment, Sojourner went up to the camp to deliver another address to the soldiers, but so large a crowd of white citizens were gathered to hear that her inspirations were devoted almost exclusively to their ears, with a promise of a future discourse for the soldiers. At the close of the lecture, a handsome collection was volunteered for the benefit of the speaker.

--Advertiser and Tribune."

In the spring of 1864, a brief article in the same journal mentioned her having gone to Washington to see Mr[.] Lincoln.

"To the Editor of the Advertiser and Tribune.

"Many of our citizens are doubtless acquainted with the name of Sojourner Truth, have seen racy anecdotes of her from time to time in the newspapers, read Harriet Beecher Stowe's narrative of her in the Atlantic Monthly, and remember her stay of several months in this city five or six years ago. Those who called upon her at that time, were richly entertained by her original remarks, her ready wit, and the stories of her wonderful life. She was then full of intense interest in the war, and foresaw its result in the emancipation of her race. It was touching to see her eager face when the newspapers were read in her presence. She would never listen to Mrs. Stowe's 'Libyan Sibyl'. 'Oh!' she would say, 'I do n't want to hear about that old symbol; read me something that is going on now, something about this great war.' She had utter faith in Abraham Lincoln. To a friend who was impatient with his slow movements she said, 'Oh, wait, chile! have patience! It takes a great while to turn about this great ship of State.' Toward spring she made ready for a journey to Washington, to see Mr. Lincoln. 'I shall surely go,' she said, 'I never determined to do anything and failed.' And she did go--the brave-hearted, indomitable old woman--despite her light purse and heavy burden of seventy-seven years."

She left Battle Creek in June, but did not immediately go to Washington. A New York paper says of her:--

"Sojourner has been some months in New York, speaking in many places with great acceptance, and is now in this city, where she will speak this evening in the lecture room of the Unitarian Church, corner of Lafayette Avenue and Shelby Street. Let those who enjoy an original entertainment hear her. She is trying to pay off a mortgage on her little house in Battle Creek. Give her a full house, and a generous contribution. Remember that here in the North, in the State of New York, she was robbed, by our race and by our laws, of FORTY YEARS of her life. Do we not owe her, from abundant fullness, some compensation for those years with their entailed sorrow?

"'There is that scattereth and yet increaseth.'
"'The soul of the liberal man waxeth fat.'
"'The Lord loveth the cheerful giver.'

"C. E. C."

From New York, she went to Brooklyn, and spoke in Plymouth Church, where a collection of $100 was taken up for her. A Brooklyn paper speaks of her as follows:--

"Sojourner Truth, whom the newspapers lately described as dying, reported herself in person to us last week, a living contradiction of the false rumor. The old lady says that, so far from being at the point of death, she has not experienced for many months any symptom of sickness. Her age is now eighty, but her spirit continues as youthful as ever. On Sunday morning she heard Mr. Beecher's opening sermon of the season, which she called 'a feast for her poor old soul.' Sojourner's conversation is witty, sarcastic, sensible, and oftentimes profound. Her varied experience during a long life gives her a rich and deep fountain to draw upon for the entertainment and instruction of her friends, and her reminiscences and comments are equally interesting both to grown folks and children. She looks and acts as if she might live to be a hundred years old. She has uplifted her voice to two generations of mankind, and may yet become sibyl and prophetess to a third."

Sojourner reached Washington during the autumn, and in due time made her long-contemplated visit to the president.

THE STORY OF HER INTERVIEW WITH THE PRESIDENT.

The following letter from Sojourner Truth, written by a friend at her dictation, was addressed to Rowland Johnson, who has kindly handed it to us for publication. Our readers will be glad to see Sojourner's own account of her visit to the president.

"FREEDMAN'S VILLAGE, VA., NOV. 17, 1864.

"DEAR FRIEND :--

"I am at Freedman's Village. After visiting the president, I spent three weeks at Mrs. Swisshelm's, and held two meetings in Washington, at Rev. Mr. Garnet's Presbyterian Church, for the benefit of the Colored Soldiers' Aid Society. These meetings were successful in raising funds. One week after that I went to Mason's Island, and saw the freedmen there, and held several meetings, remained a week and was present at the celebration of the emancipation of the slaves of Maryland, and spoke on that occasion.

"It was about 8 o'clock A. M., when I called on the president. Upon entering his reception room we found about a dozen persons in waiting, among them two colored women. I had quite a pleasant time waiting until he was disengaged, and enjoyed his conversation with others; he showed as much kindness and consideration to the colored persons as to the whites--if there was any difference, more. One case was that of a colored woman who was sick and likely to be turned out of her house on account of her inability to pay her rent. The president listened to her with much attention, and spoke to her with kindness and tenderness. He said he had given so much he could give no more, but told her where to go and get the money, and asked Mrs. C--n to assist her, which she did.

"The president was seated at his desk. Mrs. C. said to him, 'This is Sojourner Truth, who has come all the way from Michigan to see you.' He then arose, gave me his hand, made a bow, and said, 'I am pleased to see you.'

"I said to him, Mr. President, when you first took your seat I feared you would be torn to pieces, for I likened you unto Daniel, who was thrown into the lion's den; and if the lions did not tear you into pieces, I knew that it would be God that had saved you; and I said if he spared me I would see you before the four years expired, and he has done so, and now I am here to see you for myself.

"He then congratulated me on my having been spared. Then I said, I appreciate you, for you are the best president who has ever taken the seat. He replied: 'I expect you have reference to my having emancipated the slaves in my proclamation. But,' said he, mentioning the names of several of his predecessors (and among them emphatically that of Washington), 'they were all just as good, and would have done just as I have done if the time had come. If the people over the river [pointing across the Potomac] had behaved themselves, I could not have done what I have; but they did not, which gave me the opportunity to do these things.' I then said, I thank God that you were the instrument selected by him and the people to do it. I told him that I had never heard of him before he was talked of for president. He smilingly replied, 'I had heard of you many times before that.'

"He then showed me the Bible presented to him by the colored people of Baltimore, of which you have no doubt seen a description. I have seen it for myself, and it is beautiful beyond description. After I had looked it over, I said to him, This is beautiful indeed; the colored people have given this to the head of the government, and that government once sanctioned laws that would not permit its people to learn enough to enable them to read this book. And for what? Let them answer who can.

"I must say, and I am proud to say, that I never was treated by anyone with more kindness and cordiality than were shown to me by that great and good man, Abraham Lincoln, by the grace of God president of the United States for four years more. He took my little book, and with the same hand that signed the death-warrant of slavery, he wrote as follows:

"'For Aunty Sojourner Truth,

"'Oct. 29, 1864. A. LINCOLN.'

"As I was taking my leave, he arose and took my hand, and said he would be pleased to have me call again. I felt that I was in the presence of a friend, and I now thank God from the bottom of my heart that I always have advocated his cause, and have done it openly and boldly. I shall feel still more in duty bound to do so in time to come. May God assist me.

"Now I must tell you something of this place. I found things quite as well as I expected. I think I can be useful and will stay. The captain in command of the guard has given me his assistance, and by his aid I have obtained a little house, and will move into it to-morrow. Will you ask Mrs. P., or any of my friends, to send me a couple of sheets and a pillow? I find many of the women very ignorant in relation to house-keeping, as most of them were instructed in field labor, but not in household duties. They all seem to think a great deal of me, and want to learn the way we live in the North. I am listened to with attention and respect, and from all things, I judge it is the will of both God and the people that I should remain.

"Now when you come to Washington, do n't forget to call and see me. You may publish my whereabouts, and anything in this letter you think would interest the friends of Freedom, Justice, and Truth, in the Standard and Anglo-African, and any other paper you may see fit.

"Enclosed please find four shadows [carte de visites]. The two dollars came safely. Anything in the way of nourishment you may feel like sending, send it along. The captain sends to Washington every day. Give my love to all who inquire for me, and tell my friends to direct all things for me to the care of Capt. George B. Carse, Freedman's Village, Va. Ask Mr. Oliver Johnson to please send me the Standard while I am here, as many of the colored people like to hear what is going on, and to know what is being done for them. Sammy, my grandson, reads for them. We are both well, and happy, and feel that we are in good employment. I find plenty of friends.

"Your friend,

SOJOURNER TRUTH."

"The colored population of Baltimore have procured the most beautiful Bible ever manufactured in this country, to be presented to the President of the United States. The cover bears a large plate of gold, representing a slave with his shackles falling from him in a cotton field, stretching out his hands in gratitude to President Lincoln for the freedom of the slave. At the feet of the freedman there is a scroll bearing upon its face the word 'Emancipation,' in large letters. On the reverse cover is another gold plate containing the following inscription: 'To Abraham Lincoln, President of the United States, the friend of universal freedom, by the loyal colored people of Baltimore, as a token of respect and gratitude. Baltimore, July 4th, 1864.' The book is enclosed in a walnut silver-mounted box. The entire affair cost $5,800."

Although in Sojourner's estimation Abraham Lincoln was the "foremost man of all this world," yet no idle curiosity prompted her to ask this interview. From the head of the nation she sought that authority which would enable her to take part in the awful drama which was enacting in this Republic, and that being obtained, she at once entered upon her work.

When we follow her from one field of labor to another, her time being divided between teaching, preaching, nursing, watching, and praying, ever ready to counsel, comfort, and assist, we feel that, for one who is nobody but a woman, an unlettered woman, a black woman, and an old woman, a woman born and bred a slave, nothing short of the Divine incarnated in the human, could have wrought out such grand results.

In December, she received the following commission from the National Freedman's Relief Association:--

"NEW YORK, DEC. 1, 1864.

"This certifies that The National Freedman's Relief Association has appointed Sojourner Truth to be a counselor to the freed people at Arlington Heights, Va., and hereby commends her to the favor and confidence of the officers of government, and of all persons who take an interest in relieving the condition of the freedmen, or in promoting their intellectual, moral, and religious instruction.

"On behalf of the N. F. R. Association,

"F. G. SHAW, President,

"CHARLES C. LEIGH,
"Chairman of Home Com."

Sojourner spent more than a year at Arlington Heights, instructing the women in domestic duties, and doing much to promote the general welfare. She especially deprecated their filthy habits, and strove to inspire them with a love of neatness and order. On the Sabbath she preached to large and attentive congregations, and was once heard to exclaim, "Be clean! be clean! for cleanliness is godliness."

Liberty was a stranger to these poor people. Having but lately been introduced to the goddess, they had never yet so much as touched the tips of her lovely fingers, and dared not raise their bowed heads to steal even a sidelong glance at her radiant face. Thus, being wholly unfamiliar with her divine attributes, they often submitted to grievous wrongs from their old oppressors, not presuming to expostulate. The Marylanders tormented them by coming over, seizing, and carrying away their children. If the mothers made a "fuss," as these heartless wretches called those natural expressions of grief in which bereaved mothers are apt to indulge, they were thrust into the guard-house. When this was made known to Sojourner, she told them they must not permit such outrages, that they were free, and had rights which would be recognized and maintained by the laws, and that they could bring these robbers to justice.

This was a revelation indeed, for they had never known that freedom meant anything more to them than being no longer obliged to serve a master, and at liberty to lounge about in idleness. But her electrifying words seemed to inspire them with new life and to awaken the latent spirit within them which, like fire in flint, had lain torpid for ages, but, un-extinguished and un-extinguishable, awaited only favorable conditions to escape in freedom. The manhood and womanhood of these crushed people now asserted itself, and the exasperated Marylanders threatened to put Sojourner into the guard-house. She told them that if they attempted to put her into the guard-house, she "would make the United States rock like a cradle."

Soon after the Freedmen's Bureau was established, Sojourner was appointed to assist in the hospital, as the following letter will show:--

"WAR DEPARTMENT, "BUREAU OF REFUGEES, FREEDMEN, AND ABANDONED LANDS.

"Washington, September 13, 1865.

"Sojourner Truth has good ideas about the industry and virtue of the colored people. I commend her energetic and faithful efforts to Surgeon Gluman, in charge of Freedmen's Hospital, and shall be happy to have him give her all facilities and authority so far as she can aid him in promoting order, cleanliness, industry, and virtue among the patients.

"JOHN EATON, JR.,
"Col. and Assistant Commissioner."

While Sojourner was engaged in the hospital, she often had occasion to procure articles from various parts of the city for the sick soldiers, and would sometimes be obliged to walk a long distance, carrying her burdens upon her arm. She would gladly have availed herself of the street cars; but, although there was on each track one car called the Jim Crow car, nominally for the accommodation of colored people, yet should they succeed in getting on at all they would seldom have more than the privilege of standing, as the seats were usually filled with white folks. Unwilling to submit to this state of things, she complained to the president of the street railroad, who ordered the Jim Crow car to be taken off. A law was now passed giving the colored people equal car privileges with the white.

Not long after this, Sojourner, having occasion to ride, signaled the car, but neither conductor nor driver noticed her. Soon another followed, and she raised her hand again, but they also turned away. She then gave three tremendous yelps, "I want to ride! I want to ride!! I WANT TO RIDE!!! Consternation seized the passing crowd--people, carriages, go-carts of every description stood still. The car was effectually blocked up, and before it could move on, Sojourner had jumped aboard. Then there arose a great shout from the crowd, "Ha ha! ha!! She has beaten him," &c. The angry conductor told her to go forward where the horses were, or he would put her out. Quietly seating herself, she informed him that she was a passenger. "Go forward where the horses are, or I will throw you out," said he in a menacing voice. She told him that she was neither a Marylander nor a Virginian to fear his threats; but was from the Empire State of New York, and knew the laws as well as he did.

Several soldiers were in the car, and when other passengers came in, they related the circumstance and said, "You ought to have heard that old woman talk to the conductor." Sojourner rode farther than she needed to go; for a ride was so rare a privilege that she determined to make the most of it. She left the car feeling very happy, and said, "Bless God! I have had a ride."

Returning one day from the Orphan's Home at Georgetown, she hastened to reach a car; but they paid no attention to her signal, and kept ringing a bell that they might not hear her. She ran after it, and when it stopped to take other passengers, she succeeded in overtaking it and, getting in, said to the conductor, "It is a shame to make a lady run so." He told her if she said another word, he would put her off the car, and came forward as if to execute his threat. She replied, "If you attempt that, it will cost you more than your car and horses are worth." A gentleman of dignified and commanding manner, wearing a general's uniform, interfered in her behalf, and the conductor gave her no further trouble.

At another time, she was sent to Georgetown to obtain a nurse for the hospital, which being accomplished, they went to the station and took seats in an empty car, but had not proceeded far before two ladies came in, and seating themselves opposite the colored woman began a whispered conversation, frequently casting scornful glances at the latter. The nurse, for the first time in her life finding herself in one sense on a level with white folks and being much abashed, hung her poor old head nearly down to her lap; but Sojourner, nothing daunted, looked fearlessly about. At length one of the ladies called out, in a weak, faint voice, "Conductor, conductor, does niggers ride in these cars?" He hesitatingly answered, "Ye-yea-yes," to which she responded, "'T is a shame and a disgrace. They ought to have a nigger car on the track." Sojourner remarked,

"Of course colored people ride in the cars. Streetcars are designed for poor white, and colored, folks. Carriages are for ladies and gentlemen. There are carriages [pointing out of the window], standing ready to take you three or four miles for sixpence, and then you talk of a nigger car!!!" Promptly acting upon this hint, they arose to leave. "Ah!" said Sojourner, "now they are going to take a carriage. Good by, ladies."

Mrs. Laura Haviland, a widely known philanthropist, spent several months in the same hospital and sometimes went about the city with Sojourner to procure necessaries for the invalids. Returning one day, being much fatigued, Mrs. Haviland proposed to take a car although she was well aware that a white person was seldom allowed to ride if accompanied by a black one. "As Mrs. Haviland signaled the car," says Sojourner, "I stepped one side as if to continue my walk and when it stopped I ran and jumped aboard. The conductor pushed me back, saying, 'Get out of the way and let this lady come in.' Whoop! said I, I am a lady too. We met with no further opposition till we were obliged to change cars. A man coming out as we were going into the next car, asked the conductor if 'niggers were allowed to ride.' The conductor grabbed me by the shoulder and jerking me around, ordered me to get out. I told him I would not. Mrs. Haviland took hold of my other arm and said, 'Do n't put her out.' The conductor asked if I belonged to her. 'No,' replied Mrs. Haviland, 'She belongs to humanity.' 'Then take her and go,' said he, and giving me another push slammed me against the door. I told him I would let him know whether he could shove me about like a dog, and said to Mrs. Haviland, Take the number of this car.

"At this, the man looked alarmed, and gave us no more trouble. When we arrived at the hospital, the surgeons were called in to examine my shoulder and found that a bone was misplaced. I complained to the president of the road, who advised me to arrest the man for assault and battery. The Bureau furnished me a lawyer, and the fellow lost his situation. It created a great sensation, and before the trial was ended, the inside of the cars looked like pepper and salt; and I felt, like Poll Parrot, 'Jack, I am riding.' A little circumstance will show how great a change a few weeks had produced: A lady saw some colored women looking wistfully toward a car, when the conductor, halting, said, 'Walk in, ladies.' Now they who had so lately cursed me for wanting to ride, could stop for black as well as white, and could even condescend to say, 'Walk in, ladies.'"

The city of Washington was now literally swarming with a class of people who had by the war been thrown upon the surface of society like mud from a volcano, and who were not unlike that article in respect to being dirty and entirely unfitted by a want of contact with refining and favorable influences to obtain and maintain a hold upon civilization. A report from the superintendent of police will help to explain their condition:--

"CONDITION OF THE DESTITUTE COLORED PEOPLE OF THE DISTRICT.

"In the Senate, on Tuesday, while the bill reported by Senator Morrill appropriating $25,000 for the relief of destitute colored people of the District was under consideration, the following letter from Superintendent of Police Richards was read:--

"DEPARTMENT OF METROPOLITAN POLICE.
"OFFICE OF SUP'T, 483 TENTH ST., WEST,
"Washington, March 6, 1866.

"GENTLEMEN:--

"I have the honor at this time to submit a report, based mainly upon personal inspection, of the sanitary condition of certain localities in the city of Washington, inhabited by colored people, mostly known as 'contrabands,' together with certain other facts connected with the condition of these people.

"The first locality visited is known as 'Murder Bay,' and is situated between Thirteenth and Fifteenth Streets west, below Ohio Avenue, and bordering on the Washington Canal. Here crime, filth, and poverty seem to vie with each other in a career of degradation and death. Whole families, consisting of fathers, mothers, children, uncles, and aunts, according to their own statements, are crowded into mere apologies for shanties, which are without light or ventilation. During the storms of rain or snow their roofs afford but slight protection, while from beneath a few rough boards used for floors the miasmatic effluvia from the most disgustingly filthy and stagnant water, mingled with the exhalations from the uncleansed bodies of numerous inmates, render the atmosphere within these hovels stifling and sickening in the extreme. Their rooms are usually not more than six or eight feet square, with not a window or even an opening (except a door) for the admission of light. Some of the rooms are entirely surrounded by other rooms, so that no light at all reaches where persons live and spend their days and nights. In a space about fifty yards square I found about one hundred families, composed of from three to ten persons each, living in shanties one story in hight, except in a few instances where tenements are actually built on the tops of others. There is a distance of only three or four feet separating these buildings from each other--not even as convenient as an ordinary three-feet alley. These openings lead in so devious a course that one with difficulty finds his way out again. Thus pent up, not even these paths are purified by currents of fresh air. In one building visited, seventeen families were found upon the ground floor, consisting of from two to seven persons each, one restaurant, and one boarding-house. The second story is a large dance hall, where these people nightly congregate for amusement.

"Nearly all of these people came from Virginia during the rebellion, and some of them propose to return whenever they are assured that they can find work to do there, and will be well treated. It was found that from five to eight dollars per month are paid for the rent of these miserable shanties, except in some instances, where a ground rent of three dollars per month is paid for a little spot covering a few square feet--there some of the more enterprising have erected cabins of their own. These, also, are in equally close proximity to each other, so that it is with difficulty that one can crowd between them.

"On the west side of Fourteenth Street near the same locality, are a large number of small buildings, which, however, are kept in a somewhat more cleanly condition, and are opened to light and ventilation. Here some of the occupants of houses boast of small back yards, but so low and wet are their surfaces that they are a curse rather than a benefit. Filthy water here accumulates, from which, with the advent of warm weather, the seeds of disease must spread among and destroy these wretched people.

"In each of these localities there are no proper privy accommodations, and those that exist are in a leaky and filthy condition generally. Nor can the sanitary laws be properly enforced against delinquents, for they have no means wherewith to pay fines, and a commitment to the work-house is no punishment. I can see no efficient mode of remedying this evil except that scavengers be employed at the public expense, to visit these localities; though by far the best remedy would be to require that these buildings be razed to the ground.

"Under the best sanitary laws that can be enacted, and stringently enforced, these places can be considered as nothing better than propagating grounds of crime, disease, and death; and in the case of a prevailing epidemic, the condition of these localities would be horrible to contemplate.

"A similarly crowded lot of shanties exists on Rhode Island Avenue, between Tenth and Eleventh Streets, though as to fresh air and cleanliness, a somewhat better condition of things exists. Here, in a space some two hundred feet square, two hundred and thirteen persons reside, mostly known as 'contrabands.' There are several other places equally crowded within the city limits, which I have not yet had time to visit and inspect personally; for which purpose I respectfully ask for further time.

"A. C. RICHARDS, Sup't.
"To the Board of Police."

Sojourner, witnessing the afflictions of her people, and desiring to mitigate their sufferings, found homes and employment for many in the Northern States, government furnishing transportation for all. In the winter of 1867, she made three trips from Rochester to a town about 200 miles south of Richmond, to obtain laborers for those localities left destitute by the war; but she soon came to see that this was not the best mode of procedure, as it cost a great amount of labor, time, and money to locate the young and strong, leaving the aged and little children still uncared for.

The imagination can scarcely conceive a more harrowing spectacle than the vast multitude, composed of both sexes, and all ages from helpless infancy to tremulous senility, roaming about, having no possessions but the bodies, which had recently been given them by a dash of Abraham Lincoln's pen. Surging to and fro, this motley crowd could claim no more of mother earth than sufficed for standing room, and were liable at any time to be ordered, like Joe, "to move on."

Thus they were borne upon the waves of society as a wrecked ship upon the sea, stripped of spar and sail, rudder and compass, tempest tossed upon the black and sullen deep, with no ray of light to illumine its pathway of gloom. The heads of government, seeing and commiserating their hapless state, established what was called the Freedman's Bureau as a measure of relief, and by its orders each ward daily furnished to the refugees 700 loaves of bread, which served to sustain life, but was inadequate to meet the emergency; for civilization has needs which cannot be supplied by bread alone.

It was sad to see the hungry mass stretch forth its hand, seize the proffered loaf, seek a spot where it might be devoured, and idle away the time till another loaf was due. And could the Bureau have ministered to all their wants, would not this mode of life become productive of enormous evils, since the habits it fostered, having been engendered by the system of slavery, needed no such encouragement? This institution was emphatically the necessity of the hour, but neither wisdom nor prudence would advise its continuance.

The race was increasing at a rapid rate, and the drain upon the national treasury would become exhaustive. Still, justice demanded that government take efficient legislative action in the interest of these people, whom the genius of General Butler had denominated contrabands, as some reward for years of uncompensated services. Nations anxiously watching the scales in which this government and its dependent millions must be weighed, waited to render their verdict. Advancement moves with slow and feeble pace. The new hinges upon the old. In obtaining freedom, these people were separated from many things, for which, as yet, they had received no equivalent. Those who had not where to lay their heads thought of the rude cabin once their home, in pleasant contrast with the present couch of earth, canopied by the over-arching sky. Languishing with homesickness, the worst of ailments, they were a striking counterpart of those sorrowing captives who, sitting by the rivers of Babylon, hung their harps upon the willows and wept for remembered joys.

Their coarse food and clothing cost them no thought while in slavery. But in a moment comes a change. Now, all thought and action must be bent upon self-support. But from transmitted habits many were powerless to exercise the functions of the brain in planning for the future, and, though they had arrived at man's estate, must be cared for like children. As Sojourner went about the city, she soon came to distinguish these contrabands. They had a dreamy look, taking no note of time; it seemed as if a pause had come in their lives--an abyss, over whose brink they dared not look. With so few resources, with beclouded minds, with no education from books or contact with the world, aside from plantation life--strangers in a strange land, hungry, thirsty, ragged, homeless, they were the very impersonation of Despair, humbly holding out her hands in supplication.

Sojourner had known the joys of motherhood--brief joys, for she had been cruelly separated from her babes, and her mistress' children given to occupy the place which nature designed for her own. She had tasted its sorrows, too--such sorrows as Rachel, weeping for her children because they were not, could never feel. She had drained the cup of woe to the very dregs, and its fumes, like liquid fires, had dried the fountain of tears till there were none to flow.

But many years had passed since that season of affliction. The shackles had been removed from her body, and spirit also. Time dissolves the hardest substance--'tis called the great destroyer--it reconstructs as well. As the divine aurora of a broader culture dispelled the mists of ignorance, love, the most precious gift of God to mortals, permeated her soul, and her too-long-suppressed affections gushed from the sealed fountains as the waters of an obstructed river, to make new channels, bursts its embankments and rushes on its headlong course, powerful for weal or woe. Sojourner, robbed of her own offspring, adopted her race. Happy for the individual, good for humanity, when high aspirations emanate from sad experiences!

The forlorn and neglected children who prowled about the city excited her commiseration; for they had neither homes nor employment, and as idleness is the parent of crime, they were becoming exceedingly vicious. As a punishment for misdemeanors, they were sent to the station house, from which, after serving their time, they were released, only to continue the same destructive course. Slavery's teachings had bedimmed their perceptions of right, and rendered them incapable of continued moral effort; for her blighting influence, worse than a millstone about their necks, tended to drag them downward forever and forevermore.

Intelligently appreciating the law of transmitted tendencies, Sojourner looked upon them as sinned against as well as sinning. Knowing that the children were the future nation, and that those of her race would play no unimportant part in that future, she felt the need of enlisting sympathy, either human or superhuman, in their behalf. Aided by Gen. Howard, she held meetings in one of the largest churches of the city, to urge the establishment of industrial schools, remote from the city, where they might be placed and taught to become useful members of community. Had she possessed the power and influence of the humane and philanthropic Gov. Bagley, institutions such as he has recently been instrumental in establishing would have sprung into being, till homeless, neglected children would have been no more.

The past she abhorred, with its coffles, its loaded whips, auction blocks, brutal masters, overseers, and all the fearful horrors accruing from the ownership of man by his fellow-man; the sufferings of the present called out her deepest sympathies; but as she peered toward the future with sibyl eyes, her heart beat loud and fast; for she saw in it all grand possibilities. The angel of emancipation had rolled the stone away from the door of the sepulcher of slavery, and the resurrected millions, bound hand and foot in the grave-clothes of ignorance, bewildered and uncertain, awaited guidance in this transition hour.

Would a Moses appear to remove the bands from wrist and ankle, and with uplifted finger pointing to the pillar of cloud and of promise, lead them forth from this sea of troubles and plant their weary feet upon the Canaan of their desires? Would manna descend from heaven to feed this multitude, who were morally, physically, and intellectually destitute? As neither man nor miracle appeared, Sojourner said, "Lord, let me labor in this vineyard."

But how begin the work of establishing right relations where chaos reigns? Justice must constitute the bottom round in this ladder of progress, up which the race must mount in the struggle to reach higher conditions. How can justice be secured?

As she looked about upon the imposing public edifices that grace the District of Columbia, all built at the nation's expense, she said, "We helped to pay this cost. We have been a source of wealth to this republic. Our labor supplied the country with cotton, until villages and cities dotted the enterprising North for its manufacture, and furnished employment and support for a multitude, thereby becoming a revenue to the government. Beneath a burning southern sun have we toiled, in the canebrake and the rice swamp, urged on by the merciless driver's lash, earning millions of money; and so highly were we valued there, that should one poor wretch venture to escape from this hell of slavery, no exertion of man or trained blood-hound was spared to seize and return him to his field of unrequited labor.

"The overseer's horn awoke us at the dawning of day from our half-finished slumbers to pick the disgusting worm from the tobacco plant, which was an added source of wealth. Our nerves and sinews, our tears and blood, have been sacrificed on the altar of this nation's avarice. Our unpaid labor has been a stepping-stone to its financial success. Some of its dividends must surely be ours."

Who can deny the logic of her reasoning? The prophet[*]

* Parker Pillsbury.

of the nineteenth century said, many years ago, that "our nation will yet be obliged to pay sigh for sigh, groan for groan, and dollar for dollar, to this wronged and outraged race." Ah, me! what an awful debt when we consider that every mill of interest will surely be added! Did mothers and wives whose husbands and sons languished and died in Libby and Andersonville ever think of that prophecy? Does this nation realize that the debt is still unpaid? the note not taken up yet?

She knew that the United States owned countless acres of unoccupied land, which by cultivation would become a source of wealth to it. She also saw that it was given to build railroads, and that large reservations were apportioned to the Indians. Why not give a tract of land to those colored people who would rather become independent through their own exertions than longer clog the wheels of government?

It seemed to Sojourner that the money expended upon officials, in just this District alone, to convict and punish these vagabond children, would be ample to provide for them homes with the accessories of church and school-house and all the necessary requirements of civilization. With God's blessing, they might yet become an honor to the country which had so cruelly wronged them. This scheme presented itself to her mind as a divine revelation, and she made haste to lay her plan before the leading men of the government. They heard her patiently, expressed themselves willing to do the people's bidding; but manifested no enthusiasm. She regretted now, as ever, that women had no political rights under government; for she knew that could the voice of maternity be heard in the advocacy of this measure, the welfare, not only of the present generation, but of future ones, would be assured.

As it requires both the male and female element to propagate and successfully rear a family, so the State, being only the larger family, demands both for its life and proper development. As those who had the power to legislate for the carrying out of this measure, regarded it indifferently, and those who would gladly work for its accomplishment lacked political opportunity, some other measure must be adopted. She thought that whatever else had been denied to woman, she had ever been allowed to stand on praying ground, and that through petition she might be able to reach the head and heart of the government, or rather half the head and half the heart, as only in this proportion have they ever been represented in our country's legislation. She therefore dictated the following petition:--

"TO THE SENATE AND HOUSE OF REPRESENTATIVES,
in Congress assembled:--

"Whereas, From the faithful and earnest representations of Sojourner Truth (who has personally investigated the matter), we believe that the freed colored people in and about Washington, dependent upon government for support, would be greatly benefited and might become useful citizens by being placed in a position to support themselves: We, the undersigned, therefore earnestly request your honorable body to set apart for them a portion of the public land in the West, and erect buildings thereon for the aged and infirm, and otherwise legislate so as to secure the desired results."

The vitalizing forces of her nature were now fully aroused and deeply earnest. She felt that her life culminated at this point, and that all her previous experiences had been needful to prepare her for this crowning work. Being convinced of the feasibility and justice of this plan, she hastened to present her petition to the public, and solicit signatures. Her first lecture for this object was delivered in Providence, R. I., in Feb., 1870, to a large and appreciative audience.

THE VOICE OF THE PRESS.

"The renowned Sojourner Truth spoke in the town hall last evening, and gave one of her peculiar and forcible appeals, distinguished for native wit, eloquence, and religious pathos. The burden of her message was the urgent necessity for colonizing in the West, on land which she calls upon government to give them, the large number of freed people collected in and around Washington. During the war, at the request of President Lincoln, Sojourner spent much time among these people to do them good. With that clear insight and native good sense for which she is remarkable, she saw that the course pursued by government, in supporting them by charity instead of putting them in the way of sustaining themselves, was working immense mischief. True statesmanship demands that government give them lands in the West, thus paying a little of the great debt we owe this long-oppressed people, while at the same time leading them to support themselves, to enrich the nation, and become useful citizens. Sojourner wants the people to petition Congress to do this work at once. At this very time, as appears by a letter read at the meeting last evening, some of the freedmen are dying of starvation, right in sight of our national capitol. Petitions have been placed in the hands of friends of this movement, and it is hoped every person will sign as soon as opportunity is offered."--S. H., in Northampton (Mass.) paper.

FROM FALL RIVER PAPERS.

"Sojourner Truth--the colored American Sibyl--is spending a few days in our city, and will gladly welcome any of her old or new friends at the house of Robert Adams, Esq., on Rock Street. She bears her four-score years with ease, showing no signs of decay, but conversing on all familiar topics with a clearness of apprehension that would hardly be expected of one who has passed through the varied unpleasant experiences which have fallen to her lot. Give her a call, and enjoy a half hour with a ripe understanding, and do n't forget to purchase her photograph."

"Sojourner Truth--the colored American Sibyl--will speak in the vestry of the Franklin Street Church, on Monday evening. Come and hear an original."

"SOJOURNER TRUTH.--Sojourner Truth had a good audience at the Christian Church, last evening, and delivered a very unique and interesting address. Many more would have attended had they been aware how pleasantly the evening would have been spent in company with the aged philosopher. Her theme was the duty of the North to the emancipated negroes. Many of her photographs were purchased. It is not impossible that she may speak again during her stay here."

"Sojourner Truth will speak at the vestry of the First M. E. Church, to-morrow evening, Friday, Oct. 14th, at a quarter before 8 o'clock. This will probably be the last opportunity, at least for some time that our citizens will have of hearing this interesting and decidedly original character."

"Sojourner Truth had a large audience in the vestry of the First M. E. Church, last evening, and was listened to with interest for somewhat more than an hour. She will remain here a few days longer, at Mr. Robert Adams'."

"SOJOURNER TRUTH.--Your readers will notice that this eminent colored lady will discourse this evening, at the vestry of the First Methodist Church, on Main Street, on various topics. Her utterances at the Franklin Street Church, on Monday evening last, drew out quite an audience, which was exceedingly entertained by her instructive remarks; but as very limited notice was previously given, there was not the attendance from the male sex which she wished to see, as her talk is on a matter that peculiarly interests taxpayers. This ancient saint has given largely of her time to the bettering of the condition of the freedmen at Washington, and in that capacity has discovered certain abuses which should be rectified. All who come to listen will learn how some of the public money goes that is nominally appropriated to feed the black paupers in Washington. Her scheme for their improvement is practical, and should be put in operation at once.

"We hope our friend James Buffington, who has a voice in the administration of the money of the people, will be present and take note of her points on this matter.

As a nomination here amounts to an election, he may consider himself in for the next two years, and can aid immensely in straightening out this abuse. No gang of paupers should be allowed to huddle together like pigs anywhere, and be fed out of the public funds. Go and hear on the subject.

"Everybody, of course, knows of Sojourner Truth, of her sad early life as an abject slave under the old laws of New York, until she was forty years old; of her growth in wisdom which seemed born in her as an inheritance; of her active benevolences in all directions; of her shrewd repartees and wise sayings which will go down as proverbs among the intelligent for coming ages; of her goodness as a nurse to our sick and wounded soldiers when at an advanced age; of her sharp logic and pointed satire when warmed up on subjects of interest.

"All these have been set forth by pens of power in description, and will live in story for coming generations. 'The Lord never hearn tell on ye,' was her comforting remark to a young clergyman very much afflicted for fear the women would get their rights. 'Is God dead, Frederick?' to Douglas, when forecasting the sad fate of his race in the old slave days. Do n't come expecting fine rhetoric, finished grammar, or dictionary pronunciation; but if you want to hear an earnest soul of eighty or more years, on the borders of the coming world, still young in the graces of Christian charity, and ardent in the work assigned her, talk of right and justice, and set them forth with a spirit and skill that learned men might well envy, turn out to-night. Do n't forget that she has photographs of herself for sale--her only means of support for expenses of travel, livelihood, and a humble home in Michigan--and that while she 'sells the shadow to support the substance,' it will probably be the last time we shall see the lady among us. Do n't forget the hour-- one-quarter before 8 o'clock this evening."

FROM NEW JERSEY PAPERS.

"Springfield, Union County, New Jersey, and its Presbyterian Church were honored on Wednesday night by the presence of that lively old negro mummy, whose age ranges among the hundreds--Sojourner Truth--who fifty years ago was considered a crazy woman; who was wont to address street meetings and Garrison abolition conventicles. She was smuggled into the church by some pious radical to give her religious experience; and she did it--rather to the confusion and disgust of the audience. When respectable churches consent to admit to the houses opened for the worship of God every wandering negro minstrel or street spouter who may profess to have a peculiar religious experience, or some grievance to redress, they render themselves justly liable to public ridicule. The effects of our late civil war, which brought many of our divines upon the political rostrum, and converted many of our pulpits into recruiting stations, we fear will not soon be removed.

"Our Springfield correspondent writes of the visit of Sojourner Truth:--

"'Mislike me not for my complexion,
The shadowed liv'ry of the burnished sun.'

"'Thus Shakespeare. But we do most decidedly dislike the complexion and everything else appertaining to Mrs. Truth, the radical--the renowned, saintly, liberated, oratorical, pious slave. The superintendent of the Presbyterian Sunday-school, hearing such glowing accounts of her, invited her to speak to his charge. She spoke on the 1st inst., not on religion, but at random, on copperhead Jersey, hypocrites, freemen, woman's rights, etc., till the superintendent was forced to call her to order. She is a crazy, ignorant, repelling negress, and her guardians would do a Christian act to restrict her entirely to private life.'"

"SOJOURNER TRUTH DEFENDED.--Whenever I have heard the State of New Jersey stigmatized, I have always resented its being used as a mark of derision and a jest for scoffers; but a circumstance that occurred last week has proved it a fit land for missionaries to enter with books to enlighten the inhabitants, and purifiers with scourges to correct the people. The village of Springfield, that prides itself on its great age, had the honor of a visitor (no less a personage than Sojourner Truth)--a dear creature, one of the Lord's true servants, who has worked in his vineyard for forty years, and who, at the great age of eighty, instead of taking her ease during the infirmities of old age, feels that as long as the Lord gives her the breath of life she must work for his glory. Her fame went through all the land many years ago, and she numbers among her dearest friends the most intellectual, renowned, and gifted men and women of our land, and many are the weeks she has spent in the homes of those dear to our people. She has held happy converse with our lamented president, and our present one; has spoken in Beecher's Church to thousands, in many of our State capitol buildings, and our nation's senate chamber. Turn from these happy greetings and behold her welcome in New Jersey!--no, not there, but in a small, benighted corner, where the people pride themselves on their being and remaining as a century ago. They were so ignorant a people they knew not they had a great guest, and many had not even heard of Sojourner Truth. Then they had so little good breeding they left during her remarks, interrupting and showing disrespect to old age, which always commands respect. Then to show their ignorance, their lilliputian minds, they write of her as being a crazy woman, an old mummy that ought to be enclosed in an asylum. That is the testimony of Springfield, N. J., to be placed by the side of beautiful letters of cheer, volumes full of well-wishes and blessings from such personages as Lincoln, Gen. Grant, Henry Ward Beecher, Gen. Howard, Sumner, Phillips, Anna Dickinson, Lucretia Mott, &c., &c.,--men and women we all long to meet and take by the hand, and would be rejoiced to call our friends.

> "'By ignorance is pride increased;
> Those most assume who know the least;
> Their own self-balance gives them weight,
> But every other finds them light.'--Gay's Fables.

"A NEW SPRINGFIELD CORRESPONDENT."

"SOJOURNER TRUTH.--Sojourner Truth, now about fourscore years, who has devoted the whole of her time during the last twenty years of her life to the interests of the colored race, and during the late rebellion gave her personal service to the important work of educating the freed men and women in the moral, social, and domestic duties of life, without fee or reward, is now engaged in getting signatures to a petition to Congress for the benefit of a large class of dependent freedmen who may be found around Washington and other places in the South.

"Sojourner Truth is now at her home at Battle Creek, in Michigan, and writes us a letter under date of November 29. She has just returned from an extensive tour through Ohio, Indiana, Illinois, Michigan, Wisconsin, Iowa, Missouri, and Kansas, and wishes to carry her petition, to which she has obtained many signatures, to Washington this winter, and present it personally to Congress. She makes an appeal for a little pecuniary aid to defray the expenses of her journey, and gives information that a narrative of her life will soon be published which will undoubtedly be full of interest, as her life has been an eventful one.

R. J.

"Orange, N. J."

"Sojourner Truth addressed a good-sized audience at the Unitarian Church on Wednesday evening, Jan. 12. Mr. Clute, in introducing her, said that he had a three-fold pleasure in doing so. First, he was sure the audience would be entertained by her varied experience of more than eighty years. Secondly, the lecturer was a negro, and her presence on the platform was a living argument for the admission of her race to all the privileges of society. Thirdly, the lecturer was a woman who has for many years affirmed that woman's humanity gives her claim to education, labor, and the ballot.

"The lecturer spoke for more than an hour in her usual, humorous, common-sense style. She gave some account of her thoughts when she was a heathen, and said there was no little heathenism in the very heart of the churches to-day. She spoke of the Fatherhood of God, and of his loving care for all his children; of the brotherhood of man and of the duty of men to labor for each other. Her remarks were interspersed with anecdotes fitly illustrating the subject, and had such point and pungency as carried the truth home."

FROM A WILLIAMSBURGH (L. I.) PAPER.

"LECTURE OF A COLORED WOMAN.--The female lecturer, styling herself 'Sojourner Truth,' who was for many years a slave, delivered a lecture last evening in the Congregational Church, corner of South Third and Eleventh Streets, Williamsburgh. The lecturer, who is quite aged, commenced by saying that she was born a slave in this State, and resided on the banks of the North River, near Albany, until the time of her emancipation, which took place when she was--twenty-five years of age. During that time she had five different masters, some of whom were very severe, and she related with tears in her eyes the manner in which she had been tied up in the barn, with her clothes stripped from her back, and whipped until the blood stood in pools upon the floor; and scars upon her back were undeniable proofs of her assertion. She had been twice married, and had five children, the oldest being forty years of age. Her husbands and children were torn from her and sold into bondage, the youngest at the age of five years having been taken to Alabama. She said that she never had any learning, and while in bondage was not allowed to hear the Bible or any other books read. Her mother often told her of God, and her impressions were that God was a very large human being, who sat in the skies.

"'About a year previous to my emancipation, I ran away from my master, and went to live with Mr. Wagner; it was here that a change first came over my heart, and I felt that I was a sinner. I prayed to God, and he answered my prayers, and I have experienced his blessings. I said, I really believe I am a sinner, and that Jesus died for me. I had never been to church, and never heard any one say this. I believe my only sin consisted in wishing harm to the white folks; but now I love everybody.'

"After speaking of the condition of the colored race, she spoke of the white people, and their holding human beings in bondage, and asked how it would be with them when summoned before the bar of Judgment to answer for their deeds upon earth. The speaker also narrated the history of her mother-in-law, who was stolen from her native land in Africa and brought to this country and sold into bondage. The lecture was delivered in a simple yet affecting manner."

FROM BOSTON PAPERS.
"EMANCIPATION MEETING.

"Commemoration of the Eighth Anniversary of Negro Freedom in the United States--A Large Gathering and Eloquent Speeches in Tremont Temple, Jan. 1, 1871.

"The eighth anniversary of the emancipation of negro slaves in the United States was commemorated in Tremont Temple last evening by a large gathering and eloquent speeches, under the auspices of the National Association for the Spread of Temperance and Night Schools among the Freed People of the South. The admission was free, and at a comparatively early hour the Temple began to be filled, for 7 o'clock was the time announced for the services to commence, and seldom is there an occasion of more attraction or greater general interest. Every available space of sitting or standing room was crowded. Professor Gardiner was present.

"The platform was occupied by the Tremont Temple choir, the distinguished personages of the evening, such as Rev. J. D. Fulton, Rev. Gilbert Haven, and Rev. L. A. Grimes, and many others, not omitting to mention Sojourner Truth, of Jersey, and William Wells Brown, M. D., who has in numerous instances taken a leading position among New England's orators, and who has done a great deal to elevate the colored race a grade higher in the strata of civilization. Mr. Brown is president of the National Association above alluded to, and as a matter of course, he officiated as chairman of the meeting. The services were opened with the singing of a hymn by the choir, after which Mr. Brown read a portion of the Scriptures. Prayer was then offered by Rev. Mr. Grimes, the choir sang another hymn, and Mr. Brown made a half-hour's address.

"The Rev. J. D. Fulton was the next speaker. He congratulated the meeting upon the work of ennobling and elevating the black race, but while he did so he could not forget the perils which surrounded it in a city like Boston. This emancipation was but the beginning of a big job. Mental emancipation from the chains of ignorance was a felt necessity, and education must be given the black men now. The freedmen of the South without education will be cursed rather than blessed by the ballot. 'I do not believe,' he said, 'in anybody casting a vote in this land that cannot read and write.' (The meeting applauded.) 'Now don't you cheer me,' said Mr. Fulton, 'this is God's night, and I don't want to be cheered.'

"At this juncture there was a movement at the left end of the platform, and Rev. Gilbert Haven and Sojourner Truth appeared. Mr. Fulton turned around to the good old lady and said, indicating the seat he had occupied previous to taking the floor, 'Now, Aunty, you take this easy chair.' (Laughter and applause.) Mr. Fulton--'Now I do wish you would n't do that.' The speaker then concluded his remarks by an earnest advocacy of temperance, and further observations upon education; and at a quarter before eight o'clock left the Temple to take the train for New York."

"REMARKS BY REV. GILBERT HAVEN.

"A collection was then taken up, a hymn sung by the choir, and Rev. Gilbert Haven introduced. He had the misfortune, he said, of coming after the king (referring to Mr. Fulton) and before the queen (referring to Sojourner Truth), and of course a person in that position was of very little account except to get out of the way. But such things were matters of necessity, and he would endeavor to do his best. He dwelt at some length upon the emancipation proclamation and spoke particularly of the happiness manifested by Frederick Douglass upon the occasion of its declaration. The time of this anniversary meeting had been most appropriately chosen. It was fitting that we celebrate this great event upon a Sabbath evening, for in the Bible itself we find that the most sacred festival was on account of the deliverance from the land of bondage. The present situation of affairs must be accepted with all our hearts. If we do not so accept it, there is more danger in ourselves than we are aware of. As to our duty to the South and to the colored people, Mr. Haven said there must be a brotherly feeling everywhere. First, we must assist in Christianizing our emancipated brethren, both white and black, in the South. By so doing we shall be disarmed of our prejudice and hostility. Secondly, we must give them education. There is a passion of thirst for it there, and there are a great many ways of working it out. There's the Institute of Instruction in Washington, and freedmen's societies. But, some way or other, we must put ourselves in connection with the teacher of the

South. We need the school system. Thirdly, we must add to churches and schools prohibition. Mr. Haven spoke of the terrible system of intemperance, which prevails, and called for the immediate and unconditional extirpation of it by a rigid prohibitory law. They have got to have prohibition down South. The black men are becoming terribly demoralized by rum; and America has got to meet this issue or America goes to ruin. Boston is fast becoming a Sodom and a hell; on every side, this demoralization is occurring. There is also work to be done in Boston. We must have a national education and a national prohibition; and one thing more we need, and that is homes, lands for the freedmen. That I shall let my good friend chiefly dwell upon.

"Thus introduced, Sojourner Truth took the stand. She spoke about half an hour, substantially as follows, the piquancy of her remarks being greatly heightened by the inimitable patois, if it may be so called, of her expression:--

"TRUTHS FROM SOJOURNER TRUTH.

"'Well, chilern, I'm glad to see so many together. Ef I am eighty-three years old, I only count my age from de time dat I was 'mancipated. Then I 'gun ter live. God is a fulfillin', an' my lost time dat I lost bein' a slave was made up. W'en I was a slave I hated de w'ite pepul. My mother said to me when I was to be sole from her, "I want to tole ye dese tings dat you will allers know dat I have tole you, for dar will be a great many tings tole you after I sta't out ob dis life inter de world to come." An' I say dis to you all, for here is a great many pepul dat when I step out ob dis existence, dat you will know what you heered ole Sojourn' Truth tell you. I was boun' a slave in the State of Noo Yo'k, Ulster County, 'mong de low Dutch. W'en I was ten years old, I could n't speak a word of Inglish, an' hab no eddicati'n at all. Dere's wonder what dey has done fur me. As I tole you w'en I was sole, my master died, an' we was goin' to hab a auction. We was all brought up to be sole. My mother, my fader was very ole, my brudder younger 'en myself, an' my mother took my han'. Dey opened a canoby ob ebben, an' she sat down an' I an' my brudder sat down by her, en she says, "Look up to de moon an' stars dat shine upon you father an' upon you mother when you sole far away, an' upon you brudders an' sisters, dat is sole away," for dere was a great number ob us, an' was all sole away befor' my membrance. I asked her who had made de moon an' de stars, an' she says, "God," an' says I, Where is God? "Oh!" says she, "chile, he sits in de sky, an' he hears you w'en you ax him w'en you are away

SUPERWOMEN

from us to make your marster an' misteress good, an' he will do it."

"'When we were sole, I did what my mother told me; I said, O God, my mother tole me ef I asked you to make my marster an' misteress good, you'd do it, an' dey did n't get good. [Laughter.] Why, says I, God, mebbe you can't do it. Kill 'em. [Laughter and applause.] I did n't tink he could make dem good. Dat was de idee I had. After I made such wishes my conscience burned me. Then I wud say, O God, do n't be mad. My marster make me wicked; an' I of'm thought how pepul can do such 'bominable wicked things an' dere conscience not burn dem. Now I only made wishes. I used to tell God this--I would say, 'Now, God, ef I was you, an' you was me [laughter], and you wanted any help I'd help ye;--why done you help me? [Laughter and applause.] Well, ye see I was in want, an' I felt dat dere was no help. I know what it is to be taken in the barn an' tied up an' de blood drawed out ob yere bare back, an' I tell you it would make you think 'bout God. Yes, an' den I felt, O God, ef I was you an' you felt like I do, an' asked me for help I would help you--now why won't you help me? Trooly I done know but God has helped me. But I got no good marster ontil de las' time I was sole, an' den I found one an' his name was Jesus. Oh, I tell ye, did n't I fine a good marster when I use to feel so bad, when I use to say, O God, how ken I libe? I'm sorely 'prest both widin and widout. W'en God gi' me dat marster he healed all de wounds up. My soul rejoiced. I used to hate de w'ite pepul so, an' I tell ye w'en de lobe come in me I had so much lobe I did n't know what to lobe. Den de w'ite pepul come, an' I thought dat lobe was too good fur dem. Den I said, Yea, God, I'll lobe ev'ybuddy an' de w'ite pepul too. Ever since dat, dat lobe has continued an' kep' me 'mong de w'ite pepul. Well, 'mancipation came; we all know; can't stop to go troo de hull. I go fur adgitatin'. But I believe dere is works belong wid adgitatin', too. On'y think ob it! Ain't it wonderful dat God gives lobe enough to de Ethiopins to lobe you?

"'Now, here is de question dat I am here to-night to say. I been to Washin'ton, an' I fine out dis, dat de colud pepul dat is in Washin'tun libin on de gobernment dat de United Staas ort to gi' 'em lan' an' move 'em on it. Dey are libin on de gov'ment, an' dere is pepul takin' care of 'em costin' you so much, an' it don't benefit him 'tall. It degrades him wuss an' wuss. Therefo' I say dat these people, take an' put 'em in de West where you ken enrich 'em. I know de good pepul in de South can't take care of de negroes as dey ort to, case de ribils won't let 'em. How much better will it be for to take them culud pepul an' give 'em land? We've airnt lan' enough for a home, an' it would be a benefit for you all an' God would bless de hull ob ye for doin' it. Dey say, Let 'em take keer of derselves. Why, you've taken dat all away from 'em. Ain't got nuffin lef'. Get dese culud pepul out of Washin'tun off ob de gov'ment, an' get de ole pepul out and build dem homes in de West, where dey can feed themselves, and dey would soon be abel to be a pepul among you. Dat is my commission. Now adgitate them pepul an' put 'em dere; learn 'em to read one part of de time an' learn 'em to work de udder part ob de time.'

"At this moment a member in the audience arose and left, greatly to the disturbance of the lady, who could with difficulty make herself heard.

"'I'll hole on a while,' she said. 'Whoever is agoin' let him go. When you tell about work here, den you have to scud. [Laughter and applause.] I tell you I can't read a book, but I can read de people. [Applause.] I speak dese tings so dat when you have a paper come for you to sign, you ken sign it.'

"This was the last speech, and the services of the eighth anniversary concluded at half-past nine o'clock with the pronouncing of the benediction by Rev. Mr. Haven, a general hand-shaking and congratulating on the platform, and a discussion with Sojourner Truth, whom her questioners found as apt and keen at repartee as she had proved herself to be while in attendance upon the Woman's Bazar last week."--Boston Post.

For many years she has been blessed with the friendship and sympathy of the widely known and justly revered Rev. Gilbert Haven, whom she met during her last visit in Boston. At this time he made her a present of Zion's Herald, a paper of extensive circulation, to the reading of which she listens with great pleasure.

"WOMAN'S SUFFRAGE ASSOCIATION.--This morning's session of the Woman's Right's Convention was opened at ten o'clock. After the transaction of some business, Col. T. W. Higginson, of Newport, was introduced to the audience, mostly composed of ladies, whose number increased as the hour advanced. The main object of the speaker was to rally the women of our State and induce them to come forward in the defense of their own rights. As one result of female eloquence, he said, Mrs. Lucy Stone had succeeded in melting the heart of the chairman of the judiciary committee in our general assembly. At the conclusion of Col. Higginson's address a string of resolutions was introduced bearing on the question of Woman's Suffrage. Sojourner Truth, who was sitting on the platform, was invited to speak, and made one of her characteristic addresses, favoring a grant of land to the freedmen of Washington, and such a provision of educational privileges as will tend to the elevation of this unfortunate class.

"The great speech of the morning was made by Mrs. Livermore, of Boston, whose statement of facts was better than any labored argument. Her account of the restricted female suffrage in Kansas was highly interesting and instructive. The women in that State are allowed to vote in matters pertaining to public schools, and they use their privileges for the promotion of good education, and really out-wit the men in carrying their points. In the territory of Wyoming, where female suffrage is secured, the women have joined en masse in favor of temperance and morality, defeating the vile demagogues who strove for office, and electing persons whose character and principles are a guaranty of public order and security."

Another journal speaks of Sojourner Truth's presence at this meeting thus:--

"Mrs. Paulina W. Davis said they had a venerable lady on the platform who commenced her life a slave, was forty years in that condition, and since that time had labored for the emancipation of her race.

"Sojourner Truth, who seems to carry her weight of years very heartily, said she was somewhat pleased to come before them to bear testimony, although she had a limited time--only a few minutes--but as many friends wanted to hear Sojourner's voice, she thought she would accept the offer. She spoke when the spirit moved her--not when the people moved her, but when the spirit moved her--for when she was limited to a few minutes, the people moved her. She was in the woman movement, for she was a woman herself. The Friend said that woman ought to have her rights for her own benefit, she ought to have them, not only for her own benefit, but for the benefit of the whole creation, not only the women, but all the men on the face of the earth, for they were the mothers of them. Therefore she ought to have her God-given right, and be the equal of men, for she was the resurrection of them. There was another question which lay near her heart, and that was the condition of the poor colored people around Washington, remnants of the slavery which was ended by the war. Sojourner earnestly urged that land be given to these poor people in order that they might be made self-supporting, and concluded her remarks by saying, in her naive way, that she would stop before she was stopped."

"THE AMERICAN SIBYL.--Sojourner Truth, whom Mrs. Stowe has honored with the title of 'The American Sibyl,' is spending a few days in our city, and we hope our citizens will have the pleasure of listening to her graphic descriptions of the condition of the freedmen of the city of Washington, where she spent three years during the war in nursing and teaching the poor soldiers and the emancipated people who followed the army. She has been there again recently, endeavoring in her zeal and goodness of heart to help the aged colored people to find comfortable homes in some rural district. She has spoken in nearly all the cities, and has just come from Fall River, where she spoke in two of the churches to large and enthusiastic audiences, who listened with delight to the words of wit and wisdom which fell from the lips of the ancient colored philosopher. She was, as is well known, a slave in New York the first forty years of her life, and since her emancipation and remarkable conversion to Christianity, she has labored unceasingly for the good of her race and for oppressed humanity everywhere."

"PERSONAL.--'Sister Sojourner Truth' was in town yesterday and visited the Woman Suffrage Bazaar, where she could not resist the movings of the spirit to say a few words upon her 'great mission,' which now is to 'stir up the United States to give the colored people about Washington, and who are largely supported by charity, a tract of land down South, where they can support themselves.' She don't believe in keeping them paupers, and thinks they have earned land enough for white people in past days to be entitled

to a small farm apiece themselves. She says she is going to accomplish her mission in this respect before she dies, and she wants an opportunity to address the people of Boston and to get up petitions to Congress in its favor. She means to 'send tons of paper down to Washington for them spouters to chaw on.' Sojourner believes in women's voting, and thinks the men are very pretentious in denying them the right. Still she thinks there has been a great change for the better in this respect the last few years. She is rather severe on the sterner sex, and asks, by way of capping her argument in favor of her sex: 'Did Jesus ever say anything against women? Not a word. But he did speak awful hard things against the men. You know what they were. And he knew them to be true. But he did n't say nothing 'gainst de women.' And solacing herself with this reflection the old heroine retired to admire the beautiful bouquets in the flower department of the Fair."

"Sojourner Truth, now in her eighty-third year, gave a thrilling address at the Fair--in the Phillips' Street Church (Rev. Mr. Grime's) on Monday evening. It was unique, witty, pathetic, sensible; and, aged as she is, was delivered with a voice that, in volume and tone, was equally remarkable and striking.

"Rev. Norwood Damon succeeded her in a speech of great eloquence and power. The subject was the dependent condition and the hindrances to education of the blacks in Washington and the South, and the duty of the government to open avenues and furnish inducements to a better civilization and manhood. The venerable Sojourner will renew the subject at a public meeting in Rev. Mr. Grime's church this evening."

"The first forty years of her life were spent in slavery in the State of New York. She became free when slavery was abolished in that State, and has devoted the remainder of her life to the cause of the freedom of her race. She is now at this advanced age engaged in a mission for their welfare. She wants the government, instead of feeding them as now, to put them on land of their own, as it does the Indians, and teach them to work for themselves. Unless this be done, she thinks the jails and penitentiaries will have to be increased. It is the only way to prevent a large amount of misery, degradation and crime in the present and future generations. She carries with her three small books in which she has inscribed the autographs of nearly all the eminent people in America. This she proposes sometime to have printed in fac similes. She calls them the 'Book of Life.' "

FROM N. Y. AND PHILADELPHIA PAPERS.

"SOJOURNER TRUTH.--Sojourner Truth was born a slave in the family of Colonel Hardenburgh, near Swatakill, in Ulster County, New York, and sold away from her family when about ten years old. She remained in Ulster County forty years, a slave, and had, during that time, numerous owners. She obtained her freedom under the Act of Emancipation in the State of New York. After her freedom, she lived in the city of New York a number of years, and in Massachusetts, at Northampton, about twenty years. During all this time she traveled through every section of the country, laboring to promote the welfare of her race. She worked without fee or reward. She then went to Michigan, where she has resided since that time. She has devoted her life to the interest of her suffering race. During the war, under President Lincoln's administration, she spent her time among the freedmen in and around Washington, teaching the women how to perform their domestic duties. She is now over eighty years, and has secured a little home at Battle Creek, in Michigan. The past summer she purchased a barn, and had it converted into a comfortable dwelling house. It is encumbered with a mortgage of nine hundred dollars, and to clear this place of debt, she is now on a visit to her friends, and proposes to visit President Grant, at Washington. Sojourner is remarkably active and bright for a person of her age. She has endured much hardship, and deserves the aid of her friends."

--Frank Leslie's Illustrated Paper.

"SOJOURNER TRUTH.--This remarkable colored lady addressed rather a small audience in the Methodist Church on Tuesday evening. It was small because it had not been sufficiently advertised; hence, comparatively few knew of her presence. Sojourner is a perfect type of her race, uneducated, but possessed of strong common sense. She was a slave forty years of her life, and when liberated, and an attempt was made to educate her, she declares she could never get beyond her a, b, abs. She is now eighty-three years old, and has been a public speaker for a great many many years. She spoke in Phoenixville some twenty years ago, in the old M. E. Church, and has ever since been anxious to do so again. In her address that evening she stated that she had in her wanderings inquired now and then concerning her friend Elijah F. Pennypacker, because she knew so long as he lived she would if she visited this section have a place wherever she could 'put the sole of her foot.' She spoke in high terms of the Methodist people of West Chester, and especially of their minister, the Rev. Mr. Best, and said he was n't like the majority of preachers, who was n't in their element unless they were 'spouting,' but he was satisfied to sit at her feet and to learn the truth as she knew it. Sojourner was in the anti-slavery movement in its palmiest days, and was associated with the shining lights of that struggle, and now that the wildest dreams of those she considered enthusiastic have been abundantly realized, she has turned her attention to the amelioration of her race, and considers her mission to be the establishment of a home for old and feeble colored people in the far West, for which purpose she is endeavoring to arouse public sentiment and to interest the government.

"On Thursday afternoon she addressed the ladies of the neighborhood in the Friends' meeting-house, at the corner stores."

"SOJOURNER TRUTH.--Earnest, self-sacrificing devotion to principle, especially when its scope is to benefit humanity, is always an object of the deepest interest, whatever the race, color or condition of the individual exemplifying it. This fact explains why a large and highly respectable audience assembled last night in the Friends' Meeting House, on Lombard Street, and listened with the deepest attention to the utterances of an old colored woman, who was a slave for forty years. That old colored woman was so earnest, so fearless and untiring a laborer for her race during the long contest between freedom and slavery that she is known and loved by thousands in every State in the Union. Very black, and without much education, she has remarkable faith in God, wonderfully clear perceptions of moral right and wrong, the most devoted love for the poor and needy, and the most untiring determination to carry forward plans for the amelioration of the condition of her race.

"She last night gave startling pictures of the degradation and suffering among the colored people at

Washington and elsewhere; showed that it would pay the nation to transform those paupers into industrious, moral citizens, and concluded by detailing her plan for doing that work, and stating the objections made to it. She stated that she desired to hold a number of meetings here to induce the colored people who are in better circumstances to do something to further the best interests of the unfortunate of their race.

"When she had concluded, Mr. John Needles stated that the old lady paid her expenses in her present work by selling her photograph, whereupon a number of persons went forward and bought copies.

"Sojourner Truth jocularly denies that she ever nursed General Washington, but she says she 'has done quit' telling people how old she is. 'Sometimes folks just quit growing and stop as they is, and I specs that I has jis quit growing old and keeps on de same all de time.' This is Sojourner's explanation of her remarkable longevity."

A Pennsylvania paper thus mentions another of her meetings:--

"Old Sojourner Truth was here last Thursday night and preached a good sermon in the Methodist Church. A tremendous crowd assembled to hear and see her, and were all pleased with her address and the manner in which it was delivered."

FROM ROCHESTER PAPERS.

"A LECTURE BY SOJOURNER TRUTH.--This aged negress lectured in Rochester, N. Y., recently, and the Democrat and Chronicle gives this account of her effort:--

" 'Her appearance reminds one vividly of Dinah in "Uncle Tom's Cabin." A white handkerchief was tied closely about her head and she wore spectacles, but this was the only indication of her extreme age. Her voice is strong, has no touch of shrillness, and she walked about as hale and hearty as a person of half her years. She said her object was to arouse attention to the wants of the freedmen. Their condition at Washington was pitiful. No work could be found for them, and their children were growing up in ignorance. She described the treatment they had received during the war, even after they were freed. "The poor creeters were heaped together" with no food but a ration of bread. Children were taken away from their mothers, and when the latter complained, they were thrust into the guard-house. She went among them, and when she told them they were free, they did not understand her. After drawing a vivid picture of the sufferings of the freedmen and their unfortunate condition, even at the present time, she said: "You ask me what to do for dem? Do you want a poor old creeter who do' no how to read to tell edecated people what to do? I give you de hint, and you ought to know what to do. But if you do n't, I kin tell you. De government hab given land to de railroads in de West; can't it do as much for these poor creeters? Let 'em give 'em land and an outset, and hab teachers learn 'em to read. Den they can be somebody. Dat's what I want. You owe it to dem, because you took away from dem all dey earned and made 'em what they are. You take no interest in de colored people. I was forty years a slave in de State of New York, and was 'mancipated 'long wid de odder culered people of the State.

" 'You are de cause of de brutality of these poor creeters. For you're de children of those who enslaved dem. Dat's what I want to say. I wish dis hall was full to hare me. I do n't want to say anything agin Anna Dickinsin because she is my friend, but if she come to talk here about a woman you know nothing about, and no one knows whether there was such a woman* or not, you would fill dis place. You want to hear nonsense. I come to tell something which you ought to listen to. You are ready to help de heathen in foreign lands, but don't care for the heathen right about you. I want you to sign petitions to send to Washington. Dey say there dey will do what de people want. The majority rules. If dey want anything good dey git it. If dey want anything not right dey git it too. You send these petitions, and those men in Congress will have something to spout about. I bin to hear 'em; could make nothing out of what dey said, but if dey talk about de colored people I will know what dey say. Send a good man wid de petitions, one dat will not turn de other side out when he gits to Washington. Let de freedmen be emptied out in de West; gib 'em land an' an outset; teach 'em to read, an' den dey will be somebody. Dat's wat I want to say.' "

* Miss Dickinson's lecture upon Joan of Arc.

"SOJOURNER TRUTH.--Let no one fail to hear the lecture of this remarkable woman in Corinthian Hall, on Thursday evening of this week. Her subject is the condition of the freed colored people dependent on the government. Having spent several years among them, she knows whereof she speaks. She was for forty years a slave in the State of New York. Wholly uneducated, her eloquence is that of nature, inspired by earnest zeal in her Heaven-appointed mission. She speaks to crowded houses everywhere; let Rochester give her a cordial reception."

"SOJOURNER TRUTH.--The lecture of this remarkable colored woman comes off at Corinthian Hall, on Thursday evening, 4th inst. The lecturer is a child of nature, gifted beyond the common measure, witty, shrewd, sarcastic, with an open, broad honesty of heart, and unbounded kindness.

"Wholly untaught in the schools, she is herself a study for the philosophers, and a wonder to all. Her natural powers of observation, discrimination, comparison, and intuition are rare indeed, and only equaled by her straightforward common sense and earnest practical benevolence. She is always sensible, always suggestive, always original, earnest, and practical, often eloquent and profound. Her lecture will be in behalf of her people, and whoever would be edified, entertained, and even amused, without frivolity, would do well to be present."

"SOJOURNER TRUTH.--This celebrated colored woman spoke at Lyceum Hall, Sunday evening, to an audience of several hundred people. Her subject was her own experience, more particularly her religious experience. She is now about eighty-three years old, though she looks much younger. She is unable to read or write, and in her manner and style is perfectly natural and original. She acts and speaks with the simplicity and innocence of a child, and seems to have nothing to conceal. Her motives she speaks out without hesitation. Her religious experience was very beautiful, and was told in a style that defies imitation. To be appreciated it must be heard, for nobody can repeat it. Her religion is of an exceedingly practical character, and consists in doing good to others. 'How can you expect to do good to God,' she asked, 'unless you first learn to do good to each other'? In regard to God, she says she feels that he is all around her; that we live in him as the fishes live in the sea.

"Speaking of death, she compared it--her countenance fairly lighting up with emotion--to stepping out of one room into another, stepping out into the light. 'Oh,' said she, 'won't that be glorious!'

"SOJOURNER TRUTH TALKS TO LADIES.

"Sojourner spoke to a company of ladies at Association Hall, on Wednesday afternoon. She portrayed in forcible language the vice and degradation in which the war has left the poor blacks. Ignorant and debased, they cannot be made to understand that they are responsible human beings, but continue the debased practices that marked their slave life. She endeavored to enlist the sympathies of her hearers in behalf of the black women of the South, and related many incidents connected with her efforts to find homes for them in the West. She had succeeded in providing for a hundred in this manner. At the conclusion of her address the ladies present took Sojourner by the hand and gave her pecuniary aid as well as words of encouragement."

FROM A SYRACUSE PAPER.

"SOJOURNER TRUTH.

"To the Editor of the Syracuse Journal:-

"It affords me great pleasure to announce to the Christian people of Syracuse that Sojourner Truth is in this city, and will address the people upon the 'Condition of the South,' to-morrow (Friday) evening, at 7½ o'clock.

"This remarkable woman at the age of eighty years is as eloquent as ever, and all who desire to see and hear her should take this opportunity, which will probably be the last one afforded in this city.

"The officers and pastor of the Fourth Presbyterian Church have kindly proffered their fine audience room, which is so central that it will doubtless be filled very early in the evening.

"Sojourner Truth is too well known to need any endorsements, but I was greatly pleased yesterday to read that of the martyr president--so characteristic of Lincoln--'For Aunty.'

"Sojourner Truth--let the Christian people hear her.

Yours, truly,

A. F. B."

FROM BATTLE CREEK PAPERS.

"FIRST OF AUGUST.--The colored people of Battle Creek and vicinity will observe the 39th anniversary of the emancipation of the slaves of the British West Indies by a picnic at St. Mary's Lake, interspersed with boat riding, 'swinging in the lane,' &c. W. Sweeney has been invited to deliver the oration of the day, followed by 'Aunt Sojourner Truth' and others. The festivities of the day will be concluded by a grand Grant and Wilson club ball, at Stuart Hall, under the immediate supervision of the officers of the club. G. Long is the chairman of the committee of arrangements.

"Sojourner Truth asserts that if ever the Augean stables of our political temple are to be cleared, it must be done by woman, and that it never will be clean until she is admitted to full fellowship therein.

"This well-known and venerable old lady called to see us Thursday afternoon and to subscribe for the Journal. She leaves for Ohio in a few days to lecture upon her favorite topic, that of providing a home for the colored people in and about Washington by granting them a tract of land in the West. Sojourner has been stumping for Grant, and says that if such a strange occurrence as the election of Greeley should happen, she will remove to Canada."--Battle Creek, Journal.

"REPUBLICAN MEETING--SOJOURNER TRUTH.

"On Tuesday evening, Sojourner Truth addressed the people of Hillsdale upon political topics at the courthouse. The attendance was immense, not half the throng were able to get seats, and hundreds went away without even gaining admittance. The old lady was somewhat 'scattering' in her remarks but she kept firing away, and occasionally a winged duck went out of the crowd, shrieking. The principal points touched were the slanders against President Grant, the inconsistent relations assumed by Greeley, Sumner, Blair, and others, and the duties of the colored voters. The audience, in the best humor, applauded and cheered the speaker.

"Sojourner Truth, on the Saturday before the recent election, appeared before the Board of Registration, in the third ward where she resides, and claimed the right to have her name entered upon the list of electors. Upon being refused, she repaired to the polls on election day in the same ward and again asserted her right to the ballot. She was politely received by the authorities in both instances, but did not succeed in her effort, though she sustained her claim by many original and quaintly put arguments. Sojourner states that she learned one thing by her visit to the polls on the 5th inst. She verily thought before that day that a literal pole was erected to designate the voting place, and she asked the bystanders to point it out. Her astonishment on being undeceived, as described to us by her own lips and in her characteristic style, is peculiarly amusing. It is Sojourner's determination to continue the assertion of her right, until she gains it."--Battle Creek Journal.

SUPERWOMEN

FROM DETROIT PAPERS.

"SOJOURNER TRUTH.

"A veteran worker--her 'mission'--the colored paupers about Washington and what to do with them.

"For several days past, Sojourner Truth--the 'Libyan Sibyl,' as Mrs. Stowe has aptly termed her--has been the guest of Mrs. Nanette B. Gardner, on Howard Street, where many friends, and strangers as well, have called to see and converse with this veteran worker in the cause of her own race. Already past fourscore years and ten, she yet maintains a constitution and mind unimpaired, and has an amount of vigor that betokens a 'green old age' indeed. Those who have before heard her lectures, will doubtless remember well the strong, and yet well-modulated voice, and the characteristic expressions in which she delivers her addresses, as well as the pith and point of her spicy sentences.

"To all calling upon her, she asks the question, 'Do n't you want to write your name in de Book of Life?' to which query, the counter one in relation to the same 'Book of Life,' is generally put, and Sojourner is usually gratified by the chirography of her visitor, in some manner, according to the pleasure of the writer. The book in question contains scores on scores of names, of different individuals throughout the country, including many persons of note, senators, authors, politicians, etc. Foremost in the list is Lucretia Mott's, who signs herself a 'co-laborer in the cause of our race.' Also that of

Senator Revel, of Mississippi, of Senators Morrill, Pomeroy, Henry Wilson, of Massachusetts, Patterson, of New Hampshire, and numerous others.

"Among the first and most treasured is that of the late President Lincoln, who has inscribed in his hurried style, 'For Aunty Sojourner Truth. A. Lincoln, October 29, 1864.' From President Grant, who, she declares, 'was in a most drefful hurry to put down his name,' on being asked to write in the 'Book of Life;' written in his hurried manner, are the lines, 'Sojourner Truth. U. S. Grant, March 31, 1870.' There are letters from Gerritt Smith, Wm. Lloyd Garrison, et id genus omne, and also a few lines each from Vice President Colfax, Theodore Tilton, Mrs. Elizabeth Tilton, and many others. Sojourner has 'views' as well as others, and does not hesitate to promulgate them. She is in most respects radical, and believes in the temperance movement, woman suffrage, and has no faith whatever in the 'New Departure' movement, as announced of late in the main plank in the Democratic platform. The constant and repeated inquiry made by visitors, as to her age, she considers as somewhat trying, as it is what she has done and is to do, that she considers of the most importance. In connection with this, she mentions that when in Brooklyn last spring Theodore Tilton called upon her, and in the course of conversation proposed that he should write her life, a proposition which did not meet her views, and which she did not accordingly accept, but replied in effect that she expected to live a long time yet, and was going to accomplish 'lots' before she died, and did n't wan't to be 'written up' at present.

"Sojourner calls Battle Creek her home, but as she is constantly on the move, she visits that place but seldom. Her great object, she says, in visiting this city and others, is to 'stir up' the people and interest them in her long-desired object of procuring a home for the aged and infirm--particularly colored people--who are now in and around Washington, and wholly dependent upon the government for support.

"Sojourner is to remain a short time only in Detroit, going from here westward on the same mission which induced her to come here. In the course of her travels she intends visiting Kansas, in order to prospect the land."

"About a year ago, Sojourner commenced her lectures in behalf of this object, in Providence, since which time she has lectured in many towns and cities throughout the country. Concerning this, she says that not much encouragement is given her, except the constant adjuration to talk to the people, and 'stir 'em up,' and adds, 'why don't you stir 'em up? as tho' an old body like myself could do all the stirring.'

"In relation to the subject, she states that there are hundreds of colored people in the city of Washington, who, from being cared for, and clothed, and fed by the government, have become apathetic and indifferent, and all they care for is to lead the hum-drum, hand-to-mouth existence that calls for no action on their part. Hundreds of children are brought up in a shiftless manner, and, believing that the government will provide for them, they help swell the constantly increasing number of paupers. Without friends or homes, they are sent to some of the numerous asylums in Washington which are provided for them, and thus manage to exist, but have no thought or care as to how they are to do hereafter. When urged to go North, away from Washington, the invariable reply, at least of nearly all of the able-bodied men in particular is, 'What fo' I go way? gubernment feed me, gib me close, I's doin' well enuff,' and so say they all, or at least a great part of them.

"That a new order of things may be established, Sojourner proposes to excite such an interest as shall not fail in the end to accomplish her purpose.

"As showing what a large number are fed at government expense during the winter, at least when there is little or no work, she states that last season there were from 600 to 700 loaves of bread given daily in each ward, to the colored people, who had in many cases only this to depend upon for sustenance. The following extract from a letter written by Mrs. C. A. F. Stebbins, to the editor of the National Standard, shows the condition of things then existing, and which is no better at the commencement of each winter, and, as Sojourner claims, is even growing worse:-"To the Editor of the National Standard:--

"'There could be no wider possible gulf between Dives and Lazarus, in the day when the impoverished and despised craved the crumbs which fell from the rich man's table, than here this very day in the court center of the republic, where women are starving for bread, while after all the regular nourishing meals of the day, evening tables are heaped high with luxuries from every clime, and hundreds are invited to share, but they are the hundreds who have plenty upon their own boards at home. . . . .

"'I am thankful, dear Standard, that I do not believe the Dives of Washington city will ever go to the burning gulf as did Dives in the parable; or that they will ever lack for a kind and tender hand to administer the cup of cold water in the future world; but I cannot say, in the turning and constant revolutions of the wheel, that I believe all will be so fortunate in this, for experience in the valley of humility saves, no doubt, some bitter regret, and necessitates reflections on wasted opportunities which may lead to the realization that all are brothers, and human wants are ever the same.'

"Sojourner proposes to solicit government aid, in the way of having some portion of the as yet unoccupied lands of the West donated for the purpose as set forth in the petition first mentioned, and there to have suitable buildings erected, and schools established where the now dependent thousands of colored people may go, and not only attain an independence for themselves, but become educated and respectable citizens, instead of the 'trash'-- as she denominates the humbug idlers in Washington-- which their dependence on government aid and bounty renders them.

"Sojourner intends remaining in Detroit several days longer, during which time, if a hall or suitable place can be provided, she will give a lecture on the subject described, and will doubtless attract even more than on the occasion of her last appearance in Detroit, in '68."-- Detroit Post.

"SOJOURNER TRUTH.

"This remarkable woman, born a slave in the State of New York more than eighty years ago, and emancipated in 1827, will speak in the lecture room of the Unitarian Church, corner of Shelby Street and Lafayette Avenue, on Monday evening, to any who will choose to hear her. Her lecture will be highly entertaining and impressive. She is a woman of strong religious nature, with an entirely original eloquence and humor, possessed of a weird imagination, of most grotesque but strong, clear mind, and one who, without the aid of reading or writing, is strangely susceptible to all that in thought and action is now current in the world. At the antislavery and women's-rights meetings she has been one of the chief attractions, and her shrewd good sense, mixed with oddities of speech and whimsical illustrations, never fail of producing a sympathetic interest as well as exciting the curiosity of the audience. Her life has been one of extreme vicissitudes, and a great portion of it full of hardship. She has been a true and eloquent friend of her race, and a practical and efficient counselor and assistant in their moral and religious training. Her work in the freedmen's camps at Washington and in Virginia, during the war, was very valuable and much esteemed. She was a staunch friend of Mr. Lincoln, and he gave her many words of encouragement and praise. We advise our friends to attend her 'lecture,' at the Unitarian Church, if they desire to be instructed, amused, and gratified by one of the most original, if, indeed, not one of the most marvelous, persons of the time. All she does and says is, as she believes, inspired by the Almighty, and she connects with his direct agency the events and circumstances which surround and control her. She now resides at Battle Creek, Michigan."--Detroit Post.

In a notice of the lecture the Post said:--

"Sojourner mentioned that the Rev. Gilbert Haven, of Boston, had volunteered to take charge of all the petitions signed and forward them to Congress in due form, that they might be presented before Congress in such a way as to demand both attention and action. She hoped to find some one, among those assembled to hear her lecture, who would also aid her in this respect. The Rev. Charles Foote, chaplain of the House of Correction, thereupon offered to collect and forward all petitions which should be signed, to Washington, which offer was thankfully accepted by the lecturer.

"After the lecture several of those interested went upon the platform and interviewed Sojourner, to all of whom she gave a cordial welcome, and conversed in her characteristic style."

FROM THE N. Y. TRIBUNE.

"SOJOURNER TRUTH AT WORK.

"To the Editor of the Tribune:--

"SIR: Seeing an item in your paper about me, I thought I would give you the particulars of what I am trying to do, in hopes that you would print a letter about it and so help on the good cause. I am urging the people to sign petitions to Congress to have a grant of land set apart for the freed people to earn their living on, and not be dependent on the government for their bread. I have had fifty petitions printed at my own expense, and have been urging the people of the Eastern States for the past seven months. I have been crying out in the East, and now an answer comes to me from the West, as you will see from the following letter. The gentleman who writes it I have never seen or heard of before, but the Lord has raised him up to help me. Bless the Lord! I made up my mind last winter, when I saw able men and women taking dry bread from the government to keep from starving, that I would devote myself to the cause of getting land for these people, where they can work and earn their own living in the West, where the land is so plenty. Instead of going home from Washington to take rest, I am traveling around getting it before the people.

"Instead of sending these people to Liberia, why can't they have a colony in the West? This is why I am contending so in my old age. It is to teach the people that this colony can just as well be in this country as in

Liberia. Everybody says this is a good work, but nobody helps. How glad I will be if you will take hold and give it a good lift. Please help me with these petitions. Yours truly,

"SOJOURNER TRUTH.

"Florence, Mass., Feb. 18, 1871.

"P. S. I should have said that the Rev. Gilbert Haven of Boston is kindly aiding me in getting petitions signed, and will receive all petitions signed in Massachusetts and send them to Congress. S. T."

"TOPEKA, KANSAS, Dec. 31, 1870.

"SOJOURNER TRUTH.--Dear Madam: I know so much of you by reputation, and venerate and love so much your character, that I am induced to write this. I say I know so much of you, which is true, but it is only by report, as I have never had the pleasure of meeting you yet. My object in writing this is to ask and earnestly request that you make our town a visit. I would very much like to have you come to my house and make it your home as long as you can be contented. If you will say you will come, I will send you the price of your railroad fare and enough to pay additional expenses. Please let me hear from you, and, if possible, convey the good intelligence that you will come and see us. Yours, very respectfully,

"B. M. S."

SUPERWOMEN

"SOJOURNER TRUTH IN SPRINGFIELD.

"Those who remember Mrs. Stowe's graphic sketch of 'Sojourner Truth, the Libyan Sibyl,' in the Atlantic some years ago, will be interested to see and hear her. She is now visiting at Dr. Church's on Elm Street, for a few days, and will address an audience at Institute Hall, to-night, on her chosen subject, the sufferings of the old colored people and children in Washington, and how to relieve them. She is one of the most original and effective speakers, though an unlettered woman, and all her early life a slave in New York. She is now between seventy and eighty years old, and has outlived many of her thirteen children, but her eye is not dim nor her natural force abated in proportion to her years, and her deep, powerful voice has the same effect as formerly in moving an audience. She says, however, that this is the last time she shall speak in Massachusetts; she is now on her way to a friend of hers and her cause in Kansas, and at her age she never expects to return here. Her object in holding meetings is, not to raise money, but to stir up the people to petition Congress to show humanity to the old and helpless of her race. She has spent much time in Washington, and knows by observation the misery of the colored people there, and she wants Congress to provide a tract of land for them in some Western State and remove them to it, where they can live frugally and support themselves, instead of depending upon charity at Washington. We hope our citizens will avail themselves of this opportunity to see and hear one of the most remarkable women of our time--a true sibyl, as Mrs.

Stowe calls her, but a Christian sibyl, and more devoted to good words and works than to obscure predictions. Her book of autographs contains those of Abraham Lincoln, Gen. Grant, Mr. Garrison, and a great many other eminent men and women, living or dead, and is a curious memento of her life."

"SOJOURNER TRUTH'S LECTURE

"At Franklin Hall, last evening, was in the main an exhortation to all interested in the elevation of the blacks to petition the authorities at Washington for land out West whereon to locate the surplus freedmen, and let them earn their own living, which she argued would be cheaper and better for the government than to care for them in any other way. Her matter and manner were simply indescribable, often straying far away from the starting point; but each digression was fraught with telling logic, rough humor, or effective sarcasm. She thought she had a work to do, and had considerable faith in what she was accomplishing; but she said to her audience, 'With all your opportunities for readin' and writin,' you do n't take hold and do anything. My God, I wonder what you are in the world for!' She had infinite faith in the influence which the majority had with Congress and believed that whatever they demanded, good or bad, Congress would grant; hence she was working to make majorities. She leaves the East soon never to return, and goes to Kansas where the Lord had plainly called her by prompting a man whom she had never seen or heard of to invite her and pay her expenses. Her enthusiasm over the prospect was unbounded, and she said that, like the New Jerusalem, if she didn't find the West all she had expected, she would have a good time thinking about it. A good deal of sound orthodox theology was mingled with her discourse, as well as a description of her visit to the White House, and the reformation she effected in the Washington horse-car system. The whole was followed by a valedictory song in true plantation style. A large and interested audience was present to get the benefit of her remarks."

"Her views on the question of woman's dress and the prevailing fashions are interesting. They are substantially these: 'I'm awful hard on dress, you know. Women, you forget that you are the mothers of creation; you forget your sons were cut off like grass by the war, and the land was covered with their blood; you rig yourselves up in panniers and Grecian-bend backs and flummeries; yes, and mothers and gray-haired grandmothers wear high-heeled shoes and humps on their heads, and put them on their babies, and stuff them out so that they keel over when the wind blows. O mothers, I'm ashamed of ye! What will such lives as you live do for humanity? When I saw them women on the stage at the Woman's Suffrage Convention, the other day, I thought, What kind of reformers be you, with goose-wings on your heads, as if you were going to fly, and dressed in such ridiculous fashion, talking about reform and women's rights? 'Pears to me, you had better reform yourselves first. But Sojourner is an old body, and will soon get out of this world into another, and wants to say when she gets there, Lord, I have done my duty, I have told the whole truth and kept nothing back.'"

In another issue the Tribune says:-

"Mrs. Sojourner Truth, a venerable colored woman, who has been heard before, gave her testimony the other day, in Providence, against the flummery and folly of 'feminine vestments,' and specially did she rebuke the 'women on the stage at the Woman's Suffrage Convention.' Hark to her!

"'When I saw them women on the stage at the Woman's Suffrage Convention, the other day, I thought, What kind of reformers be you, with goose wings on your heads, as if you were going to fly, and dresses in such ridiculous fashion, talking about reform and women's rights? 'Pears to me you had better reform yourselves first.'"

"Just before this, Mrs. Sojourner had freed her mind respecting 'panniers and Grecian-bend backs, high-heeled shoes, and humps on the head.' We should earnestly join in Mrs. Truth's protest against the manifold absurdities of woman's clothing, if we thought reform possible; but we do n't. There has been no simplicity of attire since our grandmother Eve made her first apron of fig-leaves."

"THE FASHIONS.

"Sojourner says that 'the women wear two heads on their shoulders with but little if any brains in either.' She knew of a young woman who had her hair cut on account of an impotency in her head and eyes. After the hair was cut, she put it into a net and wore it for a waterfall--getting rest for the head only during the night. Her hair grew again but still she continued to wear the extra hair with the addition of several skeins of stocking or other sort of yarn. Her impotencies of course 'grew no better' very fast. Perhaps there is no truer saying than that 'folly is a fund that will never lose ground while fools are so rife in the nation.' The trouble of the thing is, or the reason why we have the trouble is, that the priests are dumb dogs and dare not bark or bring out the truths of the gospel against such gigantic evils, as war, slavery, and the prided fashions. We leave Sojourner Truth with her intuitiveness and without the letter, to battle almost alone these world-wide evils. May Heaven bless and sustain her in her humanitarian work and 'God-like mission.' SELAHOMMAH."

Accompanied by her grandson, Samuel Banks, she left Battle Creek in Sept., 1871, for her western trip to Kansas. Frequently stopping by the way to hold meetings, they at length reached Kansas, where she was cordially received by her new friend, Mr. Smith, as well as by friends of earlier date, whom she had known in Massachusetts and Michigan. Her stay in this State was rendered most agreeable by the attentions of kind and sympathizing people, who spared no pains to make her visit both pleasant and profitable. The newspaper reporters did not neglect her, as the following extracts will show:--

FROM KANSAS PAPERS.

"'Sojourner Truth' is the name of a man now lecturing in Kansas City. He could only be called a 'sojourner' there, for truth could not abide in that place long as a permanent resident."--St. Louis Dispatch.

"Considerable ignorance is displayed in the first sentence, and an unusual regard for truth in the last."--Leavenworth Times, Jan. 18, 1872.

"Ignorance of the sex of this noted personage, Sojourner Truth, by the writer of the above, is proof of wonderful lack of general information. Certainly, knowledge does not sojourn in that head, and truth without knowledge has but poor dispatch in the affairs of men and women."--Kansas City Journal, Jan. 19, 1872.

"SOJOURNER TRUTH'S TALK.--There was a large attendance at the Opera House last night to listen to Sojourner Truth. Her mission, although not very intelligently stated by her, is to secure petitions to Congress to set apart a portion of the public domain for the occupation of such of the blacks as are still living on the bounty of the government in and around Washington. Sojourner's plan seems to be to have this class of 'contrabands' dealt with much in the same way as are the various tribes of Indians who occupy reservations and are being taught to support themselves.

"As the lecturer announced her intention of speaking again and again in Topeka, we will not prestate her arguments but permit them to be brought out by her in her own way.

"That she is a remarkable woman, all who have kept pace with the history of the past thirty years know, and being known, her persistent efforts will undoubtedly secure thousands of names to her pet petition.

"She also gave her views upon temperance, favoring prohibition. As to woman suffrage she declared that the world would never be correctly governed until equal rights were declared, and that as men have been endeavoring for years to govern alone, and have not yet succeeded in perfecting any system, it is about time the women should take the matter in hand."

A Topeka, Kansas, paper says:--

"SOJOURNER TRUTH:--The Temperance Society of this village have secured this remarkable colored woman to lecture here on Monday evening, Feb. 24, 1872. None should fail to hear her. For years she has been widely known. As the companion and peer of the great antislavery leaders during the dark days of the nation's struggle for freedom, she has made for herself a national reputation. Born in slavery, with no opportunities for improvement save those which come of poverty and wretchedness, she is with her rich imagination and shrewd good sense but what the oppressed race might become under circumstances fitted to develop their peculiar gifts. The music, which greeted her childish ears, was the imperious voice of her pretended master and the crack of the driver's whip; but it failed to crush out the spirit of eloquence and poetry with which nature had endowed her. Says Harriet Beecher Stowe concerning her: 'I never knew a person who possessed so much of that subtle, controlling personal power, called presence, as she.' Wendell Phillips says of her that he has known a few words from her to electrify an audience and affect them as he never saw persons affected by another party.

"Come and see and hear this peculiar, imaginative, yet strong and stalwart, daughter of the tropics. The lecture will be given in the Congregational Church, and upon the subject of temperance. We hope to see a full house."

She left Kansas in Feb., 1872, and traveled through Missouri, Iowa, and Wisconsin, making many friends, from whom she received tokens of respect and affection. Her "Book of Life," which she always carries with her, contains autograph letters from the most influential and intelligent people residing in those places through which she journeyed. She returned to Michigan with scrolls of signatures as trophies of success, over which she felt as jubilant as "great Cæsar bringing captives home to Rome." The time was nearing when these petitions might be presented in due form to Congress; accordingly, she left Battle Creek in the spring of 1874, and joining her grandson in Ohio, proceeded once more toward our national capital. They stopped on their way thither in Orange, New Jersey, being entertained in the beautiful home of her much-endeared friends, Rowland

Johnson and wife. There she met the prominent and highly gifted preacher, George Truman, with whom she held meetings. One meeting is thus noticed by one of the New Jersey papers:--

"GEORGE TRUMAN AND SOJOURNER TRUTH IN ORANGE.

"The little company of Friends in Orange held a very interesting meeting yesterday morning in Association Hall, where they were addressed by two noted preachers, one a man, the other a woman, the former white and the latter colored. These were George Truman and Sojourner Truth. The former was the first speaker.

"At the conclusion of Mr. Truman's address there was a short interval of silent meditation, after which Sojourner Truth, the venerable preacher and missionary, rose to speak. Her tall form was slightly bent with age, and as she faced her audience, clad in the simple garb of a Quakeress, she looked like an aged sibyl pleading the cause of her people. At first her voice was somewhat husky, and a few words were scarcely intelligible at the other end of the room, but as she warmed up with her subject all signs of weakness disappeared. She said that she felt that she was called to her work, and that if we are inheritors of the kingdom of God there must be some work that is to be done by us. That was what she had been trying to do for twenty or thirty years. When she was enlightened by God's love and truth she wanted to know, 'Lord, what wilt thou have me to do? Now I want to go to work. Well, it came to me in the antislavery cause. I knew slavery was a curse. I had been a slave and a chattel, and I went to work then. After that there seemed to be a call for me to go to work for the poor and outcast, for they are as poor as any one on God's footstool.' She said she had tried for years to get the government to help her and give the old destitute people, left destitute by the war, and the young growing up in wickedness, a home.

"She spoke of the misery and degradation she had seen among the colored people in the South, of the Black Maria full of them driving up to the Washington police court, of their being thrown into jails, and of their children growing up in vice and ignorance, and said that it was a shame and an abomination, and that the people did not know these things simply because they did not see them. She had heard it said that these evils would die out in time, but they would not die out, 'they must be learned out.' God looks down on these things and sees them, and we all ought to feel that the world should be better because we are in it. She believed in being doers of the word, not hearers only, and in doing something to show we are workers in the vineyard. She lectured four years on this matter, and had got up a petition to Congress to set aside a portion of the public lands in the West, and put buildings thereon for a home for the destitute. People would sign her petition, but they would say that the plan could not be carried out. It was not so, it can be carried out. She said she wished the women of the place would get up a meeting and give her a hearing, as she wanted to tell them things she could not tell the men. The venerable preacher then wandered from sacred to secular matters, stating her opinion that the national government needed the administration of women to become cleaner. In conclusion she spoke of the aid she had received from General O. O. Howard, and caused her grandson to read a letter written by the general favoring the object she was working for.

"Sojourner Truth will address a woman's meeting in Association Hall, on Wednesday afternoon at 3 o'clock. It is hoped that there will be a large attendance, as she proposes to fully present the condition and needs of her race at the South to the ladies of Orange."

"WASHINGTON, June 3, 1874.

"GEN. B. F. BUTLER, M. C.,
"Washington, D. C.

"MY DEAR SIR:--Sojourner Truth began her labors for her people many years ago. Under the operations of our laws with reference to the indigent there is constant change. The government did lend a helping hand for a time, and many think no more should be done by the general government for the classes rendered helpless by the war and by slavery.

"Sojourner finds many people living in comparative beggary, and many children growing up without education in either books, or industry, or honesty, whom she believes can be properly aided by the general government into better conditions. It struck me that the number of totally disabled soldiers, &c., would grow less as time goes on, and that possibly the income for your Asylum would soon render it practicable to try an experiment in the direction that Sojourner indicates. Without much thought and without consulting with any one, I have indicated by the enclosed papers what you may be able to put into some good, practical shape.

"It is hard to steer clear of very serious objections which arise against the exercise of benevolence or charity by the general government. Yet, as in cases of sudden overflow or famine, I believe the exercise deepens this feeling of regard for our already renovated Republic.

Yours truly,

"(Signed,) O. O. HOWARD."

The year '74 brought many vicissitudes to Sojourner. Sammie Banks, her dutiful and beloved grandson, began to decline in health soon after they reached Washington, which obliged them to leave that city and return to Battle Creek, where he lingered till Feb., 1875; when he passed away from amongst us. Sojourner also suffered from serious illness during that winter, and her life was despaired of for many long weeks. But her friends now rejoice to see her convalescing. She feels that for some special purpose her life has been spared, comparative health restored, and her mind brought back from the shadowy realm where it wandered during the days and nights when that red-lipped demon, Fever, with insatiate thirst, sucked the juices from life's fountain. She says, "My good Master kept me, for he had something for me to do."

She has no means of support. The ulcer upon her limb, from which she has so severely suffered, is partially healed. She says the "Lord has put new flesh on to old bones," which is proof to her mind that he requires more work of her. She hopes to go to Washington again and get her petition before Congress. Anna Dickinson says, "I hope every one will buy the pictures I gave her, and do all they can to help the woman, poor and old, who in her prime and strength helped so many." Another earnest woman asks the people to buy her book, and by so doing make her independent in her last days. No faithful servant of the divine Master should be accounted a burden while on earth, for the earth is the Lord's and the products are doubtless designed to sustain the creatures he has placed upon it. Especially should those who have borne the burden and heat of the day of life trustfully receive every comfort.

A friend not long ago offered to write her life. She told him she was "not ready to be writ up yet, for she had lots to accomplish first." She is now ready to be written up to this date, hoping thereby to complete the great enterprise she has undertaken. Born far back in the eighteenth century, and working for nearly a hundred years for the good of humanity, we see her ready to enter the last quarter of the nineteenth century with eye of faith undimmed and strength of spirit unabated. She has sought to promote every reform that has been agitated during this century. Most of those who were associated with her have gone from "works to rewards." But few survive to witness the flowering of those free institutions which they labored so industriously to plant.

Sojourner yet lingers on the verge of time, presenting to the world the extraordinary spectacle of a woman who, by native force, arose from the dregs of social life, like a phenix from its ashes, to become the defender of her race; and she has for years struggled faithfully to extricate it from the doom of perpetual slavery, to which it seemed to have been committed by the despotism of a great nation, the gigantic atrociousness of whose laws surpassed any other in the annals of the ages. Her parallel exists not in history. She stands by the closing century like a twin sister. Born and reared by its side, what it knows she knows, what it has seen, she has seen. Her memory is a vast storehouse of knowledge, the shelves of which contain a history of the revolutions, progressions, and culmination of the great ideas which have been a part of her life purpose. She continues to keep guard over the rights of her race, to the interests of which she has so long been devoted. True to the character of sibyl, which genius has awarded her, she, while working in the present, points to the future for the fulfillment of her longings and her hopes.

Cosmopolitan in her nature, she calls the world her home, and says she could never apply to a town for aid, but would sooner appeal to the whole United States, for the welfare of which she has labored and which is more her home than any single locality of town or State. She loves her country with truest love. After the emancipation of her people, when passing the capitol buildings, she would often pause to contemplate the ensigns of liberty displayed upon them, which then admitted a new interpretation. She devoutly thanked her God that the flag proudly floating over the dome at last afforded protection to such as she, and that the stars and stripes no longer symbolized the "scars and stripes" upon the negro's back. Instinctively her soul claimed kinship with the emblematic eagle, whose glittering eye seemed to pierce the clouds, and the span of whose wings was ample to hover over four million freemen, upon whose limbs the clanking chain would drag no more. And when her free black hands were raised to heaven, invoking blessings upon her country, it was a fairer sight to see and a surer guarantee of its permanence and glory than was the imposing spectacle of that beauteous "queen of the East," upon whose snowy, perfect hands the golden chains of slavery shone, as she entered the gates of the eternal city, leading the triumphant procession of a Cæsar.

The nineteenth century towers above all preceding ones. Numberless inventions and improvements are embraced within its circle. Mechanics, agriculture, commerce, science, and arts, the world of matter and the world of mind, have budded and blossomed, so to speak, as never before. The contemplation of its achievements is at once sublime and overwhelming, and not alone for what it has done, but for what it prophecies of the coming time. The century is a sibyl, too. Upon the foundation it has laid, a superstructure may arise more symmetrical than prophet has yet dared foretell. "It builded better than it knew," can truly be averred of it. But the century has nearly run its course. Already are the "fateful Spinners" coiling the strands with which to ring its funeral knell. Its plumed hearse and sable mourners loom up like ghosts in the dim horizon of the near future. The grave-digger, sharpening spade and pick, prepares to do his part. Representatives from many nations and races hasten to join the pageant, to pay the last honors in the "City of Brotherly Love," where the obsequies are to be celebrated.

Let us accept the name as a happy omen, foreshadowing the time when brotherly love shall so abound that the relation of each to all will be so plain that "he who runs may read." The century's history is nearly written up, and Sojourner's lacks but another chapter in which she hopes to chronicle the accomplishment of her heart's desire. May her longevity transcend the century with which she has so long kept pace.

She has ever listened to the still, small voice within her soul, and followed where it led. She has clothed the naked, and fed the hungry; been bound with those in bondage, and remembered her less fortunate brother when released from chains herself. She has upheld the right and true, denouncing wrong in high places as well as low. Her barque has been carried far out to sea, and now it nears the port. May she encounter no more storms upon her homeward course, but, wafted by soft, sweet winds through placid waters, peacefully enter the harbor of the "King Eternal." And when she glides from ship to shore, may she hear the welcome, "Come unto me all ye that labor and are heavy laden, and I will give you rest."

SOJOURNER TRUTH'S CORRESPONDENCE.

But few of the autograph letters contained in her "Book of Life" will be published, as it is beyond her limited means to give all to the public. She trusts her scribe to make the selections. She holds all in dear and precious remembrance. The light emanating from their true friendship pierces the darkest clouds that obscure her horizon, and sheds its blessed rays across the path she treads. She hopes and believes that all their names are written in the "Lamb's Book of Life," and that the sweet communion begun in time will continue when time shall be no more.

LETTERS AND SIGNATURES.

"BOSTON, AUG. 6, 1870.

"Having been long acquainted with Sojourner Truth, and familiar with her eventful life and marvelous experience, I heartily commend her to the respect, hospitality, and generous good-will of those among whom her lot may be cast for the time being: first, because of the cruel wrongs and sufferings endured by her while held for so many years in slavery; secondly, because of her disinterested, timely, and self-sacrificing labors among the wounded colored soldiers and destitute freedmen at the national capitol during the late rebellion; thirdly, because of her worthy character, and her many inspirational public testimonies in the cause of truth and righteousness; and, fourthly, because of her venerable age and necessarily increasing infirmities.

"WM. LLOYD GARRISON."

"Sojourner Truth, with the best wishes of her friend,

HELEN E. GARRISON."

"About twenty years ago my acquaintance began with this great and truly estimable woman, Sojourner Truth, since which time I have never ceased to feel myself stronger in spirit, and more earnest for justice and right for knowing her. We have dwelt together under the same roof weeks at a time; we have traveled together, holding meetings, myself a silent companion, and to-day

I rejoice to subscribe my name with her chosen friends, in her 'Book of Life.'

"AMY POST.

"Rochester, N. Y., May 3, 1871."

"May God bless, elevate, and enlighten the colored race, is the humble wish of their friend. We have met and conversed with their representative, Sojourner Truth, and are very much struck with her experience, as proving the principle that God reveals himself in other ways excepting that of his word.

"JAMES E. WALLACE.

"Rochester, N. Y."

"God speed thee in the right, Sojourner.

"Thy friend,

STEPHEN ARCHER.

"Dobb's Ferry, N. Y."

"ANTI-SLAVERY OFFICE, NEW YORK, JULY 29, 1863.

"DEAR SOJOURNER:--

"Yours by the hand of J. M. Peebles came promptly. I thank you for the photographs, though they are poor compared with the one you sent me first. It is a pity you did not preserve the negative of that instead of this. Not only is the likeness better, but the work also.

The mob did not disturb the Anti-Slavery office, nor me. The fact is, the Standard is scarcely known to the vile class composing the mob, having but a small circulation in the city. But it would have taken only a hint to direct their attention to us, and then my life would have been in danger, and the office would probably have been destroyed. A good Providence seems to have watched over us. Mr. Leonard, the colored clerk, was obliged to hide, but no harm came to him. Many of the colored people were dreadfully abused, but a very healthful reaction has already set in; and I believe the condition in this city will be better than it was before. Upwards of $30,000 has been raised for the relief of the sufferers, and they will get pay from the city government for the property they lost. I shall send the Standard as you request.

"With sincere regard for you, and earnest prayers for your welfare, I subscribe myself,

"Yours faithfully,

OLIVER JOHNSON."

"BOSTON, OCT. 21, 1867.

"DEAR MADAM:--

"I inclose my check for ten dollars ($10), a donation from the Rev. Photius Fiske, for Sojourner Truth. Please acknowledge the receipt of same. Yours very truly, WENDELL PHILLIPS."

"The first time that Sojourner addressed a public meeting in Orange, some years since, she said that the first shall be last and the last first, and that she believed the colored race would yet lead the people out of darkness and ignorance. It now seems likely that the colored voters of New Jersey will redeem the State from the grasp of the ignorant and depraved democratic party. Sojourner is now laboring to consummate that glorious work. May Heaven grant her success. ROWLAND JOHNSON.

"Orange, N. J., 1870."

A LETTER OF INTRODUCTION.

"SYRACUSE, OCT. 9, 1868.

"DEAR FRIENDS:--

"The bearer of this note will be Sojourner Truth, a worthy and remarkable woman. She is going to Courtland, to visit Miss Mary E. Mudge and other friends. I shall be obliged to any persons who, on the arrival of the train at the Courtland depot, will help her to find her friend's house.

"SAMUEL J. MAY."

"WASHINGTON, D. C., MARCH 22, 1865.

"MY DEAR SOJOURNER:--

"I have made an arrangement for a meeting at the Union Baptist Church for next Sunday evening. I want you to come, if possible. Let me know if you can.

"Yours truly,

JOHN DUDLEY."

"TO MY FRIEND, SOJOURNER TRUTH:--

"The nearly thirty years' acquaintance I have had with you, all confirm your title to the name you have chosen, and its record in humanity's 'Book of Life.'

"Yours,

SAMUEL L. HILL.

"Florence, Mass., Feb. 14, 1871."

"After a wearied pilgrimage of over eighty years, she is a sojourner among us, witnessing the culmination and fulfillment of those great truths which she has humbly foretold oft-times within the last four decades. Her pilgrimage is nearly over. Sojourner Truth is resting. She quietly and proudly awaits her time to pass over among those who have performed their part. Good-by, aged friend.

"RICHARD LAMBERTH, of San Francisco.

"Washington, D. C., 1870.
"

"PHILADELPHIA, TENTH MONTH, 21ST, 1869.

"I hope people will buy her pictures, which I have given to Aunt Sojourner, and so help her. And indeed I hope every one will do all they can to help the woman, poor and old, who in her prime and strength has helped so many. I will write for you, aunty, the Arabic blessing, 'May you live to be a thousand years old, and may your shadow never grow less.'

"ANNA E. DICKINSON."

"Amen to all dear Anna has said.

"A. C. HARRIS."

"I have very pleasant memories of Sojourner Truth. She has been a faithful worker in the cause of freedom and of right. She can truly say, with Paul, 'I have fought a good fight, . . . I have kept the faith; henceforth there is laid up for me a crown of righteousness, which the Lord, the righteous Judge shall give me.' With my sincerest good wishes,

"The wisest, wittiest woman I know is Sojourner Truth. Wiser and wittier, of course, than any man. I am glad to have enjoyed many years of acquaintance with her. I hope to enjoy many ages. May she and all her friends believe on her divine Jesus, and be with him where he is. GILBERT HAVEN."

"DEAR SOJOURNER:--

"Love is the light, life, and central attraction of the universe, and will, if men yield to it, bring selfishness and misrule into harmony and law. May you ever feel its blessing.

"C. A. F. STEBBINS.

"Washington, D. C."

"GILES B. STEBBINS."

"May the Lord Jesus, who met you in the way, ever be your friend, companion, and guide.

"Your friend,

                          HENRY FOSTER."

"SOJOURNER, as you are crowning earth's children with bright and beautiful truths, so the angels will crown you, when you enter the bright Spirit Land.

               "RENINO, the little Indian squaw."

"ANTHONY VILLAGE, R. I., NINTH MONTH, 16TH, 1870.

> "God hath many aims to compass,
> Many messages to send,
> And his instruments are fitted
> Each to some distinctive end.

               "PERES PECK. Aged 84 years."

"SOJOURNER TRUTH.

"Arisen from the degradation of slavery to be one of the most noble reformers of the age. Long may her star illumine the pathway of the progressive world. MRS. M. GALE.

"East Medway, Mass."

"May the Lord bless and preserve you through life. Yours, J. MCMILLEN.

"Brooklyn, N. Y."

"That Sojourner Truth has ennobled human nature by her life, is the firm conviction of her friend,

"ALFRED E. GILES.

"Boston, Mass."

"SYRACUSE, N. Y., MARCH 25, 1871.

"Sojourner Truth was in Syracuse, laboring in the cause of Christ and humanity. Although over eighty, she still has plans for future usefulness which she seems happy to contemplate. Her life testifies to her faith in God's words that 'no man putting his hand to the plough and looking back is fit for the kingdom of God.'

J. S. LEONARD."

"With ever kind and ever loving remembrance of my dear old friend of more than thirty years' acquaintance.

JAMES BOYLE, M. D.

"No. 20 W. Broadway, N. Y., July 13, 1870."

"P. S. All the years during which we have known each other, we were co-laborers in the anti-slavery movement, and now we see our wishes accomplished in the overthrow of that horrid wall of crimes and cruelties which Church and State combined to perpetuate. The great God is leading the bondmen and bondwomen through a Red Sea to their freedom, and writing their deed of enfranchisement with the point of the sword, in the blood of their oppressors North and South.

J. B."

James Boyle made Sojourner a present of the stereotype portion of her "Narrative," which includes the first 128 pages of this volume.

"I have conversed with Aunt Sojourner, and believe her to be a child of God.

"MRS. LEWIS FAIRBROTHER.

"Pawtucket, R. I."

"DEAR AUNT SOJOURNER:--

"I thank the 'King Eternal' that he is no respecter of persons, and that we are all his children.

HENRY C. L. DORSEY.

"Pawtucket, Sept. 6, 1870."

"Slavery has gone over the battlements, thanks be to God.

JOSEPH A. DUGDALE.

"Mt. Pleasant, Iowa."

"Dear Sojourner Truth, a holy woman doing a godlike work--May she prosper in her noble undertakings.

M. L. IVES.

"Detroit. Mich."

"ROCHESTER, N. Y., MAY 3, 1871.

"MY DEAR SOJOURNER TRUTH:--

"I rejoice to find you strong in health, vigorous in mind, warm in heart, and, as usual, full of noble purposes, looking to the welfare of suffering men and women. May you long live to bless, cheer, and enlighten, and to lift up the oppressed, and smooth the pathway of the lowly, and may you see the fruit of your labors multiply more than sixty or an hundred fold.

"FREDERIC DOUGLAS."

"DEAR MOTHER IN ISRAEL:--

"You are called of the Lord and anointed by his Holy Spirit to bind up the broken-hearted, and to sway the hearts of men by a power greater than that which resides in thrones and scepters. May God bless you, and give you success in your divine mission.

DANIEL STEELE.

"Genesee College, Lima, N. Y., May 12, 1871."

"IOLA, KAN., NOV. 5, 1871.

"How easy it is to detect the spirit, however humble its garb, freed from the trammels of the world, party, or sectarianism. In you, good old Sojourner, we see it far removed above all clogs. Once a slave, now, in the highest sense a freedwoman; desiring nothing, hoping for nothing, but the truth as revealed by the Spirit, not killed by formalism. We thought we saw afar off a true spirit, and desired to meet you. At our request and invitation, you honored us with your presence at our house. We hope you have enjoyed the visit as well as ourselves. The best room, the best bed, and the best seat, we have intended to reserve for you, hoping to make you feel free and at home. Be assured, good friend, we feel grateful to you, and benefited by your counsel, and words of wisdom and truth. May your labors for the promotion of your race and our common humanity meet with abundant success, and, finally, great reward, is the earnest desire of your friends and well-wishers,

"BYRON M. SMITH,

"ELIZA S. SMITH."

"May God's blessing rest on thy labors for the elevation of thy race and the general good of mankind.

"G. KNOWLES.

"Leavenworth, Kan."

"DEAR FRIEND SOJOURNER:--

"I hope that you will live to see the day when the people of this land shall be wise, and through their government care for the poor and ignorant, both black and white, as a wise parent cares for his children.

ELIZA R. MORGAN.

"Leavenworth, Kan."

"53 BROADWAY, NEW YORK, JAN. 17, 1868.

"SOJOURNER TRUTH:--

"Dear Madam--I had the pleasure of meeting you several years ago, at my uncle's, Mr. Richard Mott's, in Toledo. I saw Mr. Mott a few days ago, and he told me where you reside. I send one dollar, inclosed, for which please send me, by mail, as many of your photographs as the money will pay for. If you have two or three different ones, please send one of each. Perhaps you may have heard of the death of Uncle James Mott, brother of Richard Mott and husband of Lucretia Mott. He died last Sunday. Mrs. Mott is quite feeble and feels her great loss very much. I shall be glad to see you again when you come to New York, and shall try to do so.

"Very truly yours,

WALTER BROWN."

"BROOKLYN, SEPT. 8, 1869.

"Your letter of the 12th inst. has just reached me. I take pleasure in seconding my husband's invitation to you for a visit at our house. He will, no doubt, be away most of the winter, therefore, if your health will permit, as soon as you can come it will be best. We live at 136 Livingstone St., Brooklyn. Write to Mr. Tilton the day of your arrival, and he will meet you at the depot.

"I am yours sincerely,

"ELIZABETH R. TILTON."

"PROVIDENCE, R. I., SEPT. 14, 1870.

"TO SOJOURNER TRUTH:--

"May your last days be your best. May your sun set in glory. Having followed in the footsteps of Jesus all the way, he will now guide your feeble steps up the mount of ascension, and when the opening heavens receive you, you shall hear his sweet voice saying, 'Well done, good and faithful servant.'

RACHEL C. MATHER,
"Teacher of Freedmen in Beaufort, S. C."

"TO SOJOURNER TRUTH, THE LIBYAN SYBIL:--

"I give thee joy, my noble friend and true,
Thou who, but yesterday, a scorned slave,
Bearing the cross within thy great, brave heart,
Wert scourged and scoffed at by the heartless crew,
And only pitied by the Christ-like few
Who seek--like Christ--the sorrowing to save,
To-day, forevermore enshrined in art!
Honor and joy be thine! How few like thee
Wear the saints' aureole on an earthly brow.
So thy wronged race, long trodden beneath the feet
Of tyrant lords, and wearing the brand of shame,
Shall yet in manhood's majesty complete
Stand proudly in the sacred halls of fame.

"MRS. C. L. MORGAN.

"Mt. Pleasant, Wis., May 2, 1863."

"Again are we privileged in having Sojourner with us. 'Tis very pleasant for us that she feels our house is her home. She speaks this evening in the Congregational Church.

                MRS. A. MONTAGUE.

"Kalamazoo, Mich., Aug. 26, 1871."

"That the evening of your life may be as calm and peaceful as the morning was dark and stormy, is the earnest wish of your sincere friend,

                "LUCINDA WALLING.

"Mt. Pleasant, Wis., Sept., 1871."

"May our friendship of many years continue for long ages after the close of this short life.

                "THOMAS CHANDLER.

"Raisin, Mich., 1871."

"MY DEAR GRANDMOTHER:--

"As the present is your first visit to Missouri, I want to put it on record in your 'Book of Life,' that there is at least one native Missourian who entertains no prejudice against colored people, but, on the contrary, values all alike according to their worthiness. Your noble labors for the freedom of the colored race are among my earliest remembrances, and your beautiful ideas of life, death, and God, will be among the last things I shall forget.

"W. H. MILLER, Journal of Commerce.

"Kansas City, Mo., June 15, 1872."

"OUR VETERAN FRIEND,

Sojourner Truth--We have known thee for a quarter of a century, heard thy clarion voice in the day when the slave power rioted in the land and trod with its iron heel upon the hearts of its victims. God has blessed the labors of his servants in a signal manner, and slavery by his mighty power has gone over the battlements and is destroyed. May thy old age be crowned by his presence, and thy trumpet join with Gabriel's in the jubilee, when the countless multitudes shall surround the throne of God.

JOSEPH A. DUGDALE.

"Mt. Pleasant, Iowa, Second Month 7th, 1872."

"Nov. 17, 1868.

"Sojourner Truth commenced her advocacy of the rights of her race during our war with Mexico, since which her travels and labors have been wide-spread, constant, and arduous. God has given her remarkable native sagacity, a ready command of strong, expressive language, and a vein of sharp wit and rich humor with which to combat the falsities and delusions among the people of her time. May God give her length of days, and free utterance on the side of right and justice.

"W. L. CHAPLIN."

"TO SOJOURNER TRUTH:--

"You say you wish to leave the world better than you found it. Posterity will give you the credit of having done so.

"R. B. TAYLOR, Editor Gazette.

"Wyandotte, Kansas, Dec. 25, 1871."

"AUNTY:--

"Accept this book to collect the scraps of your eventful life, which has accomplished so much, and is now so entirely devoted to the interests of the poor colored people in Washington and elsewhere.

"ROBERT ADAMS.

"Fall River, Oct. 16, 1870."

"MENDOTA, ILL., APRIL 22, 1872.

"TO THE METHODIST MINISTRY OF THE PARK RIVER CONFERENCE:--

"Dear Brethren--Allow me to introduce to you Sojourner Truth, and bespeak for her your friendly attentions. If her religious experience, as narrated a few years ago in the Atlantic Monthly, by Mrs. H. B. Stowe, affected you as it did me, you will feel it an honor to receive her in the Lord with all gladness.

"Your brother in Christ,

> D. F. HOLMES."

A short sermon inserted in Sojourner's 'Book of Life,' and one which she appreciates:--

> "Our ingress in life is marked and bare,
> Our progress through life is trouble and care,
>
> Our egress out of it we know not where,
> But doing well here, we shall do well there.
>
> "C. P. MORGAN.

"Leavenworth, Kan., Jan. 31, 1872."

> "SPRINGFIELD, MASS., FEB. 28, 1871.

"SOJOURNER TRUTH:--

"Dear Friend--In writing my name in your 'Book of Life,' it gives me great pleasure to say that our acquaintance of some twenty years has made me largely your debtor. Your steady devotion to the cause of suffering humanity has always commanded my esteem, admiration, and reverence. As you have spent a long and laborious life for the good of others, may you always find troops of friends to minister to your comfort while you sojourn among mortals. And when at last you pass on to the higher life, I trust you will be met by a host of immortal friends on the shores of the summer land, who will welcome you to the blest abodes.

E. W. TURING."

"Your life, commencing in the depths of slavery, opens grandly and brightly even there, and who can tell of the glorious angelhood into which it is unfolding? The 'Well done' awaits you, Sojourner, and all earnest workers for humanity.

"MARTHA L. GALE.

"East Medway, Mass., 1871."

"AUNTY SOJOURNER TRUTH:--

"We have been greatly pleased and edified by a visit from you. Having known you for about thirty years, it is with pleasure we add our testimony to your self-sacrificing labors in behalf of your despised and oppressed race, and the cause of humanity everywhere. Although far advanced in years, may you be spared to see your efforts for the elevation of your people crowned with success.

> "N. B. SPOONER,
>
> "L. H. SPOONER.

"Plymouth, Mass., 1871."

> "May she who patiently hath wrought
> Through years of earnest toil and thought,
>
> Find her best hopes fulfilled at last,
> And when her wanderings are past,
> To crown her work of love be given
> Sweet peace on earth and rest in Heaven.
>
> "J. WALTER SPOONER.

"Plymouth, Mass."

"James N. Buffum, Ruth Buffum, Abby B. Buffum--all good friends of Sojourner Truth.

"Lynn, Mass., 1870."

> "Go on, Sojourner, God speed you.
>
> "J. A. B. STONE.

"Kalamazoo, Mich."

> "Blessings on thee, my good old friend.
> "WENDELL PHILLIPS.

"Boston, Mass.'

VISITS PRESIDENT GRANT--LETTER OP INTRODUCTION FROM GEN. HOWARD.

"BUREAU OF REFUGEES, FREEDMEN, AND ABANDONED LANDS.
"Washington, D. C., March 17, 1870.

"GEN. U. S. GRANT:--

"President U. S.--Sojourner Truth, quite an aged and distinguished colored woman, earnestly working for years for her people, desires to see the president. She will pray for him surely; but more heartily if she sees him.

"Yours respectfully,

O. O. HOWARD."

Sojourner says: "I went in company with several ladies and gentlemen to see the president. While waiting in the ante-room with other visitors, a gentleman called, to whom I was introduced. During a short conversation with him, he said, 'I recollect having seen you at Arlington Heights. How old do you call yourself now?' I had felt very much annoyed by people's calling to me in the street and asking that question. I mentioned it to Dr. Howland, and he advised me to charge five dollars for answering that question; so I said to the gentleman, A friend told me to ask five dollars for telling my age. He smiled pleasantly, and invited me to call upon him at the city hall. After he left, my friends told me that that gentleman was Mayor Bowen, one of the best men in the city. Presently, a man came in, a free-and-easy sort of fellow, and asked to see the president. We were now ushered into the presence room. A very elegant lady and gentleman shook hands with the president, and after a few pleasant words were passed, took their leave.

"Then the 'hail fellow' stepped up and offered his hand, saying, 'This is President Grant, is it? You ain't as old as I thought you was. I've seen your picter, and your picter looks older than you do.' The president smilingly said, 'I am not so very old.' 'Wall, how old do you call yourself, anyhow?' The president replied that he was 49 years of age. 'Ain't you no older than that?' said the fellow. 'No, sir,' patiently answered the president. 'You look older than that,' said he, and waited to see if the president had anything more to say, but, finding that the interview was ended, turned to go, saying, 'Good-by.' 'Good-by, sir,' said the president, and the fellow walked off.

"I felt very much mortified because I had asked Mayor Bowen five dollars for inquiring of me how old I was, when I saw how kindly and politely the president treated that clownish fellow. I will here add that I subsequently called upon the mayor and apologized for my rudeness to him. He said he ought to be the one to ask an apology, for it was improper to ask a lady her age. He invited me to spend a day with his family, which invitation I accepted and was cordially entertained by his lovely wife and interesting family. It was now our turn to be presented to the president. He shook my hand, and said he was pleased to see me. After a little pleasant conversation, I expressed my gratification that the colored people had gained the right of suffrage. This he cordially indorsed. I now showed him my 'Book of Life,' which contains the autographs of Lincoln and other distinguished persons. He took the book and wrote his name in it. 'To Sojourner Truth. U. S. Grant, March 31, 1870.' I then handed him two of my photographs, which he took, and putting one in his pocket-book, he laid the other on the table and gave me a five dollar bill, for which I thanked him.

"We now left, carrying with us a pleasant impression of the president, and the memory of a delightful hour spent in the White House."

"WASHINGTON, APRIL 14, 1867.

"MY DEAR SOJOURNER:--

"I am so thronged with work, and applications for colored people, from all parts, that I cannot finish any day's work. I always go to bed tired, leaving much work undone. As to sending you people, it is impossible to promise anything. We have been trying to get some people to go the last week, but all who go incline to go to Providence, Battle Creek, or some place where already several have gone.

"One thing now you may do--send the names and residences of those who have applied to you for help, and we will make one desperate effort. We send our men to Brockport this coming week. The Bureau requires that the names of employers be sent; so if you send on the names, I will do the best I can. You need not promise any till you see whether they can be obtained. I wish much we could send a hundred men, they stand idle everywhere and will not go in any considerable numbers till after the first of June, when they will vote. With love and best wishes,

"Your friend,

JOSEPHINE S. GRIFFING."

"OCT. 16, 1874.

"MRS. F. W. TITUS:--

"Can you inform me who wrote out (or otherwise compiled) and edited the narrative of Sojourner Truth's life? I shall be much obliged to you if you can give me this information; it is desired for the library of a public institution. If you can tell me where Sojourner Truth is now, and as to her health and circumstances, I shall be glad and further obliged to you.

"Respectfully,

"SAMUEL MAY.

"Leicester, Mass."

EXTRACT FROM A LETTER.

"LEEDS, MASS., JAN. 17, 1870.

"SOJOURNER TRUTH:--

"My Dear Friend--A line from my brother received this afternoon, speaks of your being at Vineland, so I must send you a few lines to say how much pleased I was to hear from you through friend Amy Post, of Rochester, New York. Hope you have been successful in your present journey with such kind and efficient friends as Mr. and Mrs. Theodore Tilton to help you. Was very glad your mind was set at rest about your son Peter. How strange are the events of our lives. How little we know of the world we live in, especially of the spiritual world by which we are surrounded. But we may see enough to know that it is at least marvelously interesting. You and I seem to move around as easily as soap bubbles--now here--now there--making our mark, I suppose, everywhere, though mine is a very quiet mark compared to yours. I get a glimpse of you often through the papers, which falls upon my spirit like bright rays from the sun. There is a wee bit of a chapel here, pulpit supplied by a Mr. Merritt, and one evening last fall he repeated something that 'Sojourner Truth' had said. I was not there, so I cannot tell what it was. I did not think you were laying the foundation of such an almost world-wide reputation when I wrote that little book for you, but I rejoice and am proud that you can make your power felt with so little book-education.

"OLIVE GILBERT."

ANOTHER LETTER FROM THE SAME PERSON.

"MY DEAR FRIEND:--

"I may not be able to make you sensible of the heart-felt pleasure I experienced on receiving your kindly greetings once more, but hasten to thank you sincerely for them, and for your address which I have long wished for; and I assure you I am most happy in thus being enabled to return you my own greeting, fervent, fresh, and warm from the heart. It is a very long time since we have had any opportunity of communicating with each other directly, though I have been enabled to find traces of you and your labors, from time to time, which was more, I think, than you have been able to do of your old friend; for I am not so public a personage as yourself.

"Your call upon Mrs. Stowe, and our dear, sainted president, and your labors connected with the army, and the Freedmen's Bureau, gave you a publicity that enabled me to observe you at your old vocation of helping on and doing good to your fellow-creatures, both physically and mentally. I was much pleased with Mrs. Stowe's enthusiasm over you. You really almost received your apotheosis from her. She proposed, I think, that you should have a statue and symbolize our American Sibyl.

I have written more than a sheet, and have not spoken of what has been in my mind all the time, of the great deliverance of your people from the house of bondage, the wonderful work of the Lord, accomplished only through a cruel and bloody war, as was so often predicted by friend Garrison and others in days gone by. You may have witnessed many of its terrors. And oh! it makes me almost speechless when I contemplate the hosts of men, and those the flower of their country, that were thus sacrificed to Moloch. There is but one reconciling thought, and that is, The Lord is all-wise and reigneth over all. He sees and knows what we observe, and not a sparrow falls to the ground without his notice. Of the little book I wrote for your benefit, some of the copies I took are sold; others I gave to my friends as keepsakes, &c.

"Get some one to write for you soon, and believe me to be your true friend and well-wisher, now and forevermore. O. G."

"The company of our estimable friend, Sojourner Truth, will ever be cherished with feelings of love.

"SARAH T. ROGERS.

"No. 323, North Eleventh St., Philadelphia."

"3 EXETER STREET, BOSTON, MASS., Apr. 25, 1875.

"DEAR FRIEND:--

"We are sorry to hear that you are suffering from ill health, and hope you may be getting better by this time. My mother, Mary May, who was one of the earliest abolitionists, with Mr. Garrison and Wendell Phillips, wishes me to send her remembrances to you, and her best wishes, and wants you to accept ten dollars from her. Perhaps you have seen her, either here in Boston, or at the house of my brother, Samuel May, in Leicester. She is eighty-seven years of age and rather feeble, though her mind is bright, and she is able to read a little and knit a good deal. I inclose a post-office order for fifteen dollars. Please accept five from me.

"I should be glad to hear that the money reaches you safely, so I inclose a card addressed to us, for reply. I am, with very great respect, dear madam,

"Yours,

ABBY W. MAY."

"RICHMOND, IND., APRIL 15, 1875.

"SOJOURNER TRUTH:--

"My Good Sister--Mrs. Dr. Thompson and myself, on hearing of your afflictions in the death of your grandson and your own sickness, have been trying to raise some funds for you, but I am sorry to be obliged, after waiting so long, to send you so small a sum as two dollars. For this you will find inclosed a money order. In reply I wish you would tell me all about your situation and wants, and if possible I will send you more. Have you received anything from the Julians? Have your wants been supplied? Tell me all the facts. How are you getting along with your sickness?

"Mrs. Dudley sends with me our hearty good wishes, and we only regret that we cannot send you something more substantial to supply your needs. You are remembered in our poor prayers in our family. We shall never forget the light and cheer which your presence and words gave us when here. The good Lord, whom you have so faithfully served in labor for your poor race, will take you through and give you, a weary old pilgrim, a home of rest and reward. Let me hear from you soon.

"Your fellow-pilgrim and sojourner,

"JOHN DUDLEY."

"With earnest respect for your constant effort to help humanity, and to make the world better for your being in it, I want you, dear friend, to think of me in this life and the higher one as your friend and sympathizer.

ELIZA S. LEGGETT.

"Detroit, Mich., June 29, 1871."

"GRAND RAPIDS, MARCH, 1873.

"God bless Sojourner Truth, who spoke so grandly at the Second Street M. E. Church, last night, and who has been our honored guest for a few days.

"L. H. PEARCE."

"Equality of rights is the first of rights.

"CHARLES SUMNER.

"Senate Chamber, April 26, 1870."

"ORANGE, Feb. 10, 1875.

"AUNT SOJOURNER:--

"Dear Friend--I learned last evening that thee is dangerously ill, and that it is paralysis which has prostrated thee. I spent the evening with Mrs. McKinn and learned it from her. Most sincerely do I hope she has been misinformed, and that thy illness is something from which thee may recover, and that we may see thee again in the flesh; but if this cannot be I know that thee is prepared to enter that beautiful world of spirits which has seemed so near thee while here.

"Dear Aunt Sojourner, may I among the many who love thee here, be remembered by thee on that beautiful shore of the river of everlasting life, and if thee is permitted to return to the children of earth, receive from thee some token of thy presence and continued affection.

"Thee left a trunk here which we will fill and send thee as soon as we learn what will be most useful. I do not doubt but that thee has kind friends who are not only willing but anxious to make thee comfortable in every respect, I mean in Battle Creek. But those of thy friends who have not the privilege of relieving thy wants in person, would like to add their mite toward returning the kindness which thee, for so many years, has shown others. May the Infinite Love sustain thee, and that faith which has ever been thy support in the trials of life become stronger and purer as thee nears the golden gates, is the prayer of thy loving friends,

"H. W. JOHNSON & ROWLAND JOHNSON."

"STANDARD OFFICE, NEW YORK, JAN. 13, 1866.

"MY DEAR FRIEND:--

"I know you will be glad to put your mark to the inclosed petition, and get a good many to join it, and send or take it to some member of Congress to present. Do you know there are three men, Schench, Jenkes, and Broomall, who have dared to propose to amend the United States Constitution by inserting in it the word 'male,' thus shutting all women out by constitution from voting for president, vice-president, and congressmen, even though they may have the right to vote in the State for State officers. It is a most atrocious proposition, and I know Sojourner Truth will say, No, to it. God bless you, and help you to do the good work before you, is the wish of your friend,

SUSAN B. ANTHONY."

"BIDDLE HOUSE, DETROIT, JAN. 29, 1869.

"SOJOURNER TRUTH:--

"My dear Grandmother in Israel--I am sorry I cannot get time to take you once again by the hand before I leave Detroit, but I herewith inclose to you a five-dollar bill to keep you in mind of

"Your dutiful grandson,

"THEODORE TILTON."

"MY DEAR FRIEND, SOJOURNER TRUTH:--

"If we never meet on earth again, my prayer is that we may meet on the other shore.

"E. DICKINSON.

"Brodhead, Wis."

"SOJOURNER TRUTH:--

"You want the government to give land to the freed people. This would be true statesmanship, as by so doing we should be paying a little of the great debt we owe the freedmen, and at the same time putting them in the way of supporting and educating themselves, and enriching the nation.

"SETH HUNT.

"Northampton, Mass., 1871."

"BOSTON, MARCH 18, 1875.

"MRS. F. W. TITUS:--

"Dear Madam--I have your prompt reply to my note of inquiry, and hasten to inclose a check for twenty-five dollars for the benefit of Sojourner Truth. It is the contribution of Mr. Phillips, father, and myself.

"W. L. GARRISON, JUN."

"SOJOURNER TRUTH:--

"Dear Friend--Your life is a living epistle known and read of all men. You surely are a sojourner, laboring for the truth. Your life has been one of sorrow and toil, bearing in your own body and your own family the bitter injustice and cruelty that has sent you a missionary to the learned and unlearned alike for many years. You and I have cause of sympathy, each with the other. God bless and keep you ever. CALVIN FAIRBANKS.[*]

[*] Calvin Fairbanks was confined for 12 years in Frankfort prison, Kentucky, for aiding a slave to escape.

"Florence, Mass., March 20, 1871."

"NORTH TOPEKA, KAN., NOV. 20, 1871.

"It has gratified me much, Sojourner, to see your face once more, and welcome you to my home and my church. It is a dozen years since we first met, and, possibly, we may meet again in this world; if not, we will in the next. Our meeting in this far West has brought to my mind the beautiful words of Phoebe Carey:--

'As ships from far and distant ports
To distant harbors hurrying on,
Meet with each other on the deep,
And hail, and answer, and are gone,

'So we upon the sea of life,
Have met as mortals often will,
One from the prairies of the West,
One from the land of rock and rill.

'So we shall pass on separate ways,
As vessels parting on the main,
And in the years to come, our paths
May never meet or cross again.

'Yet when life's voyage all is done,
Where'er apart our paths may tend,

We'll drop our anchors side by side
In the same harbor at the end.'

"THOMAS W. JONES.
"Pastor of Cong. Church."

"SOJOURNER:--

"The words of my husband are warmly echoed from my heart, and I feel more than gratified to have had the opportunity of entertaining you in my own home. Be sure you will always be held in loving remembrance by us all.

HELEN M. JONES."

"DEAR SOJOURNER:--

"At your request I record the fact that I succeeded in registering my name in the First Precinct of the Ninth Ward, and on Tuesday, the 4th of April, cast the first vote for a state officer deposited in an American ballot-box by a woman for the last half century. After the vote was deposited, I presented a vase of flowers to the inspectors, and also handed them a large picture representing a large crowd of women in darkness, just entering the portals of an arch, which were inscribed, 'Liberty,' and upon which an eagle was perched. The gates were held open by Columbia and the Goddess of Justice. The foremost woman held in her hands a scroll, inscribed, 'The Fourteenth Amendment.' To the right were imps of darkness fleeing away, some with barrels of whiskey. On the left was pictured the Capitol of Washington, with men crowding its steps, cheering, &c. Streams of light flowed upon them, while, with the exception of this and the foreground, the picture was darkness intensified. The following lines appeared underneath:--

"'We come, free America, five millions strong,

In darkness and bondage for many years long,

We've marched in deep silence, but now we unroll

The Fourteenth Amendment, which gives us a soul.

Glory, glory, hallelujuh, glory, &c.,
As we go marching on.'

"NANNETTE B. GARDNER.

"Detroit, Mich., June 30, 1871."

"With a great deal of esteem,

"Your friend,

JOHN R. FRENCH."

"Sojourner Truth lectured before the Pewamo Temperance Society last evening. She held the audience in breathless attention for one hour. May the Lord guide and protect her in her errands of mercy, and may her days be multiplied. One great desire of my heart has been gratified, which was to meet Sojourner and converse with her face to face.

"MRS. E. A. CHADDOCK, "President Pewamo Temperance Society."

"BRISTOL, CONN., 1840.

"SISTER DEAN:--

"I send you this living messenger, as I believe her to be one that God loves. Ethiopia is stretching forth her hands unto God. You can see by this sister that God does, by his Spirit alone, teach his own children things to come. Please receive her, and she will tell you some new things. Let her tell her story without interruption, give close attention, and you will see that she has the leaven of truth, and that God helps her to see where but few can. She can not read or write, but the law is in her heart. Send her to brother Rice's, brother Clapp's, and where she can do most good.

"From your brother in looking for the speedy coming of Christ,

HENRY L. BRADLEY."

"May the God of truth sojourn with you through this world, and then give you an abundant entrance into mansions prepared for you in Heaven.

"T. B. WELCH.

"Vineland, N. J., Dec. 25, 1869."

"HOPEDALE, MASS., JULY 28, 1870.

"Faithful mother in Israel,
Raised up to bless thy people,
Fearless for God's righteousness,
Witness for Truth's almightiness,
Scourge of scornful oppression,
Shamer of vain profession,
Tender nurse of feebleness,
Helper of sad neediness,
Friend of all humanity,
And practical Christianity,
Wondrous age of thy sojournment,
Passing strange thy life's concernment,
Stranger than the tales of fiction,
Full of woe and benediction,
But crowned with rich fruition,
May thy Heavenly Father bless thee,
And guardian angels oft caress thee,
Till all thy toils are ended,
And thy spirit has ascended,
To be with Jesus mansioned,
Among his countless ransomed.

"ADIN BALLOU,

"LUCY H. BALLOU."

"Sojourner Truth is the most marvelous person we have ever had the pleasure of meeting. May God spare her, to see her heart's desire accomplished.

"MRS. L. H. PEARCE."

"VINELAND, JAN. 4, 1870.

"The Lord and good angels have blest you and your work, and will bless you in that better world where I hope to meet Sojourner Truth.

JOHN GAGE."

"NILES, MICH., OCT. 9, 1873.

"This neighborhood has been favored with the presence of Sojourner Truth among us. She dined yesterday at S. A. Gardiner's, took tea with Mrs. Henry Moore, and spent the night at M. F. Reed's. The Lord has blessed us with this angel in disguise, which has made our hearts very glad. May he bless her most abundantly.

MRS. H. MOORE."

"WEST MEDWAY, DEC. 21st, 1870.

"DEAR AUNTY SOJOURNER TRUTH:--

"We intended to ride down to see you before you left Dr. Gale's, but shall not be able, for Mr. Ray has been to Woonsocket twice this week, and the rest of the week he is so much engaged that we cannot come. I am rather disappointed, for I wanted to see your dear face once more. Mr. Ray wishes me to tell you that he saw brother Gilbert Haven on Monday, and he said that he had been looking for news from you for some time, but did n't know your whereabouts. When Mr. Ray told him that you would spend Christmas with him, 'God willing,' he said, 'That's good. Now we'll have a big time.' Mr. Haven is anticipating your visit with a great deal of pleasure, and I know you will have a nice time. We are all well. Our circle met this week, P. M. and there were many kind inquiries for you. I am sorry you could not have stayed longer with us. May God bless you. I feel that the conversations we had, did me a great deal of good, particularly the relation of your experience on Sunday evening after meeting.

"Yours in Christian love,

JUSTINA B. RAY."

"PHILADELPHIA, MAY 9, 1870.

"MRS. TITUS:--

"We were made glad last evening by the return of our old friend, Sojourner, from Washington, where she has been for two months. She looks very well and bright, and is in her very best spirits as you will see by the following statement:--

"She has received from the government, through the influence of Gen. Howard, three hundred and ninety dollars, being fifteen dollars per month for twenty-six months. She has collected other funds to the amount of four hundred and fifty dollars, for which I send my check payable to your order, which you will please to pay to William Merritt on acc't of her mortgage, and get him to send the receipt to me with a statement of her accounts.

"She has lived to see her people delivered, and we may all rejoice with her.

"Yours truly,

"HENRY T. CHILD, M. D.

"634 Race St."

"FLORENCE, MASS., MARCH 8, 1871.

"SOJOURNER TRUTH:--

"Dear Friend--Mr. Hunt informs me to-day that Mr. Wheedon, Methodist minister in Northampton, will appoint a meeting for you in his church, next week Tuesday evening, and will himself cause notice thereof to be given next Sunday in all the churches in town, or in such of them as will give the notice. Mr. Hunt will also have the notice in the Free Press printed next Friday, and in the Gazette printed next week, Tuesday. Now if you will inform me on what evening next week you wish to have a meeting in Florence, I will also have notice given here next Sunday, by the Methodists, the

Congregationalists, and in our meeting. Will also have the notice given in the Free Press of next Friday (if I get your reply in season), and in the Gazette of next week, Tuesday. You will be welcome to the use of our hall next week, either Wednesday, Thursday, or Friday evening. Please send me word to-morrow, if you can, which evening you will occupy. If not to-morrow, send word the next day, and oblige,

"Yours truly,

SAMUEL L. HILL."

"On Saturday, Jan. 1st, 1870, our house received a new baptism, through Sojourner Truth, whose voice is continually praising God for the blessings bestowed upon her, and never murmuring because of hardships endured. She has been a wonderful teacher to me. I thank my God that I have met Sojourner Truth.

"PORTIA GAGE."

"WASHINGTON, APRIL 10, 1867.

"ISAAC POST, ESQ.:--

"Dear Sir--Inclosed find a post-office money order for $20, which is intended for Sojourner Truth, it being the amount due her from the New York Freedmen's Commission for December last. Please assure her of my regards, and that we shall be glad to see her when she returns.

"Yours truly,

A. E. NEWTON,
"Sup't of Schools, &c."

"Sojourner Truth has been very acceptably received by the people of Vineland, and I trust that the many earnest words she has uttered, both in public and private, for the cause of woman and the abolition of the death penalty, will be like seed cast upon good ground.

"DEBORAH L. BUTLER.

"Jan. 17, 1870."

Sojourner was most cordially and hospitably entertained whilst in Lawrence, Kansas, by a family of the name of Simpson, bankers in that place.

The following testimonials of their respect are transcribed from her "Book of Life":--

"May your future, Sojourner, be ever brighter than your faith.

W. A. SIMPSON."

"I wish you the same, Sojourner.

"LAURA B. SIMPSON."

"SOJOURNER:--

"May our faith be like thine, and our duty as well done.

KATE L. SIMPSON."

"The Lord bless you, Sojourner, and may your immortal crown be studded with many stars.

"HANNAH P. SIMPSON."

"The Lord bless you, sister Sojourner. I believe you are endued by the Spirit of the Lord in your efforts for the elevation of your race.

"SAMUEL SIMPSON.

"Lawrence, Kansas, Dec. 1, 1871."

"PETERBOROUGH, N. Y., DEC. 11, 1868.

"MY DEAR SOJOURNER TRUTH:--

"I cannot let you go without telling you on paper how highly we have prized your visit to us. We have enjoyed your wit and powers of description, we have been instructed by your wisdom, and we have welcomed your religion. I trust that this is not your last visit to Peterborough, and that the good Lord and Father will spare you to come again to us. Wherever you shall go, there will, I trust, be good friends to receive you, to bless you, and to be blessed by you. I know that wherever you go you will be useful, for the head and heart that you carry with you are continually doing good.

"With much love to you from my dear wife and myself, your friend,

GERRITT SMITH."

"SOJOURNER TRUTH:--

> "With weary hand, yet steadfast will,
> In old age as in youth,
> Thy Master found thee, sowing still
> The good seed of his truth.

"REV. E. MARBLE.

"Schoolcraft, Mich. Conference."

"FRIEND SOJOURNER:--

"It would be folly in me to ask the Great Spirit to bless that which he has already so abundantly blessed. Why should I invoke him to shower blessings upon thy head, or strew thy pathway with flowers? Do not all these jewels naturally belong to and sparkle around the footprints of those who, like you, go about doing their Master's business? 'T is not race, profession, or position, but knowing the right and doing it, which shall entitle an individual to a safe passport to the home of the angels.

"WARREN SAMSON.

"Hammonton, N. J., 1870."

"TOLEDO, OHIO, Jan. 12, 1866.

"SISTER SOJOURNER:--

"I have received my commission to return to Washington and Richmond as soon as I can possibly get ready, i. e., collect about $300 more to go with. I want to be ready the latter part of next week. Oh, how I want to know how you are getting along. I have not been to Battle Creek, and hardly think I can reach it; but I have written them and hope they will send money and clothes by me to you. I cannot set precise date, but may, in a week or ten days, see Washington.

"Our Home is getting along finely. The colored people of Adrian placed $40 in my hands to buy a cow for the little folks at the Home. I have bought a good cow for them, which gives eleven quarts of milk per day, and Mr. Don gave them another, so they are nicely provided for. The colored people also gave us a Christmas donation for the Haviland Home, valued at $113.84, mostly in provisions and clothing, with some money to purchase hens for the Home.

"I must close with earnest desire for your prosperity in all things.

"Yours for the poor and needy,

"LAURA S. HAVILAND."

"WASHINGTON, MARCH 18, 1874.

"DEAR, BLESSED SOJOURNER TRUTH:--

"I must address you from the heart, mother of love and truth as you are. I am blest and thankful that I have held your hand in mine, been greeted by you, and heard your voice, which, longer years than I have known, has been lifted up throughout the land against oppression and sin, say to me, 'I know your soul!' Blessed words! Cheering me on my path and to be proved thrice blessed in the spirit world, where you and I will learn the deep import of your greeting, 'I know your soul.' God grant me strength also to 'be faithful unto the end,' even as you have been.

"When Christ the Lord makes up his jewels, you then exalted will receive the crown eternal, and clothed in white rise upward in joy unspeakable and full of glory. Thanks be unto God who giveth us the victory. Reverently and lovingly,

"Your child and sister,

"JENNIE LEYS."

"PAWTUCKET, Nov. 10, 1870.

"DEAR SOJOURNER:--

"I hope there yet may be found ten righteous people to save us this way. At any rate, perhaps you'll help us to hunt them up when you come. There is a nice little hall here which the temperance people occupy only

Wednesday evenings. In applying for it, I found old friends of yours who knew you in Bensonville, and it was at once tendered to you in your behalf, free of any expense whatever.

"Yours in haste,

"J. ADAMS."

"BENZONIA, MICH., Nov. 8, 1864.

"DEAR MOTHER, SOJOURNER TRUTH:--

"We have received your 'shadow' all right--very beautiful. We esteem it very much. May God bless you and make you very useful, and prepare you for your higher life, and rest, and glory. Today we suppose Father Abraham is again elected. May God bless him and give him all needed wisdom and grace.

"We all unite in much love to you.

"Yours for the good cause,

"GEORGE THOMPSON."

"FROM THE LION'S DEN, MOUNT GLENDEL."

"He who feedeth the ravens, careth for thee, true Sojourner, and blesses all thy labors of love abundantly. Go on proclaiming glad tidings. Preach the true gospel, and curse the follies and sins of this world.

"Your Old Lion S,

DOLLIE LION."

"SCHUYLKILL, CHESTER CO., PA.
"APRIL 5, 1863.

"TO SOJOURNER TRUTH:--

"Dear Sister--I saw, this morning, in the Anti-slavery Standard, an extract from a letter written by Mrs. Stickney to our mutual friend, 'Uncle' Joseph Dugdale. I was glad to learn that you are among kind friends. Although my sympathies were moved at the thought of your poverty and bodily afflictions, yet it was not with feelings of sorrow or regret. I rather rejoiced that your needs should have been the medium through which I learned your whereabouts, and that you still breathe in the atmosphere of truth, and feel an interest in the welfare of your race and all mankind. That notice will unquestionably bring you all needed temporal help as far as pecuniary aid can supply your wants. I will inclose a mite in this letter for you. It would be more only I that feel assured it will not be needed, as, no doubt, hundreds will feel glad of the opportunity of contributing to your needs.

"Let us bless and praise God for his manifold goodness. God's goodness is none the less displayed in his abused mercies turned into curses by a wicked people than in the fruition of divine joy by his obedient children. May his spirit in such fullness as thy vessel can contain and enjoy, ever be with thee. With fond Christian affection,

"Farewell.

"ISAAC PRICE."

"PETERROROUGH, MAY 4, 1869.

"MY DEAR SOJOURNER:--

"I was very glad to receive a letter from you, but sorry to learn that you are suffering from indisposition. I hope you will soon be well enough to go to Brooklyn and call here on your way. We very often talk of the pleasant visit we had from you, and when I am alone I frequently recall the words you spoke to us and feel refreshed and strengthened by them. I send you ten dollars, for food and fire as far as it will go. Wish it were more, but it must suffice now.

"God bless you always, and keep you in his own peace. In much love,

"ANN C. SMITH."

"ALEXANDRIA, MAY 3, 1866.

"SOJOURNER TRUTH:--

"Dear Friend--The bearer of this note is desirous of going North and taking thence his family, consisting of wife and daughter. I have known him since my stay here, and recommend him to your consideration. If anything can be done as regards transportation, &c., it will be thankfully received by him.

"Very respectfully, your obedient servant,

"A. W. TUCKER,
"A. A. Surgeon, U. S. A."

"Glad to see our dear co-laborer, Sojourner Truth, again.

LUCRETIA MOTT.

"Road Side, Philadelphia, Eleventh Month, 1869."

"Ever yours,

HENRY WILSON,
"Senator, Mass.

"April 20, 1870."

"This is my first interview with Abraham Lincoln's 'Aunty' Sojourner Truth. A pleasant season.

"GEORGE TRUMAN.

"Philadelphia, Eleventh Month, 1869."

"I hope, dear Sojourner, that you will be enfranchised before you leave us for the better land.

"Your true friend,

"ELIZABETH CADY STANTON.

"New York, May 4, 1870."

"Very truly yours,

"MARY A. DODGE--GAIL HAMILTON."

"My friend, Sojourner Truth, the friend of the human race--God bless you.

"JACOB WALTON.

"Adrian, Mich., 1871."

"Your brother in the hope of glory,

"B. SUNDERLAND,
"Pres. Minister, Wash. D. C."

"May God bless and guide you!

"ANNE G. PHILLIPS.

"Aug. 1."

"Your true friend and co-worker,

"LUCY N. COLEMAN.

"Syracuse, N. Y."

"Your old young friend,

"W. F. MORGAN.

"Leavenworth, Kan."

"S. C. POMEROY, Senator, Kan.

"April 20, 1870."

"J. M. THAYER, Senator, Neb.

"April 20, 1870."

'A. McDonald, Arkansas."

"Most sincerely your friend,

"GEORGE W. JULIAN."

"HENRY E. BENSON, Lawrence, Kansas."

"JACOB M. Howard, Michigan Senator."

"T. M. MORRELL, Illinois Senator."

"Yours truly,

J. W. PATTERSON."

"J. M. BOWEN, Mayor of Washington."

"GEORGE E. SPENCER, Senator, Ala."

"D. D. PRATT, U. S. Senator, Ind."

"H. R. REVELS, Senator, Miss., Colored."

"J. S. ADAMS, Louisiana."

"Z. CHANDLER, Mich."

"R. E. FENTON, N. Y."

"JAS. S. FOWLER, Senator, Tenn."

VISITS WESTERN NEW YORK.

"We met Sojourner at Angola Station, stopped at Joseph Linton's to dinner, then took her to Alonzo Hawley's, a few rods distant, where she spent the night. The next afternoon Mrs. Hawley brought her to our house. Sunday, the 6th, called a meeting for her at Hemlock Hall, where, at 10 o'clock A. M. she addressed an appreciative audience of four hundred people. Wednesday morning we carried her to George W. Taylor's, distant six miles. The afternoon of the same day, Mr. Taylor and wife carried her five miles farther into the town of Collins, to the comfortable home of Isaac and Lydia Allen, aged people like herself, who extended to her a hearty welcome. In the evening she spoke to a good audience in the Rosenburgh schoolhouse near by. The following day, Thursday, was spent by Sojourner with the family of Mrs. Cook, who are relatives of the Allens. The next night, Mr. Cook took her four miles, to Collins Center. There she addressed a large audience in the new Free Church, and felt that her labors were not in vain. Returned with Mr. Cook to the house of Isaac Allen.

"Friday night, Mr. Allen and wife went with her to Mr. Rosenburgh's, who took her to Gowanda, where she addressed an intensely interested audience. Saturday she was conveyed to G. W. Taylor's, and Sunday brought to Kerr's Corners, to the home of Lewis Baldwin, where she remained until the 14th, and then spoke to a large gathering in the Methodist Church. After the meeting she came home with us once more.

"She seems very quiet and happy here, and we are enjoying a feast which we may never be privileged to enjoy again. It is a blessing to be with her and receive her experience from her own lips. Wednesday night, James Varney carried her to Bront Center, where was assembled an appreciative audience in the new Methodist Church. On Friday night, the school-house in Pontiac was filled with people eager to listen to her teachings. Since that time she has been very quiet until the 22d, when she accompanied us to a political pic-nic at Hemlock Hall, where was convened an audience of probably three thousand people to listen to able speakers. I have endeavored in a hurried manner to write a little diary for Sojourner, to show to such of her friends as are anxious to know where she has been and what has been her success.

"PHEBE MERRITT VARNEY."

"James Varney conveyed Sojourner Truth to our house fourth day, the 23d of ninth month, 1868, where she remained till the following sixth day, when we carried her to the house of our son-in-law, P. Paxton, where she remained till seventh day evening, when she went to Potter's Corners to attend a large republican meeting in which she made a few remarks. This caused such enthusiasm among the people that it opened the way for a very large meeting the next evening. The large hall was nearly filled with an attentive audience, which she addressed for more than an hour, in her usually impressive and sarcastic manner, much to the satisfaction of the majority present. From thence, she went home with Alfred Moore and wife, with whom she spent several days, to the edification of the neighboring people who came to see her. In conclusion, we rejoice in the opportunity of becoming partially acquainted with Sojourner Truth. May she yet survive long to combat in her peculiar and impressive manner the errors with which this nation is enthralled.

ISAAC BAKER.

"East Hamburg, Erie Co., N. Y."

"On the 29th of ninth month, 1868, J. B. C. Eddy went to Harry Abbot's after Sojourner Truth to attend a meeting held in Dr. Dolin's neighborhood, which was very well attended, and to good satisfaction to those in favor of liberty. On the first day of tenth month, she held a meeting at Griffin's Mills, in the lecture room, speaking to a good and attentive audience, telling them many truths. Friend Sandford took up a collection for her. I can say on our part that her company has been very acceptable, and I hope she may live to have her wishes gratified in seeing Grant sit in the presidential chair.

"J. B. C. EDDY."

"On Monday, Oct. 19, 1868, Sojourner Truth, being in Courtland village, was sent for by C. P. Grosvenor, and brought to Mr. Granville's. Tuesday eve she addressed a crowded assembly in the Methodist Church with good effect. She had been several days at Courtland, and lectured to a multitude, having her home at the house of the younger Dr. Goodyear, who was happy to have her company and make her acquaintance. Here she was visited by many ladies and gentlemen.
CYRUS P. GROSVENOR. "McGranville, N. Y."

SUPERWOMEN

MEETING IN NEW LISBON.

"Sojourner Truth interested an audience in New Lisbon, Ohio, at the Methodist Episcopal Church, for nearly an hour, talking of slavery in this country, and the suffering and injustice inseparable from it. If earnestness is eloquence, she has a just claim to that appellation; for she makes some powerful appeals, which cannot but strike a chord of sympathy in every human heart.

"She sang the following original song at the close of the meeting:--

"I am pleading for my people--
A poor, down-trodden race,
Who dwell in freedom's boasted land,
With no abiding place.

"I am pleading that my people
May have their rights astored
For they have long been toiling,
And yet had no reward.

"They are forced the crops to culture,
But not for them they yield,
Although both late and early
They labor in the field.

SUPERWOMEN

"Whilst I bear upon my body
The scars of many a gash,
I am pleading for my people
Who groan beneath the lash.

"I am pleading for the mothers
Who gaze in wild despair
Upon the hated auction-block,
And see their children there.

"I feel for those in bondage--
Well may I feel for them;
I know how fiendish hearts can be
That sell their fellow-men.

"Yet those oppressors steeped in guilt--
I still would have them live;
For I have learned of Jesus
To suffer and forgive.

"I want no carnal weapons,
No enginery of death;
For I love not to hear the sound
Of war's tempestuous breath.

"I do not ask you to engage

SUPERWOMEN

In death and bloody strife,
I do not dare insult my God
By asking for their life.

"But while your kindest sympathies
To foreign lands do roam,
I would ask you to remember
Your own oppressed at home.

"I plead with you to sympathize
With sighs and groans and scars,
And note how base the tyranny
Beneath the stripes and stars."

TOBACCO VICTORY--THE BRANDED HAND.

The habit of smoking was contracted by Sojourner in early youth. Not many years since, whilst traveling in Iowa, a gentleman asked her if she believed the Bible, to which she readily assented. Her friend said, "The Bible tells us that 'no unclean thing can enter the kingdom of Heaven.' Now what can be more filthy than the breath of a smoker?" "Yes, child," she answered, "but when I goes to Heaven I spects to leave my breff behind me." But as time passed on she became convinced that the habit was wrong. She had not courage to chide people for using spirituous liquors while indulging in the use of tobacco, herself. Accordingly she discontinued the habit. She was told it would affect her health. She said, "I'll quit if I die." She did quit and lived!

"ROCHESTER, JAN. 11, 1869.

"DEAR FRIEND SOJOURNER:--

"The announcement in the Anti-slavery Standard of thy having laid aside the pipe, is receiving considerable attention. I received a letter from Dr. Trask, of Fitchburg, Mass., who rejoices greatly over thy grand and triumphant effort, and says, 'It ought to be proclaimed far and near to strengthen others to cast aside the abomination.'

"Also a letter has just come to me from our old and highly esteemed friend, Jonathan Walker, the original of 'The Branded Hand.' Thou wilt probably remember him.

He was captain of a small vessel running from New York to the Gulf States. He secreted several slaves and brought them to the free States, was taken and imprisoned, and the letters S S branded on his right hand, signifying slave stealer; but in our vernacular we should interpret it slave savior. This vessel with its entire cargo was confiscated, and he lay in a filthy jail in Florida for several months.

"AMY POST."

"MUSKEGON, MICH., JAN. 1, 1869.

"MY DEAR AGED AND VENERATED FRIEND:--

"Your earnest and effectual devotion, for so long a time, to the cause of human redemption, has, from my first knowledge of your missionary services to the present time, impressed me (as well as many others) with the warmest fraternal regard for your welfare and usefulness. When I saw it announced by Amy Post, in the Antislavery Standard, that you had abandoned the pipe at your advanced age, I could form no other conclusion than that you had done it under the influence of the keenest moral and religious sensibilities.

'I have known ministers and many professors of religion, as well as other good people, who tried hard and long to abandon the use of tobacco, yet made a failure, and confessed that they could not conquer the habit. I distinctly remember, also, the tedious and desperate struggle I had to emancipate myself from twenty years' slavery to the foul weed. Considering the effect its long use has upon the nervous system, I could hardly suppose you could have achieved so great a victory at your age without a break-down; nor do I look upon so heroic an act as much short of a miracle. May the example of such self-sacrifice in you, indeed stimulate and encourage (as Amy says) 'others to do likewise,' is the earnest desire of your

"Sincere friend,

"JONATHAN WALKER."

"P. S. I am not sure, but I think I met you twenty-five years ago at Bronsonville, North Hanston, Mass., soon after my return from imprisonment in Florida. J. W."

The heroic deeds of Jonathan Walker have rendered his name immortal; and our prince of song has paid them a just and noble tribute in the exquisite poem entitled, "The Branded Hand," from which the following is an extract:--

"Why, that brand is highest honor! than
  its traces never yet
On old armorial hatchments was a

prouder blazon set;
  And thy unborn generations, as they tread our rocky strand,
  Shall tell with pride the story of their father's branded hand!

"Then lift that manly right hand, bold ploughman of the wave!
  Its branded palm shall prophesy, 'Salvation to the Slave.'

  Hold up its fire-wrought language, that whoso reads may feel
  His heart swell strong within him, his sinews change to steel.

  "Hold it up before our sunshine, up against our northern air.
  Ho! men of Massachusetts, for the love of God, look there!
  Take it henceforth for your standard--like the Bruce's heart of yore,
In the dark strife closing round ye, let that hand be seen before!

"And the tyrants of the slave-land shall tremble at that sign,
  When it points its finger southward along the

Puritan line:
Woe to the State-gorged leeches, and the church's locust band,
When they look from slavery's ramparts on the coming of that hand."

SOJOURNER TRUTH'S AGE.

Sojourner is often asked her age. She is as ignorant of its date as is the fossil found in the limestone rock, or the polished pebble upon the sea-shore, which has been scoured by the waves ever since the sea was born.

It was the diabolical scheme of those dealers in human flesh to so stultify the brain of the slave that it might become incapable of reason, reflection, or memory. The slave child followed the condition of its mother, and seldom had any knowledge of father, or date of birth. They were Pompey or Cuffee, Dinah or Chloe, as the case might be, having no permanent second name, but taking the surname of the master; consequently they received a new cognomen with each new owner.

Sojourner counts her years from the time she was emancipated--says she began to live then. She thinks it is what we accomplish that makes life long or short, and says that some have been on earth scores of years, yet die in infancy.

The following account is well authenticated:--

The act of 1817 in the State of New York emancipated all slaves of the age of 40 years. From this time all became free as fast as they arrived at the age of 25 years, till 1827, when all were free. Sojourner became free in 1817. This statement is corroborated by an old gentleman by the name of Miller, who was brought up in the vicinity of Sojourner's birthplace. He recently died in Green Co., Wisconsin.

HER PARENTAGE.

Mrs. Stowe was mistaken in regard to Sojourner's ancestry. Her mother's parents came from the Coast of Guinea, but her paternal grandmother was a Mohawk squaw. The "whoop" Sojourner gave in the horse-car at Washington was probably a legacy from her Mohawk ancestor.

EXTENT OF HER LABORS.

Sojourner Truth has traveled and lectured in the following States:--

New York, Massachusetts, New Jersey, Maine, Pennsylvania, Michigan, Wisconsin, Minnesota, Ohio, Illinois, Missouri, Indiana, Iowa, Kansas, Connecticut, Vermont, New Hampshire, Rhode Island, Delaware, Maryland, Virginia, and the District of Columbia.

ANECDOTES.

SOJOURNER TRUTH AT ABINGTON.

About 20 years ago Sojourner attended a grove-meeting at Abington, Mass., to celebrate negro emancipation in the West Indies. Many of the old line abolitionists were there,--Pillsbury, Garrison, Phillips, Stephen and Abby Foster, Henry C. Wright, Charles Lenox Rimond, and a host of others. Two fugitives from southern slavery, who were traveling over the underground railroad to Canada, stopped off a train to enjoy a day with friends before going to that "cold but happy land." They sat upon the platform with the speakers. One, a very large man, was squeezed into a coat much too small for him. The other, a diminutive man, wore a coat of such ample proportions that it hung in folds about his liliputian form. But as these garments had been given them by employees on the underground express, and were the first of the kind they had ever owned, the fit did not appear to disturb them, judging by the pleased look upon their faces. The contrast between their present condition and what might have been, had they been overtaken in their flight and dragged back into slavery, filled them with bliss. They were comparatively happy.

These coat collars were nicer than the iron collars which might now have been on their necks; and the cuffs, softer than the iron cuffs which they knew the captured fugitive was made to wear. The voice of bloodhounds baying in the distance, was superseded by kindly human voices. Traveling toward the North Star by night, they had hidden in dark caves and underbrush during the day, avoiding the light of the sun. Now, streams of golden sunlight flowed around them. Surely, they were receiving "beauty for ashes and the oil of joy for mourning."

One of them arose, and in a brief manner expressed his appreciation of this mighty change, and his deep gratitude to the people of Massachusetts for their kindness and generosity. At the close of his remarks, which were received with applause, Mr. Garrison said, "Sojourner Truth will now address you in her peculiar manner, and Wendell Phillips will follow." Sojourner began by improvising a song, commencing, "Hail! ye abolitionists." Her voice was both sweet and powerful, and as her notes floated away through the tree-tops, reaching the outermost circle of that vast multitude, it elicited cheer after cheer. She then made some spicy remarks, occasionally referring to her fugitive brethren on the platform beside her. At the close of her address, in which by witty sallies and pathetic appeals, she had moved the audience to laughter and tears, she looked about the assemblage and said, "I will now close, for he that cometh after me is greater than I," and took her seat. Mr. Phillips came forward holding a paper in his hand containing notes of Sojourner's speech, which he used as texts for a powerful and eloquent appeal in behalf of human freedom. Sojourner says, "I was utterly astonished to hear him say, 'Well has Sojourner said so and so'; and I said to myself, Lord, did I say that? How differently it sounded coming from his lips! He dressed my poor, bare speech in such beautiful garments that I scarcely recognized it myself."

As Sojourner was returning to the home of Amy Post in Rochester, one evening, after having delivered a lecture in Corinthian Hall, a little policeman stepped up to her and demanded her name. She paused, struck her cane firmly upon the ground, drew herself up to her greatest hight, and in a loud, deep, voice deliberately answered "I am that I am." The frightened policeman vanished, and she concluded her walk without further questioning.

During the war, Sojourner met one of her democratic friends, who asked her, "What business are you now following?" She quickly replied, "Years ago, when I lived in the city of New York, my occupation was scouring brass door knobs; but now I go about scouring copperheads."

At a temperance meeting in one of the towns of Kansas, Sojourner, whilst addressing the audience, was much annoyed by frequent expectorations of tobacco juice upon the flour. Pausing and contemplating the pools of liquid filth, with a look of disgust upon her face, she remarked that it had been the custom for her Methodist brethren to kneel in the house of God during prayers, and asked how they could kneel upon these floors? Said she, speaking with emphasis, "If Jesus was here he would scourge you from this place."

Previous to the war, Sojourner held a series of meetings in northern Ohio. She sometimes made very strong points in the course of her speech, which she knew hit the apologist of slavery pretty hard. At the close of one of these meetings, a man came up to her and said, "Old woman, do you think that your talk about slavery does any good? Do you suppose people care what you say?" "Why," continued he, "I do n't care any more for your talk than I do for the bite of a flea." "Perhaps not," she responded, "but, the Lord willing, I'll keep you scratching."

Sojourner was invited to speak at a meeting in Florence, Mass. She had just returned from a fatiguing trip, and not having thought of anything in particular to say, arose and said, "Children, I have come here to-night like the rest of you to hear what I have got to say." Wendell Phillips was one of her audience. Soon after this he was invited to address a lyceum, and being unprepared for the occasion, as he thought, began by saying, "I shall have to tell you as my friend Sojourner Truth told an audience under similar circumstances, I have come here like the rest of you to hear what I have to say."

Autographs of Distinguished Persons,

WHO HAVE BEFRIENDED SOJOURNER TRUTH BY WORDS OF SYMPATHY AND MATERIAL AID.

AUTOGRAPHS.   313

Autographs of Distinguished Persons,

WHO HAVE BEFRIENDED SOJOURNER TRUTH BY WORDS OF SYMPATHY AND MATERIAL AID.

Wm. Lloyd Garrison.
A. Lincoln
Parker Pillsbury,
Gilbert Haven
Susan B. Anthony
Calvin Fairbanks.

314   "BOOK OF LIFE."

Wendell Phillips

H B Stowe

Charles [S White]

Lucretia Mott.

L. Maria Child.

Geo. Thompson

Gerrit Smith

Wendell Phillips
H B Stowe
Charles [S White]
Lucretia Mott.
L. Maria Child.
Geo. Thompson
Gerrit Smith

Jonathon Parker
J. S. Griffins
Samuel J. May
O. O. [Howard]
Rowland Johnson
Lydia Mott
Amy Post
[Autographs]

SUPERWOMEN

NOTES ON THE AUTOGRAPHS.

In Sojourner's correspondence are found names of such weight and power that it seemed fitting to have them engraven for her "Book of Life." Here are names that are indelibly stamped upon the pages of their country's history, and inseparably connected with it--names which will reverberate adown the centuries, and the echoes be caught by the generations in the coming time--"immortal names that were not born to die," but which are synonyms of all that is most exalted in human life and character--names of men and women, the luster of whose lives shed a light on humanity's page, pure and sparkling as the shimmer of a white wing flashing through the yellow sunlight--names of those who manifested their love to God by tender compassion for the lowliest of his children.

The name of one who was dragged through the streets of a populous city with a halter about his neck, will be remembered when that city which permitted the outrage, would be forgotten but for the immortality attained through his sublime heroism. Boston with its moving atoms will fade away, but the waves of progress received an impetus from the breath of this true devotee of freedom, which will help to cleanse and purify the streams of life till they are engulfed in the ocean of eternity.

The name of one is written who only "awaited the opportunity to enfranchise millions."

SUPERWOMEN

I read the name of one who traveled many winters among the hills of New England, braving its snow drifts and piercing winds, to preach the gospel of freedom to those whose hearts were harder than the granite rocks over which he toiled, and chillier than the snows and breath of winter. Abandoning a situation of honor and profit, he consecrated his giant intellect, and the best years of his life, to a cause that brought neither honor nor profit, despised by mammon worshipers and all who seek the applause of such. Beyond the turmoil of the present hour, when its noise and uproar have died away, the refined and polished future will render his verdict. He can afford to wait. The present never knows its saviors; retrospection clears the vision.

The influence of another, who labors with deep earnestness in the Master's vineyard, confined to no locality, knowing neither North nor South, but imparting his loving spirit to all races and conditions of society, will be felt upon the tide of civilization whilst its waves break upon the shores of time.

Here is the name of a noble woman who has gone up Calvary bearing the cross, and gained the mount of ascension with bleeding feet; who has labored for the rights of her race and for the rights of her sex, braving the scorn and obloquy of conservatism. Bold iconoclast! endure a little longer. "The hour for your ideas has not yet struck."

One, languishing twelve years in prison, found compensation for his sufferings in the words of the divine Master, "Sick and in prison ye ministered unto me."

One of these, a world-renowned orator, said, "The age of reading men has come. The age of thinking men has come. The age of the masses has come."

One of Sojourner's friends, by her genius in the delineation of character, opened the world's eyes to perceive that irresponsible power vested in a Legree was a dangerous thing, and that Uncle Toms and Topsies were human beings after all.

Another inscribes this formula in Sojourner's "Book of Life": "Equality of rights is the first of rights."

A woman whose four-score years are so replete with good words and deeds that the name falls like a benediction upon the listening ear, has taught her sex that old age need not be desolate, but may be fragrant as a garden of roses. White hairs, like a saint's aureole, encircle her brow. We involuntarily bow our hearts in worship when the honored name of Lucretia Mott is pronounced.

Another is the name of Lydia Maria Child, the key note of whose useful life and brilliant intellect has ever been attuned to freedom's cause.

One crossed and recrossed the Atlantic, to blend his efforts with the little band of reformers which eventually slew the giant, Slavery, with a pebble of truth, and demolished his castle, the corner stone of which was lies, and its superstructure the bleeding hearts of crushed humanity. Landing upon our shores he was pursued by the hooting mob, as if the Plutonian regions had been emptied at his heels.

G. S., meaning "Great Soul," gave farms to poor blacks and whites, carrying out Sojourner's idea of encouraging industry, and making wild lands a source of revenue to the government. In Congress he said, "Truth lives and reigns forever. In proportion as we obey the truth, are we able to discern the truth." If all that is wrong within us was made right, not only would our darkness give place to a cloudless light, but like the angel of the Apocalypse we should "stand in the sun."

Another could bear the torture of the branding iron rather than be false to his convictions of duty.

Josephine S. Griffing labored for years to ameliorate the condition of the black race, and in her system were sown, by overwork, the seeds of consumption which bore speedy fruit.

Another in the sacred desk ever insisted that humanity was of all things under heaven the most sacred. A marble bust of this good man adorns the city of Syracuse, and a friend writing of it says, "It is eminently fitting that one of the purest of the once proscribed abolitionists should now be thus publicly honored."

Another, who holds a high position under the government, is Sojourner's friend, and unites his efforts with hers to promote the welfare of the race which has been so mercilessly tossed about by our Ship of State. He encourages her to persevere in her efforts to obtain a grant of land for the freedmen, and lends his influence to the cause.

And last but not least are those royal souls who sheltered and comforted the flying fugitive, who fed and clothed him, who warmed him by the sacred fires of their own domestic hearth-stones. The money they have so freely given to the poor and needy, is out at an interest whose profits are beyond the power of arithmetic to calculate. Their names are engraven upon human hearts as with a pen of fire; and to them will the beatitude apply, "Blessed are the pure in heart, for they shall see God."

APPENDIX.

SOJOURNER TRUTH.

[The following interesting sketch came to hand after this volume was printed, this will explain why it is given in the form of an appendix.]

"BATTLE CREEK, MICH., APR. 14, 1863.

"OLIVER JOHNSON:--

"Dear Friend, Permit me, through the columns of The Standard, in behalf of Sojourner Truth, whom your readers so well remember, to acknowledge the receipt of the several donations from her many generous friends, all of which have been gratefully received by her. Printed words can never convey such deep and heartfelt gratitude as she feels. The donors needed but to have seen the expression of her dark, care-worn face and heard her words of genuine thankfulness, to have realized that indeed it is 'more blessed to give than to receive.'

"As we opened the letters, one by one, and read the words of sweet remembrance and kindness, she was quite overcome with joy, and more than once gave utterance to her feelings through her tears praising the Lord who had so soon answered her prayers, which was, in language from the depths of her soul as she sat weary and alone in her quiet little home 'Lord, I'm too old to work--I'm too sick to hold meetings and speak to de people, and sell my books; Lord, you sent de ravens to feed 'Lijah in de wilderness; now send de good angels to feed me while I live on thy footstool.'

"No sooner had the appeal gone forth, than the answers came from the East and West, accompanied with material aid to supply her physical needs. Then again she exclaimed, in words of deepest gratitude: 'Lord, I knew dy laws was sure, but I did n't t'ink dey would work so quick.' The words of friendship and sympathy that filled every letter were a source of great joy and consolation to her, and when the comforting message from Gerrit Smith came, saying, 'Sojourner, the God whom you so faithfully serve will abundantly bless you, he will suffer you to lack nothing either in body or soul,' she threw up her hands, and, in her deep-toned voice, said: 'The Lord bless the man! his heart is as big as de nation, and if he had'nt sent a penny, his words would feed my soul, and dat is what we all want.' Then she mentioned Samuel Hill, of Northampton, Mass., where she lived 15 years, saying that his noble, generous heart had done a great deal for her. Ofttimes the full ecstasy of her soul would gush forth in all its original vigor and freshness at the thought of her many friends and their quick responses. She once said to me: 'I tell you, chile, de Lord manages everything; you see when you wrote dat letter, you did n't think you was doing much, but I tell you, dear lamb, dat when a thing is done in de right spirit, God takes it up and spreads it all over de country.'

"She wishes the friends to know that the 'little curly-headed, jolly grandson,' whom Mrs. Stowe so graphically describes, is now grown to a tall, able-bodied lad, and has just enlisted in the 54th Massachusetts Regiment; gone forth with her prayers and blessings, she says, 'to redeem de white people from de curse dat God has sent upon them.' The glorious news of old Massachusetts leading in the van for the right of the colored man to fight, has just reached here, and she seems at times to be filled with all the fire and enthusiasm of her former years. She says if she were only ten years younger, she would be 'on hand as the Joan of Arc to lead de army of de Lord; for now is de day and now de hour for de colored man to save dis nation; for dere sin have been so great dat dey do n't know God, nor God do n't know dem.' I never heard her speak with greater force and power than she did the other day when some friends called to see her. She says this is all the way she has now to preach. She often speaks of T. W. Higginson and Frances D. Gage--thinks 'dey are appointed of God to fill de position dey have taken.' As I closed the interview Sojourner called down many blessings on all who had helped her to live, and 'do good in de world.'

"I will give the names of the donors, so far as I know them, and if any have sent whose names do not appear, perhaps they will write, or they will yet come to hand.

"Yours truly,

       "PHEBE H. M. STICKNEY."

Names of Donors.

- JOSEPH A. DUGDALE, Iowa.
- RUTH DUGDALE, Iowa.
- SARAH B. DUGDALE, Iowa.
- WILLIAM BARNARD, Chester Co., Pa.
- MARY L. BARNARD, Chester Co., Pa.
- PHEBE HOUSE, Chester Co., Pa.
- SARAH M. BARNARD, Chester Co., Pa.
- MARIA AGNEW, Chester Co., Pa.
- HANNAH COX, Chester Co., Pa.
- DINAH MENDENHALL, Chester Co., Pa.
- ELIZA AGNEW, Chester Co., Pa.
- ISAAC PRICE, Chester Co., Pa.
- SAMUEL HILL, Northampton, Mass.
- H. B. STOWE, Andover, Mass.
- GERRIT SMITH, Peterboro, N. Y.
- S. P. TOWNSEND, New York.
- A friend, New York.

--Antislavery Standard.

www.ingramcontent.com/pod-product-compliance
Lightning Source LLC
Chambersburg PA
CBHW080048190426
43201CB00036B/2272